IN SEARCH
OF LOST FROGS

IN SEARCH OF
LOST
FROGS

Robin Moore

THE CAMPAIGN TO REDISCOVER
THE WORLD'S RAREST AMPHIBIANS

FIREFLY BOOKS

A FIREFLY BOOK

Published by Firefly Books Ltd. 2014

First printing

Publisher Cataloging-in-Publication Data (U.S.)

Moore, Robin.
 In search of lost frogs : the campaign to rediscover the world's rarest amphibians / Robin Moore.
[256] pages : col. photos. ; cm.
Includes bibliographical references and index.
Summary: "On August 9, 2010, 33 teams from 21 countries were dispatched to search for a host of "lost frogs" identified by Conservation International, many not seen for more than a century. This new book tells the story of the expedition -- several species were rediscovered; two totally new species were found. However, one third of the world's amphibians remain threatened with extinction" — Provided by Publisher.
ISBN-13: 978-1-77085-464-2 (pbk.)
1. Frogs – Identification. 2. Frogs – Conservation. I. Title.
597.8/9 dc23 QL668.E2.M667 2014

Library and Archives Canada Cataloguing in Publication

Moore, Robin, 1975-, author
In search of lost frogs : the campaign to rediscover the world's rarest amphibians / Robin Moore ; Lisa Thomas, editor.
Includes bibliographical references and index.
ISBN 978-1-77085-464-2 (bound)
1. Frogs--Identification. 2. Frogs--Conservation. I. Title.
QL668.E2M655 2014   597.8'9   C2014-900853-8

Published in the United States by
Firefly Books (U.S.) Inc.
P.O. Box 1338, Ellicott Station
Buffalo, New York 14205

Published in Canada by
Firefly Books Ltd.
50 Staples Avenue, Unit 1
Richmond Hill, Ontario L4B 0A7

Cover design: Erin R. Holmes, Soplari Design
Interior design: Nicola Liddiard, Nimbus Design

Printed in China by C & C Offset Printing Co Ltd

Developed by Bloomsbury Publishing Plc,

50 Bedford Square, London WC1B 3DP

FOREWORD

Comedy writers are supposed to be cynics. We're meant to squint at life's ragged parade with a sardonic eye, as we satirise human folly.

I was in California writing for 'The Simpsons' – satirising away, squinting and sneering at one and all. My guiding principles? Life is ridiculous; people never learn; let's have a few laughs before it all goes KABLAM! Then I met Robin Moore.

Robin was young and energetic and bafflingly free of cynicism. His passion was to protect the rare and gemlike frogs of the world from disappearing forever. Not only was he going to hurl his entire life at this quixotic mission; he fully expected to succeed.

What was wrong with this guy?

Didn't he know that people are selfish, materialistic, shortsighted and rapacious? Didn't he know that laptops and smartphones suck up all our time now, leaving nature tapping at the window like an old forgotten boxcar tramp?

Sure. Robin knows what he's up against. But he's also resourceful, and tenacious, and he has allies. Millions around the world – I'm one of them – have an enduring crush on frogs and toads and salamanders. We can safeguard these captivating critters and revel in their pursuit of hoppiness.

I know we can do it, because one night I rode in one of those funky cars that's shaped like a cube. Its owner proudly showed me the illuminated cup holder, which lit up in seven blazing colours. At that moment I thought, "Human beings are WIZARDS!"

This book will dazzle you with the elegance and allure of amphibians. After that, if you want to help us conserve these charmers, splash on in!

GEORGE MEYER
Seattle

CONTENTS

PROLOGUE

On a late September day in 2007, three miles above the equator in southern Ecuador, I joined a team of scientists on a quest to find a small black frog. We hiked across windswept peaks under cotton-wool clouds billowing in a sapphire sky – the air so thin that it made my head pound and my lungs ache – in search of a creature no bigger than my thumb. The frog had not been seen in two decades; its disappearance had been as sudden as it was mysterious. The frog was posthumously named after the Quechua word for sadness, to lament the loss of frogs from cool streams and glassy pools across South America and

beyond. It was my first search for a lost frog, but just one step of a bigger journey.

The following year in the shallows downstream I saw my first corpse. She was also a harlequin frog, but a different kind – with brilliant yellow on black, she was as beautiful in death as in life. Her stillness was broken only by the rhythmic wash of water on splayed limbs, and onto her back clung a male – oblivious to her passing – trying to mate. They were among the last of a species new to science. As her rigid limbs were squeezed into a jar filled with frogs like pickled eggs back at the lab in Quito, she took her place in a growing queue of species to be named and mourned. Her companion would join her just weeks later; both of their lives taken by a silent killer that was on the move, from Costa Rica to Ecuador and Australia to California.

The slow tug of nostalgia for lost amphibians punctuated by jolts of grief at the sight of dead frogs transformed a childhood passion, nurtured in the peat bogs of the Scottish highlands, into a global quest to unravel one of the most compelling mysteries of our time: what was happening to the amphibians?

My quest led me in 2010 to spearhead an unprecedented coordinated and global search for frogs, salamanders and the lesser-known caecilians. Over six months more than a hundred biologists slashed through thick jungle, waded up rivers and hiked remote mountain passes, from Borneo to Brazil, Colombia to Congo and Israel to India, faced with long odds and often miserable conditions and armed with boots, headlamps and dogged determination to find some of the most elusive creatures on earth. I was lucky enough to join some of these searches, to feel the pangs of disappointment and the thrill of discovery in some of the most remote and uncharted corners of the world.

On the following pages I invite you to join me on my journey as it unfolds in three parts. It begins in the back gardens and remote moors of Scotland, where my search for elusive frogs and newts in garden ponds to misty peat bogs ignited a passion that fueled a quest to unravel the mystery of vanishing frogs from Central and North America to Australia; their disappearance sometimes so rapid that not even a corpse was left to mark their existence. In the second part of the story we embark on a journey with scientists around the world in search of frogs and other amphibians not seen in decades, before taking a step back to consider, in the final part, what the successes and the failures mean in the grander scheme of things. It is a story of rediscovery, reinvention and hope; a story about the fine line between life and death, and what it is telling us about the sixth mass extinction on earth.

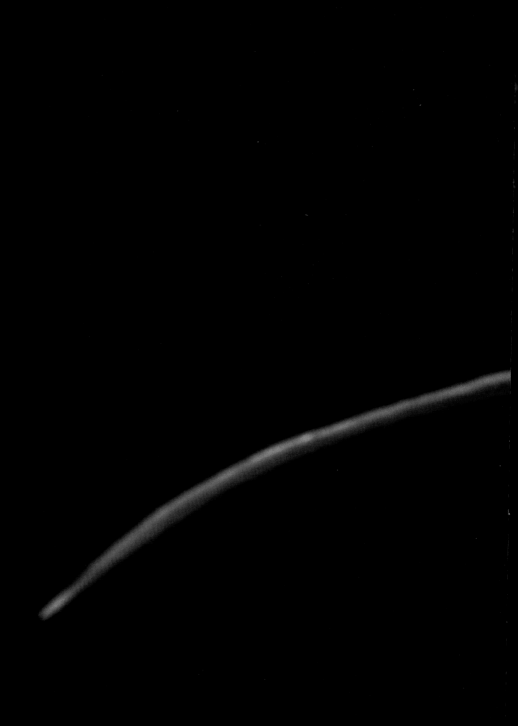

PART ONE

CHAPTER 1

SPAWNING A PASSION

"I have always liked frogs. I like the looks of frogs, and their outlook, especially the way they get together in wet places on warm nights and sing about sex."

ARCHIE F. CARR, *THE WINDWARD ROAD*

Edinburgh, April 1981

It is a crisp April afternoon in Edinburgh, filled with the comforting hum of distant lawnmowers and the sweet scent of freshly cut grass. I am six years old, buzzing with the thrill of exploration as I track glistening snail trails on the grey stone wall that lines my grandparent's garden, when an unusual sound breaks the silence. *Raaack raaaack raaaack, waaaaaarp.* I wiggle my fingers into the cracks between sun-warmed stones and scale the wall that separates me from the sound. As I flop belly-first onto the top of the wall and peer into the neighbour's garden, I am treated to a sight that I will not forget.

A small pond fringed by untamed grass thrums with life. The water bristles as frogs plop and wrestle in the shallows. I slide backwards down the wall into the neighbour's garden and, as my feet make contact with the ground, a frog springs from under me, skidding to a halt next to the pond. I steal closer before pouncing to clasp the frog's bulbous

Common Frog, *Rana temporaria*, Scotland.

waist. Her soft belly folds around my slender fingers like Play-Doh; she is loaded with eggs. She is resigned to this intrusion without struggle, and fixes me with what I take to be a look of mutual curiosity.

And this is when it happens. Her large inquisitive eyes and half-smiling mouth speak to me. Her primal form exudes the untold wisdom of a creature that has roamed the earth long before humans were even a distant promise; a creature that has rubbed ankles with the dinosaurs. The animal is as intriguing in life as in mythology; a mystique that is amplified by evanescence. After their explosive performance in the pond the frogs disappear as quickly as they arrived, spending the remainder of the year in the landscape of my imagination. Upon their disappearance they leave behind, bubbling from the surface of the pond, tickets to one of the most miraculous shows

A self portrait of Robin collecting frog spawn, drawn at the age of seven.

on earth. To snag my ringside seat, I return to the pond the following Sunday to plunge a hand into one of the cold, quivering masses. It feels like soft jelly marbles running through my fingers as I detach a small clump of spawn and plop it into a jam jar filled with water. Back home I transfer it to an aquarium, carefully lined with pebbles and decorated with sprigs of pondweed, to witness the magical transformation.

Over the following days the small black dots lengthen, from full stops to commas, until one day the commas jerk to life in an asynchronous choreography to a dozen different rhythms. Their dance leads them free of their jellied cocoons to roam the tank on their singular mission to eat and grow, rasping invisible algae off the sides of pebbles and rising belly-up to the surface to gulp with smiling mouths at floating fish flakes. Over the weeks they swell and lighten in colour and their skeletons harden. Into their smiling mouthparts grow jaws and teeth. Gills shrivel, lungs form and legs grow to propel them to a different life. The seamless transition from one realm to another echoes the primordial exodus of life from the water to the land. It is a metaphor for the evolutionary history of life on Earth, but also for my own transformation from curious child to intrepid naturalist.

It is with more than a pang of nostalgia that I release the tiny froglets into the grass beside the neighbour's pond. I watch as they hop into the tangle of grass to start their new life. From aquatic beings to denizens of the land in a matter of weeks – the transformation would never cease to amaze me.

The Axolotl is a type of salamander that never grows beyond the larval stage. It has big feathery gills, and even breeds in this juvenile form.

This, my first encounter with frogs, prompts further research. As I crack the spine on books about amphibians, a whole new world opens up, and frogs are just the beginning.

‍ॐ

Let's consider, for a moment, the frog. Unchanged for more than 200 millions years, the frog is an exemplar of evolutionary design. With porous skin stretched like an inverted lung across a delicate frame, frogs are intimately connected with their environment; in many ways they are an integral part of it. Some frogs have done away with lungs altogether and breathe only through the skin. Porous skin compels frogs to live near water to avoid dehydration, making them effective predictors of coming rains in some parts of the world. In India frogs often mark the arrival of the monsoon, and when the rains don't arrive the rain gods are summoned through a ritual that involves uniting two frogs in marriage. A severe rain shortage in 2011 prompted residents of the Indian region of Nargund to pool their money to pay for the wedding of two frogs in front of more than 500 guests. *The Times of India* reported the events, noting that "after marriage, the 'newly-weds' were taken out in a procession from Bhavani temple amidst beating of drums and blowing of trumpets". The report didn't indicate if the celebrations were cut short on account of rain. But when water is in seriously short supply, some frogs get creative in their efforts to conserve moisture. Few

Glass frog eggs, *Cochranella resplendens*, develop on a leaf overhanging a stream in southern Ecuador. Upon hatching the tadpoles will drop into the stream below to complete development.

Emerald Glass Frog, *Espadarana prosoblepon*, metamorph on a rock in the Chocó Department of Colombia.

are as impressive as the Water-holding Frog of Australia, which can survive underground for up to five years with nothing but a full bladder. The bladder serves as a convenient thirst-quencher for Aborigines, who in desperate times unearth the frogs to wring their liquid contents into parched mouths.

Frogs are joined by toads, newts, salamanders and strange worm-like caecilians to form a class of vertebrates called the Amphibia. The Amphibia (the name is derived from ancient Greek meaning 'both kinds of life') are ectothermic (cold-blooded) creatures found on every continent except Antarctica, and need water for reproduction (although some species have evolved creative ways of skipping the aquatic stage). More than 7,000 known species of amphibians present a kaleidoscopic cacophony of colours, shapes and sizes, and indulge in an equally eclectic pot-pourri of behaviours. Caecilians, of which there are around 160 species worldwide, are the most cryptic group. These curious creatures look like large worms, spend most of their time in leaflitter or underground and, as author Kathryn Philips notes, "The number of people in the world who study them could fit into a standard-sized hot tub." Nine-tenths of all amphibians are tailless, being frogs or toads, and among this group some of the most incredible behaviours can be observed. Take the ability of some frogs (five species to be exact) to freeze solid and, upon thawing, bounce

The skin of poison arrow frogs, such as this Andean Poison Frog, *Ranitomeya opisthomelas*, carrying its tadpole on its back, contains many compounds with potential medicinal benefits for people.

back to life. The Wood Frog can even, in this frozen state, suspend its heartbeat for several weeks before jumpstarting it. But the feature that elevates amphibians to symbolic status in cultures worldwide, and gives the class its name, is the remarkable transformation from one realm to another. Amphibians are the largest animals to undergo a metamorphosis as dramatic as that from egg through tadpole to adult. As Charlotte Sleigh, in her book simply titled, *Frog*, asks: "Who would not desire the frog's powers of total transformation? Who would not wish to metamorphose from the realm of frustration and subordination to another world altogether: from the murky pond to the clear, bright air?" As they move from water to earth, she continues, "so perhaps they signal the human possibility of moving from earth to air: in short, resurrection." In many cultures around the world, frogs have independently ascended to totems of resurrection and transformation.

But in a group known for such a transformation, it may be surprising to note that many amphibians skip metamorphosis, and one species famously avoids growing up altogether. The Axolotl (pronounced ACK-suh-LAH-tuhl) – a type of salamander that lives in the murky canals and lakes of Xochimilco near Mexico City – spends its entire life underwater as a feathery-gilled juvenile. It is the Peter Pan of the animal world, and is even able to breed in this juvenile form through a phenomenon called neoteny. There are also many frogs that skip the tadpole stage, laying eggs that develop directly into froglets, and even a couple of frogs that give birth to fully formed froglets through their mouth (don't try this at home). The diversity of reproductive modes in amphibians is astounding, but it is their propensity for explosive breeding (not as messy as it sounds) that has made them symbols of fertility in cultures from Japan to Egypt. In Egyptian mythology there is a goddess called Heget who represents fertility and is typically depicted as a frog, or a woman with a frog's head, or even – for those on whom subtlety is lost – as a frog on the end of a large phallus. Charlotte Sleigh explains the widespread occurrence of frogs as symbols of fertility as being because "tadpoles are a most vivid symbol of nature's irrepressible urge to reproduce." The fact that they also resemble large sperms probably helps.

A quick spin around the globe reveals that the symbolic value of amphibians is not limited to transformation and fertility. Frogs and toads appear widely throughout Asia as totems of healing and fortune. The Japanese word for frog is *kaeru*, which also means return; for Japanese travellers carry a small frog amulet with the intent of returning safely home. In Korea, amphibian tales and drawings often portray the animal as an intelligent person of good mind. In China the frog represents the lunar yin, and the frog spirit Ch'ing-Wa Sheng is associated with healing and good fortune in business. Feng Shui practices recommend putting an image of a frog in the east window of your home to encourage childbirth or happy family life (it is unclear if you get to choose which). A frog in a well, however, is symbolic of a person lacking in understanding and vision.

Frogs are also known for their medicinal properties throughout Asia. In Korean culture, the Gold-spotted Pond Frog has been prescribed to cure infectious diseases from wild animals and burning Japanese Tree Frog oil was believed to heal wounds. The book, *Chinese Magical Medicine,* tells of madness being cured by, "having the patient drink, thrice daily, a spoonful of calcined toad steeped in wine."

If you think it all sounds a little like hocus pocus, the science suggests that there may be method in their madness, as more than 70 amphibian species are known to have some kind of medicinal value for people (and these are just the ones that have been tested). The skin of frogs and toads has been used successfully for medicine by many cultures since ancient times. More recently, the peptides from the skin of frogs have been shown to inhibit the growth of cancer cells, and an alkaloid from the skin of the Phantasmal Poison Frog from Ecuador has produced a painkiller 200 times more potent than morphine. Not to mention the Gastric-brooding Frog of Australia, which as we will find out later, possessed a unique behaviour with potential implications for treating stomach ulcers.

Growing up in Scotland, my first introduction to amphibians was through folklore, and the characters that permeated popular culture in the forms of Kermit the frog, Mr Toad of Toad Hall from *Wind in the Willows* and the Frog Princess. Frogs in folklore often seem to be cast as fairly likeable characters, but toads have not fared so well. As Kathryn Phillips writes in *Tracking the Vanishing Frogs,* "This poor animal has been horribly maligned over the years by virtually everyone, credited with every evil known to man. In light of this history, it is almost surprising that there are any toads still alive." Even the father of modern taxonomy, Carl Linnaeus, was less than flattering when he penned the following account

The Solomon Islands Eyelash Frog, *Ceratobatrachus guentheri,* is one frog that skips the tadpole stage, instead laying eggs on the forest floor that hatch directly into fully formed froglets.

of amphibians in the 1750s: "Animals that are distinguished by a body cold and generally naked; stern and expressive countenance; harsh voice; mostly lurid colour; filthy odour; a few are furnished with a horrid poison." The most famous of the anthropomorphised toads has to be Mr Toad of Toad Hall – a narcissistic and impulsive character imprisoned for theft, dangerous driving and impertinence to the police. Mr Toad was concocted by author Kenneth Grahame to entertain his troubled son, Alastair, when he left home for boarding school. Instead of receiving letters from his father, Alastair would receive letters penned by Mr Toad – a device that Grahame used to shirk the responsibility of being an emotionally supportive parent. But the troubled Mr Toad, for all his character flaws is, underneath it all, a kind-hearted and ultimately loveable character that succumbs to bouts of remorse for his arrogant behaviour. Even toads, it seems, aren't all bad. And no, they don't give you warts.

But while fictional frogs and toads fuelled my childhood imagination, they bore little resemblance to my first real-world encounters in the neighbour's pond. It was the creatures themselves, not their fictional representations, that opened my eyes to the wonderful world of amphibians, and instilled in me a desire to dig deeper. I knew that to quench my curiosity I would need to venture beyond the manmade confines of the neighbour's garden. Setting was important, and in order to continue my journey I would need to become a visitor to their realm; to travel to a land of majestic mountains and squelchy bogs that had been sculpted over timescales that made my brain hurt. And so it was: I secured *A Field Guide to the Reptiles and Amphibians of Britain* and hummed with excitement at the prospect of exploring the remote reaches of the Scottish highlands. I wouldn't have long to wait.

⚬

Drumbeg, Scottish Highlands, July 1982

A fine drizzle blurs land and sky like a smudged canvas, as heaving mountains loom in and out of focus with every swish of a straining windscreen wiper. Clearly someone forgot to tell the weather gods that it is summer. But while the persistent drizzle would tempt many holidaymakers south to warmer climes, I am thrilled, for it is perfect for my mission. I wind down the window to breathe in the humid, peaty air and scan valleys strewn with tantalising bogs.

Our mauve Datsun Cherry car brims full of anything you could need for a couple of weeks in the Scottish highlands; we are prepared for rain, shine and everything in between. The whole family – my parents and two brothers – had bundled into the car before it spluttered out of our driveway in Edinburgh as night was falling some hours earlier. All plans to stay awake the whole journey were abandoned after 30 minutes as the burr of the engine and swish of the windscreen wipers overcame me like a potent sleeping draught, my head slowly nodding onto a rucksack bulging with nets, jam jars and other necessary hunting equipment.

But now I am wide awake – the rugged scenery too commanding to miss – as we wind along single-track roads hugging vertigo-inducing cliffs upon which waves crash a hundred feet below, running like spilt milk down the dark rocks to rejoin the sea. My heart races at the wildness of the land; the endless possibilities that stretch further than the eye can see. I pull out my well-thumbed field guide and it naturally falls open at illustrations of a strange and exotic creature accompanied by maps of where it may be found and descriptions of its habitat and behaviour. We are in newt country during breeding season. This fact seems to be lost on my family who stare out the window hoping for a crack in the clouds as I read aloud in an excited voice, "Males develop flaps on their toes and, most prominently, an undulating crest up to 10mm tall running down the length of the back and tail…" My brother nudges up the volume of 'Here Comes the Sun' to subtly drown out my unsolicited natural history lessons. Their indifference fuels my fascination, which becomes mine and mine alone, like a tightly held secret.

Eventually we pull into a rough farm-track that leads us to a small bleached-white house perched on a grassy hill. The Datsun stops with a creak and my mother turns round to address us before we disappear: "Don't forget to …." Clunk – the car door is already closed behind me as I run, scattering grasshoppers like spray from the bow of a boat, to the edge of the knoll. Here I stop to scan heather-dappled mountains plunging into lush, boggy vales. I can almost touch the sky; a low blanket of cloud forming a ceiling that is disregarded by mountains hell-bent on pushing skyward. A stiff breeze carries the sweet odour of damp bracken, and the air tastes cool and clean. I run back to the car, fish out my welly boots and rucksack bulging with jars and ice cream tubs. "Don't forget your…" my mother offers, but it is too late – I am barrelling down the hill in the direction of the peat bogs as fast as my gangly legs will carry me, wellies flapping as I run.

At the edge of the bog I stop. I watch as my breath dissipates as fine mist into moist air and admire unfurling fronds of lime green bracken dotted with a thousand tiny spherical mirrors. After a long moment I transfer my attention to a blanket of spongy moss under my wellies, and watch how the brown water, which looks like tea, seeps in and out like a miniature tide as I bounce up and down. I move slowly to the edge of a pool of open water

Smooth Newt, *Lissotriton vulgaris*, undulating towards the surface to gulp air.

and crouch to observe the reeds gently agitating the surface as they whisper in the gentle breeze, scattering ripples like radiowaves from tiny masts. A dragonfly glides into the scene, navigating its silent landing onto a reed. The sun cracks through the grey patchwork of clouds and glints off its paper-thin, translucent wings. I squint as a thousand lights bounce off the rippled water.

I sit and breathe slowly, as life unfolds in front of me, to take the pulse of the land. I pick out the distant calls of birds against the chirp of grasshoppers; if I listen closely I can hear the grinding of teeth as sheep slowly roll grass in their mouths on a nearby hillock; the occasional buzz of a passing dragonfly; the plop of some creature rising from the depths of the pond to gulp air. A stiff breeze mixes the sweetness of wet bracken, a wisp of fragrant heather and the subtle bitterness of peat. Clouds in a thousand shades of grey skit through the sky, sculpting the ever-changing light as it dances on the water and illuminating wings and stems.

I find mounds of frogspawn lumping at the edges of the pool, telling the story of the previous evening's eager chorus; I wish I could have been here to hear the sounds that must have filled the night air. Under the water's surface I see a pair of toads weaving black pearl necklaces around the reeds, performing a silent slow-motion dance.

My senses are alert as I scour the pond for a creature that has captured my imagination – the elusive and exotic cousin of the frogs and toads. An unusual movement and flash of colour catches the corner of my eye and I turn to see an orange ribbon undulating upwards from the depths of the peaty water. The flash of orange grows more vibrant as the creature rises until, breaking the surface, it takes a gulp of air before turning and disappearing, silently and as quickly as it appeared. That was it! A newt! My very first newt. I pull out my field guide and it falls open at the male Smooth Newt in dapper mating regalia. The dragonfly helicopters from its perch, leaving a stillness in its wake.

Over the next two weeks, and then every summer throughout my childhood, I roam the moors and marshlands of the Scottish highlands in search of frogs, toads and newts. Each year I eagerly await my exploration; each year I see the world through slightly different eyes. And each year the heartbeat of the wild, untamed land pulses through me a little stronger and the belief grows that, for those who are willing to stop and listen, the amphibians have something important to say.

♋

The seed planted, my childhood passion for frogs and newts grew into research projects on amphibians. First I swapped the moors of Scotland for the ephemeral pools of Trinidad, where I studied foam-nesting frogs for my Masters thesis, and then, under the inspirational tutelage of Dr Richard Griffiths, for the craggy limestone mountains of Mallorca where I measured thousands of Mallorcan Midwife Toad tadpoles to document a shape-shifting response to the presence of predatory snakes. I evoked the changes, from short fat tadpoles to long, thin turbo-tadpoles, over the course of weeks by dunking snakes in mesh bags daily into remote plunge pools, a behaviour we dubbed the Laurel and Hardy effect. I was on course to complete my metamorphosis into a researcher – to immerse myself in the world of callipers, spreadsheets, statistics and academic journals, but something was nagging at me like an insistent child tugging at my sleeve. As I learned more about what was happening to the amphibians I felt the urge to do something other than simply documenting it.

So what exactly *was* happening to the amphibians?

THE GREAT DISAPPEARING ACT

Monteverde cloud forest, Costa Rica, 1964

When biologist Jay Savage came upon a male Golden Toad in the elfin cloud forest of Costa Rica in the spring of 1964, he thought he was the subject of an elaborate practical joke. The two-inch long creature looked as if it had been dipped in a tin of paint the colour of a ripe Florida orange. And then there were the female toads, which were as different as they were striking in their own right, as bright scarlet spots jumped off an olive and black background. You could hardly invent a more striking pair if you were let loose with a bucket of frogs in a paint shop. The toad was, according to author Scott Weisenhaul, a "standout even among an order that includes psychedelically coloured poison-dart frogs and other eye-popping wonders". But far from being the subject of a hoax, Dr Savage had just discovered a new and extraordinary species confined to a single mountain ridge. Little could he have known at the time, but the beautiful toad was destined to become the poster child for an alarming global phenomenon.

⚬

Even more impressive than the sight of the Golden Toad was, by all accounts, the sight of hundreds of them – like tiny orange figurines – during their annual breeding frenzy. One of the lucky few to have been privy to this spectacle is field biologist Marty Crump. After several visits to Monteverde, and without ever seeing the toads, late one rainy night in April 1987 Crump heard pounding on her door. She opened it to find a wet but excited man by the name of Wolf Guindon, who said: "Marty, the Golden Toads are out. You've got to come see them!" Guidon was one of the 41 original Quakers who settled in Monteverde in 1951; he was also one of the first to ever see the toad in the 1960s, and his land was one of the first to be preserved to protect the toad in 1972. Crump had been waiting anxiously for this moment, and penned her diary entry of 6 April 1987: "I can hardly contain my excitement. I'm finally going to see the Golden Toads." The next day, after a cold, wet and downright miserable hike into the elfin cloud forest of Monteverde, she describes in her book *In Search of the Golden Frog* rounding a corner to be greeted by, "over a hundred dazzling bright

A male Golden Toad, *Incilius periglenes*, an impossibly bright orange species from the cloud forests of Costa Rica.

orange toads, poised like statues – jewels scattered about the dim understory." The cold and wet that had been seeping into her bones on the long muddy hike evaporated as she marvelled at the scene.

Almost a quarter of a century later the sense of wonder drips from every word as Crump recounts the experience for me. "I was absolutely floored the first time I saw those guys in the wild," she says. "I remember it was a miserable cold dark day in April. It was drizzling and I was *freezing* cold. We rounded the bend and here were all these glowing orange toads on the forest floor. They were glowing. I felt so fortunate to have been there. I loved it. I was just there, at the right place at the right time."

Like clockwork, the toads had been summoned from their underground retreats by the rains to indulge in an explosion of breeding activity that would span from a couple of days to, at most, weeks. The males, outnumbering females by up to 30 to one, were necessarily undiscerning in their choice of mates: if it moved, it was fair game. Even if a male fought and coaxed his way onto the back of a female, fatherhood was far from guaranteed, as he ran the gauntlet of being pried from her back by another male. There were no unwritten rules of loyalty here and the result was a writhing orgy of orange. At one point Crump describes seeing, "an orange blob with legs flailing" that turned out to be three males clambering around one female. The spectacle was, as Crump notes, "the ultimate for a field amphibian biologist". Any male that managed to cling on would remain attached for hours, sometimes an entire day, releasing his grip only after he had billowed sperm over a string of jellied eggs ejected like a train of sausages by the female below. Mission complete, the male and female would go their separate ways.

Crump counted more than 1,500 toads across five breeding pools in the spring of 1987, and estimated that 48,500 eggs were deposited in the pools that had formed around the dank base of trees stunted by a constant wind. But despite all the activity, nearly all of the eggs died before they developed as the pools dried up one by one. The weather was abnormally dry that year because of El Niño, a climatic fluctuation that occurs across the tropical Pacific roughly every five years. "The toads will need better luck next year," Crump concluded hopefully in her diary as she snagged a National Geographic grant to study their breeding behaviour over the next two years.

But luck was not awaiting the toads, nor Crump, the following year. After a long wait for the rains, on 21 May 1988, the first Golden Toad of the season appeared; a reddish-orange male perched beside one of the breeding pools. Wolf Guidon later spotted nine Golden Toads at a pool some three miles from the main breeding area, but the following week there was no sign of toads, eggs, nor tadpoles. It was a far cry from the breeding frenzy of the previous year, and it was the first year since discovery that the toads had skipped a breeding season. Crump was growing concerned – "a feeling of Golden Toad catastrophe" nagging at her. In a nearby site she had also noted that her beautiful yellow and black harlequin frogs had disappeared as suddenly and mysteriously. Along a stream at which she had found 700 the previous year, this year she saw not a single one. It was not a good year.

The following April, hoping once more for a reversal of fortunes, Crump hiked up to the elfin forests every day to catch the toads as they arrived. The bounce in her step became heavier with every successive outing. Although pools formed in the base of gnarled trees where they had been in previous years, they remained dark and silent. Other frogs, such as the beautiful and fragile glass frogs, were now also missing. Crump was mystified as she returned to Florida for a family emergency, leaving her graduate student Frank Hensley in charge. Then, one rainy day in mid May, Hensley was at the pool where Crump had found the lone male Golden Toad the previous spring when, out of the darkness, he made out a small orange figure. Less than three metres from where Crump had seen her last toad the previous year was a single male Golden Toad. The toad sat in an eerie stillness on the black soil until he also disappeared. He was the last Golden Toad ever seen.

In 2001 the International Union for the Conservation of Nature (IUCN), the authority on all things extant and otherwise, made the verdict official when it declared the Golden Toad extinct, and speculation swirled around the causes of its vanishing. Links were drawn between the disappearance of the toad and climatic fluctuations, making it the first terrestrial extinction to be linked to climate change. But something didn't quite add up. Amphibians are survivors; they have been around for hundreds of millions of years, and have made it through at least 60 glacial periods over the past 60 million years. It didn't make sense that the recent shifts in climate had pushed the Golden Toad over the brink single-handedly. Something else had to be at play. Far from being the end of the story, this was just the beginning.

Unbeknownst to Crump and colleagues at the time, the disappearance of the Golden Toad was an eerie echo of something happening on the other side of the world, and would be echoed further still across other parts of the world in the coming years and decades.

⚭

In May 1973, an Indonesian researcher named David Liem was visiting Australia when he found something in the wet rainforests of Queensland that Australians claimed not to have – a fully aquatic frog. Liem described the aquatic frog as *Rheobatrachus silus* (Rheo in Greek referring to its association with water, and batrachus meaning frog). Like the Golden Toad, it was locally abundant, with up to 100 frogs appearing along a stream on a single night of frog-hunting. Large protruding eyes and a short, blunt snout along with complete webbing of the toes were adaptations to a largely aquatic lifestyle – the frog was never found more than 4 metres from the water.

Although its aquatic lifestyle differentiated the frog from other Australian frogs, what truly stood this frog apart from all other frogs, and indeed all other animals, was a unique and bizarre way of producing offspring. It was about a year after the frog's discovery that the behaviour revealed itself. Two of the frogs were being kept in an aquarium in Brisbane when one day one of the frogs spat out a tadpole. No eggs had been seen in the tank, and so quite where this tadpole came from was a mystery. Mike Tyler from the University of Adelaide was contacted immediately to provide his frog expertise; his first reaction was that the species must be related to the Darwin's frog of Chile, which broods tadpoles in its throat. Upon further examination, however, Tyler found an entirely new way of reproducing.

The Southern Gastric-brooding Frog, *Rheobatrachus silus*, from Queensland, Australia.

The frog – promptly named the Gastric-brooding Frog – was the only animal in the world to develop embryos inside its stomach. In a behaviour reminiscent of the alien in the eponymous Ridley Scott film, the female would ingest around 40 ripe eggs, which would hatch into tadpoles to grow and develop in her stomach and emerge out of her mouth some weeks later as fully formed froglets. Scientists were baffled as to how this was even possible, and identified a compound in the jelly surrounding the eggs that switched off the production of hydrochloric acid, paralysed the muscles in the stomach wall and increased the number of small blood vessels. The compound effectively converted the stomach into a womb. Recognising the potential benefit to humans with gastric ulcers of understanding exactly how the compound was produced and activated, a team of researchers set their sights on figuring it out.

And then the research abruptly stopped.

The last living Gastric-brooding Frog (later renamed the Southern Gastric-brooding Frog) was seen in the Blackall Range of Queensland in September 1981, and the last captive specimen died in November 1983, a mere decade after the species was discovered.

But this was not the end of the gastric-brooding frog story. In January 1984 another gastric-brooding frog was found in the undisturbed rainforests of Eungella National Park in northern Queensland. It was a different species from the one that had disappeared, and was named *Rheobatrachus vitellinus* – the Northern Gastric-brooding Frog. Curiously, the Northern Gastric-brooding Frog did not display the same physical changes during reproduction as its southern cousin – while eggs were ingested in a similar way, hydrochloric acid production continued as normal and the muscle walls of the stomach were not paralysed during incubation. It is assumed that the eggs and young were protected from the acid by a mucous coating. But again, we may never know. Only eighteen months after its discovery, the Northern Gastric-brooding Frog was seen in the wild for the last time. Like the Golden Toad would do just a few years later, it disappeared without trace from a protected and pristine forest. With the death of the last individual went the opportunity to understand a unique behaviour and its implications for human medicine.

So what caused the two gastric-brooding frogs to vanish? Some attributed the decline of the frogs to climate change, but the suddenness of the disappearances was hard to explain by a gradual shift in climate. No drought or notable changes in the environment were detected – but there was one shred of evidence to suggest that something in the environment had played a role. A small colony of Southern Gastric-brooding Frogs in a laboratory in Adelaide survived for three years after the last individual was seen in the wild. There were also curious things happening to other frogs in Eungella National Park – the Eungella Torrent Frog disappeared alongside the Northern Gastric-brooding Frog, while other species in the same habitat were spared. The silent killer, whatever it was, appeared to be selective in choosing its victims.

⚘

The greater significance of the disappearance of the gastric-brooding frogs, the Golden Toad and the harlequin frogs of Monteverde was not immediately recognised by those who witnessed these events. This was in the days before things spun through the Twittersphere the minute they happened, and nobody was truly aware what was going on beyond the confines of their study sites until things were published in the scientific literature – a process that could take years. Nobody at the time was in a position to put the pieces together, or to see the storm that was brewing.

Until, that was, just months after the last Golden Toad was sighted in 1989, when the First World Congress of Herpetology brought together almost 1,400 herpetologists – the slightly unflattering name for someone who studies reptiles and amphibians – from 60 countries at the University of Kent in Canterbury. It was here that Crump, for the first time, shared her story about the Golden Toad to an international audience. And when she did, a curious thing happened. People started coming up to her in the hallways and conference rooms to share stories about their study animals. "I remember the moment of realisation," Crump tells me, "I'll always remember talking to Dave Wake (an eminent amphibian biologist from the University of California at Berkeley) and telling him of my frustration; I had been given this grant money by *National Geographic* and I had to produce results or I wouldn't get another grant. But the toads just weren't there. When Dave talked about his own observations in Central and North America things just clicked. It wasn't just my population." Wake had observed salamanders and frogs disappearing from Costa Rica, and had also witnessed the rapid decline of the Mountain Yellow-legged Frog from the pristine and protected lakes in the Sierra Nevada of California. I ask Crump how it felt the moment she realised that what she had observed may be one piece of a bigger phenomenon. "It was a combination of good and bad," she says. "On the one hand I realised I wasn't alone. It was somehow reassuring to hear others' stories – misery loves company. We loved our animals, so you really took their disappearance personally. But by far the strongest feeling was horror. A sense of 'what *is* going on?'" Frog by frog, country by country, a global picture was emerging, and it was alarming. Amphibians were disappearing, rapidly and without warning, from pristine and protected areas around the world. A mysterious and silent killer appeared to be acting quickly and decisively. Perhaps most alarming of all, nobody knew what it was or how to stop it.

⚬

Around the time that legwarmers were going out of style and Rick Astley was limbering his vocal chords for a denim-clad assault on the world of music, news of the alarming decline and extinction of amphibians hit the headlines. In a nifty piece of marketing the amphibians were likened to canaries in the global coalmine, sounding an early warning that something was wrong with our ecosystems. The analogy struck a chord with the public, and amphibians were cast as the bellwethers of ecosystem health. But some scientists were not so eager to adopt the analogy. As James Collins and Marty Crump point out in their book *Extinction in Our Times,* in order to designate a group as indicators of ecosystem health, you need to know exactly what they are indicating. The problem with the enigmatic decline of amphibians was that it was just that – enigmatic. Nobody knew exactly what it was indicative of. Others challenged the notion that amphibians, by disappearing, were acting as an early warning – suggesting that it was, in fact, a rather late warning for the amphibians that were already gone.

Canaries or not, early warning or late, it is true to say that amphibians are typically

30

sensitive to changes in the environment, and can be sentinels of environmental health. Their life in the realms of both water and land exposes them to a wide variety of environments, while their unprotected gelatinous eggs and moist, porous skin place them in intimate contact with those environments. Imagine if our lungs were spread across our skin – we'd likely be mindful of what we touch. In addition, amphibians rely on environmental temperature to regulate their own body temperature, making them vulnerable to abnormal fluctuations – this may be especially important for species inhabiting relatively stable environments like tropical cloud forests. Add to this the typically small range of many amphibian species, particularly in the tropics (the Golden Toad was only known from three square miles – some species are restricted to single streams), and it is not surprising that some consider amphibians to be sentinels of environmental change.

The sudden disappearance of amphibians jump-started the scientific community as they rose to the challenge of unravelling the mystery. A meeting of bright minds was convened in Irving, California, just five months after the Canterbury Congress, where 40 scientists hand-picked by Dave Wake, by now a leading figure in the quest for answers, pored over the reports of amphibian declines from Central, South and North America, Europe and Australia. They agreed that, although much of the evidence was anecdotal, it was sufficient to conclude that something very real and very serious was happening to amphibians. But as hard as they looked, they could find no compelling evidence for a single or consistent cause. Habitat destruction was highlighted as the most pressing threat to amphibians worldwide, but this could not explain the sudden and rapid disappearance of amphibians from protected areas. There had been unusual weather patterns in Costa Rica following El Niño; but again, this did not explain the rapid and simultaneous declines across the globe, and it was later concluded that El Niño was unlikely to have directly caused amphibian deaths. There was a big piece of the jigsaw puzzle that just seemed to be missing. A hidden threat seemed to be at large, and it was continuing to wreak havoc as its impact spread like lines of toppling dominoes.

The Irving meeting crystallised the focus of the herpetological community, now with its sights firmly set on unmasking the silent killer. Within a year the International Union for the Conservation of Nature had established a body called the Declining Amphibian Populations Task Force (DAPTF), with the mission to determine the causes of declines and promote ways to halt or reverse them. Over the following years the DAPTF provided seed grants to researchers and consolidated disparate shreds of evidence to advance our understanding of the scale and cause of declines and extinctions worldwide, which was by now being recognised by many, such as Peter Daszak and colleagues at the University of Georgia, as "perhaps one of the most pressing and enigmatic environmental problems of the late 20th century".

Over the following years the mystery would be unravelled slowly through a series of observations, experiments and coincidences pieced together by scientists around the world.

⚛

"I have been put in a unique position, to have seen the Before, and to have seen the After," says Dr. Karen Lips. She seems unsure of whether to count herself lucky or unlucky to have been in the right place at the right time – or the wrong place at the wrong time – to witness something quite out of the ordinary.

Karen Lips grew up in the small town of Jensen Beach in Florida watching sea turtles emerge to breed on beaches and scouring sun-baked scrub for Gopher Tortoises, Indigo Snakes and rattlesnakes. She relished growing up in a place so rich with unusual plants and animals and unique environments. But it was also a place that was changing fast, moving further from a pristine wilderness as development ravaged Florida from the coast to the Everglades and invasive species displaced native ones.

It was after graduation, during a one-year internship at Archbold Biological Station in Lake Placid, that Lips discovered the excitement of field biology and the allure of exotic rainforests as she lived vicariously through the experiences of the other interns. One girl she befriended had even seen the mythical Golden Toad in Monteverde; this, among other stories, seemed to make an impression on her. And so, drawn to the diversity and mystique of tropical frogs, Lips enrolled in a graduate programme in the lab of none other than Dr. Jay Savage who had, 24 years previously, been the first person to record the Golden Toad. This was also the year before the Golden Toad would be seen for the very last time.

Lips set about designing a basic research project on stream frogs in Las Tablas, one of the most remote and unexplored areas of Costa Rica, oblivious to events that were about to unfold. "In 1991 I moved into a four by four metre shack without electricity or running water located at the top of a mountain in the cloud forest," she says. She lived alone in this shack for two years to study the spectacular Spiny Treefrog. "I saw quetzals every day as they floated across the open pasture, showing off their long, green iridescent tails. I was stalked by Jaguars and Mountain Lions, and collected many new species of amphibians and reptiles."

In the winter of 1992, with mountains of precious data on the frogs of Las Tablas under

The Spiny Treefrog, *Isthmohyla calypsa*, from Panama, was Karen Lips' first study subject.

her belt and with a feeling that her research was going well, Lips returned to Florida for Christmas. She could not have imagined what was about to happen, nor could she have predicted the significance of the data she had collected so far. When she returned to her cabin in the woods in January, things had changed. "I had trouble finding enough frogs. It was a mystery," she says. She pondered the possible reasons for the lack of frogs – for she had a lot of time to ponder – and the only explanation she could come up with was that it was because the rains were late that year.

But it was not simply because of the late rains that the frogs had not showed up. They did not turn up at all that year, nor would they turn up several years later when Karen Lips returned to look for them under ideal weather conditions. She had just witnessed the rapid disappearance of multiple frog species from one of the most remote and pristine sites in Central America. And, like Crump several years earlier, she was flummoxed.

Lips had not planned on studying amphibian declines. "I was a first-year graduate student, and even the experts did not know what was happening, or the causes of these declines, where or when they might occur, or how to recognise them, much less how to study them." But like it or not, she had something worth its weight in gold, one of the missing pieces in the puzzle. She had data. Years of observations and measurements of the

Before and After. But she was missing one vital shred of evidence – without which it was like turning up at a crime scene moments too late to solve the case. That piece of the puzzle was corpses, for without bodies there could be no post-mortems, and with no post-mortems there could only be speculation about the causes of death.

At the time, Karen Lips could not appreciate the significance of all the measurements and observations she had scribbled in her fieldbook. She was living in a hut, trying to study frogs, and there were no frogs to study. And so, to continue her studies she decided to relocate, setting up camp at a nearby location in western Panama called Fortuna. She did not find the Spiny Treefrog in the new site – the species that had been the main focus of her study – but within the Forest Reserve she found more than 36 species in two days and concluded there would be plenty for her to study here. In 1995 Lips began her studies at Fortuna. Now with a full-time job in the US, she no longer lived at the site, and limited her fieldwork to summer and winter breaks.

It was around this time that Lips recalls telling Dr. Stan Rand, the resident herpetologist at the Smithsonian Research Station in Panama, that she had a hunch; that what she had witnessed at Las Tablas was the same thing that had happened to the Golden Toad and harlequin frogs in Monteverde. If the pattern continued – that is, if the disappearances were moving in a predictable path – then she expected them to show up soon in western Panama. But despite her hunch, she concedes that, "nobody was more surprised than I when, in December 1996, I returned to Fortuna and found dead and dying frogs along every transect". With the find came the missing piece of the puzzle: corpses. Lips and team moved fast, and in three weeks they hoovered up 50 dead frogs, which she sent to Dr. Earl Green, a veterinary pathologist at the US National Wildlife Health Centre in Maryland, to determine the cause of the deaths.

ஃ

Minnesota, USA, Summer 1995

In the summer before Karen Lips returned to Las Tablas, a group of schoolchildren were on a field trip to a local farm pond in Minnesota when they stumbled upon something quite bizarre. Lumbering in the shallows were frogs with between three and six legs; abnormalities so grotesque that their images were immediately splashed across worldwide news sites. Once the word was out, just as happened in Canterbury six years previously, it became clear that this was not an isolated case, and reports of deformed frogs flooded in

– the tally stands at deformities reported in 50 species of frogs in 44 states across the USA.

In *A Plague of Frogs: the Horrifying True Story*, journalist William Souder takes us on a detective hunt for the cause of the deformities. The initial obvious suspect was toxicity, but when public health officials tested the Minnesota ponds for toxic chemicals, they found none. They did confirm, however, that almost half of all the frogs they fished out of the ponds were deformed. Further scientific studies similarly found no significant relationship between toxicity levels and deformities.

Despite the wave of hysteria around deformed frogs that ensued after the Minnesota discovery, deformed frogs have actually been reported since the 1940s, and biologist Stanley Sessions as early as 1987 suggested that parasites are capable of causing amphibians to develop abnormally. Certain trematodes – also known as flatworm – live in the digestive tract of birds and transfer their eggs into the environment via the bird's faeces – these hatch into a stage called a mitacidium that infects some pond snail species. Having multiplied inside the snail, the parasite is released into the pond as a free-swimming stage. These free-swimming parasites can infect tadpoles, embedding near the developing hind limbs and forming a cyst that disrupts normal development. "It's about as close to using an egg beater on the limb bud cells as you can get," Sessions wrote in a *Science* report in 1999. Abnormal frogs are easy prey for birds – it's tricky hopping to safety with four hind legs – neatly completing the life cycle of the parasite. Tests in the laboratory confirmed that tadpoles could be stimulated to grow extra legs through infection, and it is generally accepted that trematodes caused the abnormalities found by the Minnesota schoolchildren.

But the case of the deformed frogs was not entirely closed. Some abnormalities have been found, like missing eyes, that are not consistent with the parasite explanation, and in areas without trematodes. Other culprits have been put forward that include radiation and agricultural chemicals. Nitrogen fertilisers could also influence the density of trematodes by increasing algal growth, which in turn results in more snails. Some recent studies have indicated that hot spots of grotesque deformities are shifting across the western United States, suggesting that the parasites may be moving in response to some environmental cues. "A lot of it is about what's underlying the change in parasite abundance," biologist Pieter Johnson told *National Geographic News* in August 2011, continuing, "I don't think this story is just about frogs."

Deformed frogs continue to appear across the United States, and research continues into the interactions between trematodes, amphibians and the environment – but in many ways the hysteria surrounding the grotesque twisted forms in the 1990s was a momentary distraction from the bigger mystery at play, for it did little to shed any light on what was driving the mass declines and extinctions of amphibians around the world.

⚛

Southern Ecuador, April 2007

As we pick our way up the banks of a small stream near Cuenca in southern Ecuador, Dr. Luis Coloma turns to me and says, "They used to be so abundant here, you would have to watch your step. Now, it is empty." Coloma is a stocky scientist with the demeanour of someone who has witnessed something profoundly sad. Born in the small town of Guaranda, in the shadow of the Chimborazo volcano in the Ecuadorian Andes, Coloma grew up playing on the shores of a crystal-clear river that ribboned through the town. He recalls finding glass frogs and an orange harlequin frog in the stream, early encounters that had a profound impact on the young Coloma and developed his relationship with frogs. "Promptly I fell in love with them and repeatedly they appeared in my dreams," he says. The orange Guaranda Harlequin Frog holds particular significance for Coloma, even today; it was the beauty and abundance of this animal that triggered his passion for frogs. But as Coloma was beginning his graduate studies in the late 1980s to become an amphibian biologist, the Guaranda Harlequin Frog suddenly disappeared from the banks of the river. Having witnessed its extinction, he would go on to describe it in 2002, an exercise he refers to as forensic taxonomy. "It was too late," he says. He would go on to witness the loss of more harlequin frogs.

Harlequin frogs – which belong to the genus *Atelopus* – are the jewels of the frog world, capturing the imagination of children like the young Coloma throughout Central and South America. The *New York Times* described them as "extraordinarily charismatic," a rare honour for a frog. Despite being true toads (often referred to as stubfoot toads), they are typically promoted to frog status on account of their slender elegance and colourful appearance; with yellows and deep blacks, reds and even purples competing for attention. And because toads are types of frogs, whereas frogs are not types of toads, it is not uncommon for herpetologists to use frogs when referring to both.

Of all the different types of frogs hopping through the forests of Central and South America, the harlequin frogs have been the hardest hit by the silent killer sweeping through their habitat. They feature prominently in stories of vanishing frogs told by Luis Coloma, Marty Crump and Karen Lips, from Ecuador to Costa Rica to Panama. Of 96 recognised

36

Dead frogs preserved in a jar of formaldehyde in the lab of Coloma and Ron in Quito.

National Geographic photographer Joel Sartore expesses delight at the prospect of tucking into a guinea pig in Ecuador.

species of harlequin frogs, more than 90 per cent are threatened with extinction and three quarters are classified by the IUCN as critically endangered.

I experience the loss of these beautiful frogs through the eyes and memories of Coloma and his colleague Dr. Santiago Ron, and feel the slow tug of sadness as I sit by silent streams and stare into empty pools. It is a strange nostalgia for a time and a place I will never know.

Back at the lab in Quito, Coloma takes me to a poster pinned to the wall: it is filled with illustrations of over a dozen species of striking harlequin frogs. "Extinct, extinct, extinct," he says as his finger moves from one frog to the next. He pauses, his finger hovering over a yellow and black harlequin frog. "Possibly extinct," he says, pausing as if mentally plotting his bid to find the frog. He is clearly not ready to give up hope entirely.

I find it galling to stare into jars of frogs that are now extinct, but the feeling does not compare to witnessing the demise of a beautiful creature with my own eyes, as I discover when I join Coloma, Ron and *National Geographic* writer-photographer team Jennifer Holland and Joel Sartore (working on their April 2009 story 'The Vanishing') on a quest to find a rare and beautiful yellow-and-black harlequin frog in southern Ecuador.

Road works hurl rocks and debris down a ravine into the last home of the Limón Harlequin Frog.

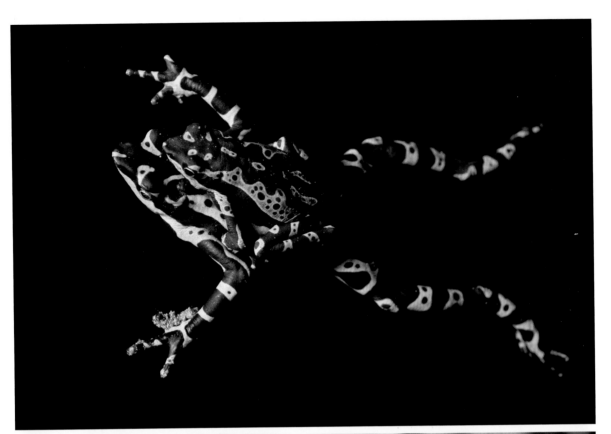

Limón, southern Ecuador, April 2008

It is a crisp and cloudless April morning as we set off from Quito to embark on the ten-hour drive to Limón. Our only stop is to sample guinea pig, or *cuy* as it is known locally, which tastes like a greasy, chewy duck with a hint of chargrilled hair (the buck-toothed head staring back at me will haunt my dreams for years to come). We roll into Limón after dark

ABOVE: *National Geographic* writer Jennifer Holland holds a Limón Harlequin Frog with a latex glove.

LEFT: A male Limón Harlequin Frog – a species new to science that has yet to be described – attempting to mate with a dead female below.

and find a very basic bed and breakfast (without the breakfast) in the small town.

I wake the next morning giddy with excitement; our destination for the morning is a small stream, the last known home of a harlequin frog that has yet to even be named. The stream is a short drive from the town, but as we round the final bend on our approach, our stomachs collectively turn. A cloud of dust kicked into the air by pneumatic drills obscures our view of a bulldozer tumbling rock and debris down the banks of a ravine. Coloma and Ron look pensive as they stop the vehicle and climb out, powerless to stop the tragedy that is unfolding in front of them. There is nothing for it but to see if any frogs have survived the assault on their home. We pick our way up the stream over flattened vegetation and branches. "Normally we would find half a dozen frogs in this stretch alone," says Ron. But damp spirits spike when we find one frog nestled in the nape of a plant – a beautiful and delicate frog, yellow mottled on black, it looks almost like a toy. It is a thrill to find a frog that I have waited long to see, but it is with mixed emotions that we make our way back down the stream, unsure of the brittle future of this incredible creature.

And this is when we happen upon the body. Her taut yellow and black skin is stretched

The Panamanian Golden Frog, *Atelopus zeteki*, is one beautiful species of harlequin frog which has disappeared from the forests of Panama.

42

over stiff outstretched limbs as she lies strewn in the shallow water, her mate clinging to her leathery body in a desperate attempt to hold onto something already lost. We take him back to the lab in Quito where he will live out his last days in a tank in an air-conditioned room. Two weeks later he will take his place among jars of pickled frogs that line dusty shelves. I scan jars of ghost frogs – species that blinked out of existence before they were even named, and 60 recently discovered species waiting to be named. Coloma pulls out a jar, stares at the contorted bodies, and tells us that this species went extinct in his hands. Here, I think to myself, is a scientist clearly dedicated to saving the frogs that coloured his childhood and breathed life into his dreams. "We're becoming paleontologists, describing things that are already extinct," Ron says.

જી

What had killed the Limón Harlequin Frogs? It seemed fair to conclude that the decimation of their habitat was playing a role, but without any signs of physical damage to the frogs there seemed to be another, more insipient menace at play. Coloma and Ron ran some tests that would confirm that it was the same silent killer that had likely pulled the trigger on Karen Lips' frogs in Costa Rica and Panama. The same killer, it would turn out, that was by now wreaking havoc across the Americas, Australia and Europe.

THE SMOKING GUN

Sequoia National Park, Sierra Nevada of California, August 2008

The packer – our guide for the next two days – slaps the brown leather saddle strapped to the back of a muscular tan and white horse. His thick moustache twitches as he drawls at us to "Climb aboard." A royal blue necktie frames his angular face, and cowboy boots curl from faded jeans. In the shade of a large cowboy hat, piercing blue eyes fix me with a look that says, "What are you waiting for?" as he holds the leather strap taut around the horse's neck.

I look anything but graceful as I attempt to mount the horse; positioning my right boot in the right stirrup I launch two false starts, my left leg making it to the top of the arc before coming back down to land on the same side, until the third hoist achieves enough momentum to swing it up and over the saddle. The packer is patient with me – he has clearly seen it all before. Dust billows between my fingers as I pat the thick neck in front of me and look down at the first horse I have sat on for 20 years; his sleek tan-and-white coat taut over a muscular frame. Butterflies flutter in my stomach as I mentally prepare for the day-and-a-half ride into the Sierra Nevada. All this way to find a frog. But this is not just any frog: the Mountain Yellow-legged Frog has gone from one of the most abundant to one of the most imperilled animals in the western United States in a matter of decades, and we have received reports that die-offs are currently sweeping through the lakes. I look round to see the *National Geographic* team of Jennifer Holland and Joel Sartore saddle up to continue our quest to unravel the mystery of the vanishing frogs.

Two packers lead the way as our train of horses and mules, laden with everything we will need for six days, snakes out of the stables. Light-hearted banter slowly subsides as the blazing sun – tipping the scales at 40 degrees Celcius – frazzles our sense of humour and our undercarriages begin to feel like punching bags. As we slowly climb into the mountains and further from civilisation I forget about my tender underside and focus on my horse as he navigates razor-thin rocky trails that drop off sharply on the side. As we enter more stable ground I soak in the splendour of Sequoia National Park.

Riding on horseback into Sequioa National Park and high into the Sierra Nevada.

After a long day in the saddle it is music to my ears when the packers announce that we will stop to set up camp. I dismount stiffly, aching in places I never knew I had, and pitch my tent in a clearing. Stretching my joints, I enjoy the evening light as it warms the mountains rising majestically in front of us.

Later that evening I look on enviously as the packers feast on grilled steaks washed down with cold beers while we scoop boil-in-the-bag 'Tasty Bites' out of foil bags with plastic sporks and wash them down with tepid water. Contrary to the name, the Tasty Bites are not particularly tasty and have as much bite as soggy cardboard. The spork, however, does live up to its name as a convenient cross between a spoon and a fork. All in all it is fair to say we look like amateurs next to the seasoned packers.

The following morning I lower tender skin onto a hard saddle as we continue our journey into the mountains. The discomfort slowly eases as the landscape grows increasingly rugged. We wade through rivers and climb past ancient, twisted trees into thinning air. Finally, the rocky path doubles back on itself as it winds steeply from the spectacular Rae Lakes for the final leg of our journey. I glance back to enjoy the train of horses weaving their way against a backdrop of snow-capped peaks thrusting from shimmering lakes into deep blue skies. The air is clear and crisp, the light golden.

It is the pristine setting that makes what happens next all the more jarring. As we crest the final climb into an area known as Sixty Lakes Basin, we are greeted by the sight of a deliciously clear lake the size of half a football pitch. We eagerly dismount our horses to splash cold water on our faces before ambling round the lake edges, circling mounds of snow spilling from the shadows. The tranquility of the scene is broken as Joel summons us urgently from the other side of the pool. I race round the pond to see the corpse of a frog, its pale belly and outstretched limbs shimmering beneath the surface. And then I see another. And then more; some half a dozen dead frogs hang like ghostly statues in the crystal waters.

"You should have been here last week. There were dozens of them," a husky voice surprises us from behind. I turn to see amphibian biologist Dr. Vance Vredenburg approaching to greet us. "This is Die-off Lake," he adds. Vredenburg is a young, charismatic

Packer and mule-train climbing into the Sierra Nevada with our gear for six days.

figure with reddish stubble and a lightly freckled skin weathered by the high elevation. He speaks passionately and with authority, for few know these lakes and what is happening here as well as he does.

Vredenburg, a professor at San Francisco State University, has been working since 1995 to unravel the mystery of the disappearing Mountain Yellow-legged Frogs. When he first arrived in the Sierra Nevada the frog was nearly ubiquitous in the high-elevation lakes, able to thrive in an environment that other frogs could not tolerate. The frog is in many ways the pinnacle of evolutionary design, pushing the boundaries of conditions tolerable by cold-blooded creatures. Adult frogs have adapted to spending harsh winters under ice by lowering their metabolism so much that, for nine months straight, they can go without food and live off the oxygen diffusing through their skin from the icy lake water. Tadpoles have adapted to spending two or even three winters under ice before leaving the pools as

froglets; this long, slow growth produces some of the largest tadpoles in North America, up to almost 10cm in length. The slow growth also means the frogs are long-lived – a Mountain Yellow-legged Frog can live for 15 to 20 years.

The frogs used to be so abundant in the high lakes of the Sierra Nevada that researchers would have to watch their step for fear of squashing them. But then, several decades ago, frogs began vanishing from many of the lakes. An early culprit in the declines was introduced fish. The lakes, historically fish-free, had been seeded with fingerling trout for sport fishing since the 1850s. Initially lugged in by mule, by the 1950s the fish were being dropped into remote lakes from airplanes. "Some missed," deadpans one of the rangers we meet as he describes scenes of fish flapping on the shores. Fish and frogs don't mix well, as fish eat tadpoles, and the fish started wiping out frogs from lake after lake. In response, fish stocking was stopped in the early 1990s in the national parks of Sequoia, Kings Canyon and Yosemite and fish were painstakingly gill netted out of some of the lakes. The frogs, given a second chance, came back and started to thrive again in the fishless lakes.

In 1997 Vredenburg and colleagues counted 512 thriving populations of the Mountain Yellow-legged Frog throughout the Sierra lakes. As Karen Lips had been in Costa Rica some six years previously, Vredenburg was in the right place at the right time to witness what happened next. Frogs started dying out, lake after lake, in a deadly wave sweeping through the Sierra. It was an echo of the silent killer sweeping through Central America and Australia. By 2009, 214 of Vredenburg's study populations were gone. Some potential culprits were considered – like pesticides blowing upwind – but they did not explain the extent or speed of the disappearances.

And then, one spring day in 2001, Vredenburg found the evidence he was looking for when he fished a tadpole that was lacking pigmentation around the mouth from one of the lakes. He ran some tests on the tadpole that confirmed his worst fears; the silent killer that he had heard about from Central America and Australia had reached the remote peaks of the Sierra Nevada. "I have to admit," he tells me later, "while I had heard about this killer wiping out populations in Central America and Australia, I didn't expect it to wipe out my study populations until I saw first-hand what could happen." In 2004 he witnessed his first die-off, as frog carcasses piled up in Milestone Basin, one of the most remote areas in

TOP LEFT: Climbing out of Rae Lakes on the final ascent into Sixty Lakes Basin, high in the Sierra Nevada.

BOTTOM LEFT: Early morning in Sixty Lakes Basin in the Sierra Nevada of California. A slow shutter speed was needed in order to avoid capturing mosquitoes in the shot.

Dead frogs shimmer ghost-like beneath the surface of the water in Die-off Lake.

California. It was a chilling reminder that nowhere seemed too remote or too pristine for this killer.

⚯

So what was it that was killing the frogs in Costa Rica, Panama, Australia and now California? A breakthrough in the investigation came in the mid 1990s when Dr Green inspected the carcasses sent to him from Panama by Karen Lips. Although he could not immediately confirm the identity, he found the same thing on the skin of every frog from both of Lips' study areas, and he could confirm that it was some form of infection. His first reaction was that it resembled a pathogen that had been killing oysters in Chesapeake Bay. He also proposed a mechanism by which the disease could cause rapid death in the frogs; by inhibiting respiration through their permeable skin. "We began to wonder if we had found the smoking gun," says Lips. And so, apparently, did the *New York Times,* which broke the news in a story on 16 September 1997 in an article entitled: 'New Culprit in Death of Frogs.'

Meanwhile, on the other side of the world, researchers had independently implicated a rapidly spreading disease in the decline of at least 14 species of frogs in the rain forests

The Mountain
Yellow-legged Frog
(*Rana muscosa*).

of eastern Australia. They suspected a virus, but when Dr. Green shared his images of the infections on the skin of the Panamanian frogs with an Australian pathologist, she was struck by the similarity to what she had seen on their frogs. Could it be that the very same disease was killing frogs thousands of miles apart in the forests of eastern Australia and Central America?

The short answer is: yes. Scientists quickly identified the pathogen as a fungus capable of causing a disease called chytridiomycosis. In 1999 the fungus was given a name: *Batrachochytrium dendrobatidis*, *Bd* for short. *Bd* – or chytrid as I shall refer to it from hereon – belongs to a group known as the chytrid fungi, of which there are around 1,000 species, but this was only the second species known to parasitise vertebrates (most chytrid fungi feed on dead and decaying organic matter, although one species is known to parasitise a fish). Chytrid acts by blocking the pores in the frog's skin, ultimately leading to death by cardiac arrest. Stream-breeding frogs living at higher elevations were soon identified as being particularly susceptible to the disease. Tadpoles such as that fished out by Vance can carry the fungus in their mouthparts like a ticking time bomb – as soon as they turn into frogs it attacks their skin and kills them. Time from infection to death depends on the dose and strain of the pathogen, the species and age of the frogs and environmental temperature among other things. What made this particular fungus different from any other before it was its devastating impact on an entire class of animals. The *Amphibian Conservation Action Plan*, a blueprint for action produced by the world's leading amphibian experts, characterised chytridiomycosis as, "the worst infectious disease ever recorded among vertebrates in terms of the number of species impacted, and its propensity to drive them to extinction".

So where had the fungus come from, and how had it spread among hundreds of species of frogs thousands of miles apart and separated by vast ocean? An Out of Africa hypothesis quickly emerged, pointing the finger at the African Clawed Frog as Typhoid Mary, the primary carrier of the fungus. The earliest record of the fungus was found on the skin of an African Clawed Frog collected in 1938 and preserved in the South African Museum, and at that same time the clawed frog was being shipped around the world as a human pregnancy test. While I could not recommend you try this at home, female clawed frogs will, within 8 to 12 hours of being peed on by a pregnant woman, produce eggs.

LEFT: A Park Ranger empties a net full of introduced trout in Sixty Lakes Basin. Attempts to eradicate introduced fish have been successful for some lakes.

Also, unlike rats, you do not have to cut the frogs open to see the results. The frog can also, it turns out, survive with the fungus in tow, making it the ideal carrier to ship it around the world. But the Out of Africa hypothesis had its doubters, and some suggested that the fungus originated in North America and was transported around the world by the American Bullfrog, while others claimed that Japan was the source. A paper just published at the time of writing again challenges the Out of Africa idea, reporting the presence of the chytrid fungus on the skin of frogs collected in Brazil as long ago as 1894 and preserved for the past 116 years as museum specimens. Recent studies led by Lee Berger of James Cook University in Australia indicate that the fungus may actually be a descendant of an ancient strain (at least 1,000 and as much as 26,000 years old) that has only recently escaped its niche thanks to globalisation.

☙

When the chytrid fungus was discovered in 1999, although it was clearly on the move, it had yet to be caught in the act of killing frogs, and much of its impact was speculative. And so the following year, armed with a hunch that it was spreading in a predictable wave through Central America, Karen Lips began plotting her move to catch the killer red-handed. In order to do this she knew she had to get ahead of the wave and wait. Unlike her first years in Costa Rica, when she was caught unawares, this time she knew exactly what she was doing. This didn't mean the mission was without challenges, however – the first of which was finding a suitable patch of pristine forest in the right area and with good access to monitor frogs in front of the wave. Lips later describes frustrating days spent driving into small towns that abruptly ended in pastureland, only to see forest off in the distance. Eventually, she found her site – Parque Nacional Omar Torríjos, a National Park above the town of El Copé in Central Panama. The forests paled in comparison with the pristine wilderness of Costa Rica, as monkeys and large mammals had been hunted out, and there were other challenges to contend with. "The road sucked. It was hot. And boy, those trails were steep!" But there was a small house where Lips and her team could sleep and store their gear; it was practical and it was where she needed to be. She also conceded that on clear days they were treated to a spectacular view of the Atlantic Ocean to the east and the Pacific Ocean to the west – it beat the view out of most office windows. They also found a staggering 74 species of amphibians in the area during their first surveys, including striking harlequin frogs and glass frogs.

And so, with her site chosen, she waited.

The view from our camp site in Sixty Lakes Basin.

Clouds of mosquitoes make head nets a permanent accessory during our time in Sixty Lakes Basin.

Vance Vredenburg scales a waterfall to search for salamanders in Sixty Lakes Basin.

Our packer enjoys a beer after the long journey down from Sixty Lakes Basin.

While Karen Lips was patiently waiting it out in El Copé, the first comprehensive assessment of 5,743 described species of amphibian was being conducted by some of the heavyweights of conservation: the International Union for the Conservation of Nature (IUCN), Conservation International and Natureserve, with input from scientists worldwide. The ambitious undertaking was appropriately called the Global Amphibian Assessment, or GAA. In late 2004 the results of the assessment were released, and they made for a sobering read. A third of known amphibian species were threatened with extinction – a further quarter were too little known to assess, and 120 species were believed to have gone extinct since 1980. "It was much worse than we expected," said Simon Stuart, who led the project. While the main threats to amphibians were identified as habitat loss, disease, pollution and invasive species, a large category of rapid declines – affecting some 435 species – was classified as "enigmatic." Although disease and climate change were implicated and interactions between the two suspected, the exact mechanism behind these declines had not been pinpointed. "Enigmatic-decline species have never previously been recorded at a level comparable to that currently observed in amphibians," said Stuart and colleagues when the findings were revealed in the high-profile scientific publication *Science*. Until the culprit behind these rapid declines was caught in the act, they would remain enigmatic.

At the time that the findings were released, Lips had been waiting for four years at El Copé – but her wait was nearing an end. It was September 2004 when she found a discoloured and lethargic frog – two of the clinical signs of chytridiomycosis. It was exactly what she had been waiting for. Within a matter of weeks, corpses were littering the forest floor. Over the following three months, Lips and team swept up 400 dead and dying amphibians, until there was nothing left to collect. "This, unfortunately, was the proof we were looking for that *Bd* was an invasive pathogen, spreading through naïve populations of amphibians from southern Mexico to Central America," she wrote afterwards. In her mind there was no longer any question. They had found the smoking gun, and with this she was able to chart the movement of the fungus from Costa Rica south through Panama over the course of the preceding years, at an average rate of 17km/year (in coastal Queensland the pathogen was estimated to have spread at a relatively speedy 100km per year).

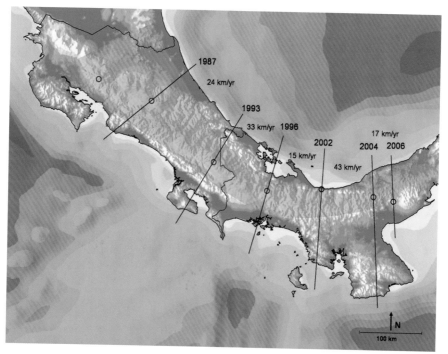

Map of Central American spreading wave (Wave 1) with date of decline (DOD) sites indicated along with rate of spread. DOD sites are indicated by open circles. Black bars indicate the hypothesised leading edge of the wave of chytridiomycosis in the year indicated.

How exactly was the fungus spreading? Nobody could be sure, but various theories emerged based on what was known about the fungus. A form of the fungus, called a zoospore, could propel itself through wet environments with a kind of tiny tail, like a microscopic tadpole. The zoospore could also survive in wet environments for several months, allowing it to travel via water, on the skin of amphibians or even on birds or flying insects. As long as it was moist and moving, the fungus could probably hitch a ride. And this seems to be what it was doing, continuing its relentless march through Central America, crossing the Panama Canal in 2007. This wave-like spread was also happening in other locations such as the Sierra Nevada of California.

Just as it seemed that the riddle had been solved, some prominent scientists voiced caution against jumping to hasty conclusions, noting that a pandemic pathogen wiping out otherwise healthy frogs was likely far from the end of the story. Some observations simply didn't fit neatly with the idea that a wave of disease was sweeping through new habitats and killing every frog in its path. Some species seemed to be more susceptible to the fungus than others and, even within species, individuals were responding differently. Why were some species, and some individuals, able to survive while others died around them? Simultaneous die-offs miles apart were being observed in Australia, suggesting that perhaps something else was at play. Rather than closing the case of the vanishing frogs, the suggestion that a novel pathogen hitting naïve frogs was the smoking gun invigorated scientists. The debate had only just begun.

⚇

Dr. Alan Pounds was a graduate student of Marty Crump's when he travelled in 1982 to Monteverde to start a research project on the Variable Harlequin Frog, *Atelopus varius*, that dotted the streams in the headwaters of the Rio Lagarto. Pounds planned to study the breeding habits of the harlequin frogs – for this frog certainly had a curious ritual. Male harlequin frogs would indulge in a frenzy of hand-waving (known as semaphoring) – as if directing planes onto a runway – to send a warning to other males not to enter their territory. Should a bold male ignore the warnings and cross an invisible threshold, the defending male would simply roll on top of them and pin them to the ground in a wrestling move reminiscent of Hulk Hogan, until they threw in the towel. Should it be a female that wandered into his territory, the male would instead grasp her behind her front legs and cling on for dear life until he had fertilised her eggs – a process called amplexus that could last for a week or more.

When Pounds turned up in Rio Lagarto in 1982, the beautiful yellow and black harlequin frogs were everywhere, decorating moss-cloaked boulders and peering out from crevices among rocks and tree roots, and so he set up camp and waited for breeding to commence. But he waited in vain – for the harlequin frogs never bred that year. After this disappointment, and fearing the onset of a disastrous research project with no data, Pounds switched his research focus to lizards.

Despite the rather ominous start to his research, Pounds was enamoured with Costa Rica, and in particular Monteverde, and so he stayed. He became involved in various research initiatives and over time became something of an authority on the area. In 1990, after the Golden Toad had failed to turn up to breed for three successive years, he was invited to reignite his interest in amphibians and look into its disappearance. He had been lucky enough to see the Golden Toad in the wild a few times, but he had never studied it – and its sudden vanishing intrigued him. And so, in the spring of that year, he began hiking into the forests of Monteverde to diligently check the Golden Toad breeding pools, but no toads turned up. He also went to check on the Rio Lagarto population of Variable Harlequin Frogs and they, too, had disappeared after the 1987 breeding season. Many other frogs – such as glass frogs – had also declined dramatically, and he set about seeking an explanation.

Pounds spent a lot of time thinking through different scenarios and discarding one theory after another. But there was a coincidence that he found hard to dismiss, and it involved the weather. Frogs, because of their porous skins and reliance on the environment for moisture, are somewhat at the mercy of the elements. The year that Pounds' harlequin frogs had failed to breed, 1982, was in the middle of El Niño (a periodic disruption to normal weather patterns that can result in unseasonable droughts and storms). The 1982–83 El Niño was one of the harshest on record, and Pounds and Crump had collected data at Rio Lagarto that showed that the harlequin frogs had been clumping together on the riverbank near waterfalls, a behaviour that frogs often adopt to conserve water. The following El Niño arrived in 1986–1987, the year the Golden Toads and harlequin frogs vanished. But it was, by all accounts, more moderate than the 1982–83 El Niño, and to Crump it still felt cold and wet. It simply didn't make sense that the frogs would survive the 1982–83 El Niño only to be knocked off by a more moderate fluctuation in 1987. Or did it?

Pounds began to pick apart the weather data for Monteverde in the hopes of finding a causal relationship with the disappearance of the frogs. With only 20 years of rainfall data available, he didn't have access to enough figures to run a long-term analysis. When

Crump sent him her data on the harlequin frogs of Rio Lagarto from 1987 he said, "It fit with the idea that something was terribly wrong." As he considered, and ruled out, many other theories, he kept coming back to the weather. In order to make sense of the data, he tried to "think like a frog", according to Kathryn Philips in her book, *Tracking the Vanishing Frogs*. He abandoned the human calendar – which means nothing to an amphibian – and instead defined seasons depending on rainfall or cloud mist that fell on the area; cycles that were more relevant to the frogs. Slowly he formulated a theory that he published with Crump in 1994 in *Conservation Biology*, in an article entitled 'Amphibian Declines and Climate Disturbance: The Case of the Golden Toad and the Harlequin Frog'. When the year was divided into four seasons based on precipitation, they reported, 1987 turned out to be the only year out of the past 20 with abnormally low rainfall in all four periods, and temperature anomalies reached record highs. "This climate disturbance, associated with the 1986–1987 *El Niño*/Southern Oscillation, was more severe than a similar event associated with the 1982–1983 *El Niño*, though this earlier oscillation was the strongest of the past century." But despite the severe climate disturbance, Pounds and Crump indicated that climate alone was unlikely to be the only culprit (amphibians have, after all, survived more dramatic climatic changes in their time on our planet), and offered two causative agents that could have colluded with climate to kill the frogs; microparasites and contamination. It was the best explanation based on available evidence at the time, for it would be another five years before the pathogenic chytrid fungus was discovered and implicated in the decline and extinction of amphibians in Costa Rica and Panama.

Upon its discovery, the chytrid fungus provided the missing piece of Pounds' theory. And so he revisited his data, plugged in this new information and, in 2006, published in *Nature*, the most prestigious of all science periodicals, an article with 13 co-authors (Crump was not amongst them) entitled "Widespread amphibian extinctions from epidemic disease driven by global warming." The title of the paper presented a bold claim that polarised scientists into a heated, and public, debate, and thrust amphibians headfirst into climate change discourse. In the manuscript, Pounds and colleagues presented a case that climate change and disease had conspired to spell the death knell for the Golden Toad and harlequin frogs of Monteverde. Pounds and colleagues analysed the last year observed for each harlequin frog species (Jason Rohr from the University of South Florida and colleagues later said this "represents perhaps the most comprehensive dataset on the timing of a modern day mass extinction within a single genus") against a number of possible factors. Four out of five missing harlequin frog species, they reported, had disappeared after a relatively warm year – the chances of this happening by coincidence were less than one in 1,000. Returning to the gun analogy, they proposed that, although disease was likely the bullet, it was climate change that had pulled the trigger – supporting what was being called the "climate-linked epidemic hypothesis." They concluded with "very high confidence that large-scale warming is a key factor in the disappearances." In an essay entitled 'Clouded Futures', Pounds and Robert Puschendorf offered a mechanism, suggesting that climate change could hamper amphibian defences against the fungus to pull the trigger on sick frogs.

A media-frenzy ensued, as outlets from the BBC to *The New York Times* reported that global warming was the driver of global amphibian declines, leading to controversy among eminent amphibian scientists. Some voiced concern about drawing such bold conclusions from the available evidence. Amphibian biologist Cynthia Carey said that the paper "failed to offer anything beyond circumstantial evidence". (Carey did, however, warn in a previous manuscript that changes in climate would pose challenges for surviving amphibians.) Stanford University climatologist Stephen H. Schneider, who had collaborated on the study, acknowledged that uncertainties remained. But few were more vocal in their disagreement with Pounds and colleagues' conclusions than Karen Lips who, two years after the paper by Pounds *et al* was published, co-authored a reply that ripped into their analysis of the available data, reporting that, although "climate change seriously threatens biodiversity and influences endemic host-pathogen systems," the authors found "no evidence to support the hypothesis that climate change has been driving outbreaks of chytridiomycosis." Lips and colleagues questioned the use of 'last year observed' as a proxy for date of disappearance of a species, and used instead the 'year of population decline' (including only species for which there was good data on the year of population decline) because, they suggested, this was a more accurate representation of the arrival of the amphibian chytrid fungus at a location. Analysed in this way, Lips and colleagues reported that the data supported the "spatio-temporal spread hypothesis", concluding that chytrid-related declines were caused by several discrete introductions of the exotic pathogen and its subsequent wave-like spread through naïve populations – not, as Pounds and colleagues had claimed, because of any interaction between chytrid and climate change.

In a November 2008 review evaluating the links between climate and disease in amphibian declines, Jason Rohr from the University of South Florida and co-authors addressed "unsettled controversy and possibly misconceptions over the causes of these declines," with a review of the data analysis presented by Pounds and subsequently attacked by Karen Lips. Rohr and co-authors acknowledged that the correlations between harlequin frog extinctions and mean tropical air temperature in the previous year presented by Pounds and colleagues were valid, but warned that correlation does not necessarily equate to causation, highlighting their point with the observation that regional banana and beer production were better predictors of the frog extinctions than temperature. Picking apart correlation from causation requires careful analysis and prudent interpretation of results, making research into the respective roles of climate change and disease in driving extinctions challenging. Rohr and colleagues concluded that "although climate change is likely to play an important role in worldwide amphibian declines, more convincing evidence is needed of a causal link".

So what evidence is there of a causal link between climate change and amphibian declines? In 2007, the year sandwiched between Pounds' and Lips' opposing papers, the findings from a long-term study of frogs and lizards in Costa Rica revealed that both groups had experience precipitous declines over the preceding 35 years. An amphibian-specific disease alone could not be solely responsible. The authors, although perplexed by the findings, proposed a mechanism that could ultimately be traced to global warming – a gradual reduction over the years in the amount of leaf litter on the forest floor. Simply put, in response to rising temperatures, trees held onto their leaves longer and decomposition rates were faster, leading to less leaf litter for the frogs and lizards to live in.

In Australia, Ross Alford and colleagues at James Cook University presented evidence based on a study that involved meticulously measuring treefrogs to look for signs of stress (which manifests itself in asymmmetrical development) in response to climate change. And they found it, some two years before chytrid-related declines were observed. Their findings, discussed in the same volume of *Nature* in 2006 as the article by Pounds and colleagues, lent support to the idea that climate change could be the trigger, with disease the bullet, in the disappearance of some frog species. They also noted that "the earliest possible arrival date of [the fungus] in north-eastern Australia is completely unresolved", and that El Copé is probably the only locality in the tropics for which a clear link between the arrival of chytrid and the decline of an amphibian fauna has been shown. With new techniques now available with which to detect the fungus in old museum specimens, it may soon be possible to fill in this piece of the puzzle.

Further support for the role of climate in triggering losses came from scientists in Italy who detected the chytrid fungus in pool frogs as far back as 1999; they appeared to live quite happily alongside the fungus until a Europe-wide heatwave in 2003 coincided with die-offs. The authors of the study concluded that stress probably raised the susceptibility of the frogs to the pathogen. More recently, in August 2012, a study by Thomas Raffel and colleagues from Oakland University supported the idea that unpredictable fluctuations in temperature could decrease frog resistance to the fungus. The fungus, as a simpler organism, they said, was able to adapt faster than the frog's immune system and stay one step ahead of the game. In 2013 the International Union for the Conservation of Nature (IUCN) released a report indicating that 670 to 933 amphibian species (11 to 15 per cent) – a higher percentage than birds and corals, the other groups analysed – were both highly climate-change vulnerable *and* already threatened with extinction on the IUCN Red List.

Evidence continues to accumulate for both the impact of climate change and the impact of disease on amphibian populations, and the interaction between the two remains an active area of research. It is clear that disease dynamics are influenced by a multitude of interacting factors that relate to the host, the pathogen, the environment and climate, and deciphering these, especially after a species has gone extinct, is rarely straightforward. The controversy that erupted following the 2006 publication by Pounds and colleagues polarised scientists eager to defend one hypothesis or the other, and threatened to distract from the urgent need to do something to save the hundreds of species that were disappearing. Amphibian biologist Ross Alford of James Cook University in Australia said that "arguing about whether we can or cannot already see the effects is like sitting in a house soaked in gasoline, having just dropped a lit match, and arguing about whether we can actually see the flames yet, while waiting to see if maybe it might go out on its own". And so, without further ado, let's get back to the subject of extinction and what can be done to avert it.

CHAPTER 4

THE GRAND CURTAIN OF LIFE

*"There will always be [passenger] pigeons in books
and in museums, but these are effigies and images,
dead to all hardships and to all delights. Book-pigeons
cannot dive out of a cloud to make the deer run for cover,
or clap their wings in thunderous applause of mast-laden
woods. Book-pigeons cannot breakfast on new-mown
wheat in Minnesota, and dine on blueberries in Canada.
They know no urge of seasons; they feel no kiss of sun, no lash
of wind and weather. They live forever by not living at all."*

ALDO LEOPOLD

Edinburgh, Scotland, 1982

As I was learning more about the frogs in my grandparents' garden, my interest was piqued in the incredible diversity of life that once lived alongside the frogs but was now gone. Mesmerised by the thought that some of these life forms were still preserved in stone, when I turned seven I formed a rather exclusive group called the 'Fossil Club' with my across-the-street neighbour Neil. Once Neil and I tired of our attempts to connect our back gardens with a secret underground tunnel, we turned our attentions to digging up the flowerbeds with hand trowels in search of remnants of long-lost species. You may be surprised to learn that we never found any. Call it cheating, but when I learned that there was a shop in Edinburgh called Mr Woods' Fossils, I took the easy route to acquiring my preserved dinosaurs. With my 50-pence weekly pocket money I was able to buy an ammonite curling from a rock and an armoured woodlouse-like creature called a trilobite. The creatures took pride of place on my bedside table and were the perfect petrified pets; easy to care for representatives of a lost world. I was fascinated with creatures that no longer were, and my imagination ran riot with the idea of living in a world with trilobites and ammonites. At the time, extinction was something I associated with creatures long gone and far away.

In order to be one of two active members of the Fossil Club I had to brush up on the subject of fossils and dinosaurs. I learned that 99 out of every 100 animal species to have roamed the earth were now gone; and only a fraction of these were preserved as rock forms like my trilobite and ammonite. I learned about five mass extinctions, triggered by cataclysmic events such as meteorites and ice ages, that had wrung species out of the earth as though it were spring-cleaning; the most recent bringing about the end of the dinosaurs and half of all other species some 65 million years ago. I learned that the amphibians had made it through the last four of those mass extinction events; they were the survivors of the planet. This discovery fuelled my fascination for these curious creatures – they became, in effect, living dinosaurs. But what I did not learn was that I would live to enter what many scientists would refer to as the sixth mass extinction on earth (a 2011 study in the journal *Nature* concluded that if all species listed as threatened on the Red List, maintained by the International Union for the Conservation of Nature (IUCN), were lost over the coming century, and that rate of extinction continued, we would be on track to lose three-quarters or more of all species within a few centuries – such rapid loss of species has occurred only five times in the past 540 million years). I did not know that at the forefront of that mass extinction event would be the biggest survivors of them all – the amphibians. I did not know that when my son would read about extinction it would not just be about dinosaurs and Dodos, but about animals that had taken their last breath within his own lifetime. With every passing year, my perception of extinction changed with the reality of the world in which I was living.

What we see now is a snapshot in the great unfolding dynamic that is life on earth. It is a vastly different snapshot to that of 100 million years ago, and different to the one that will be seen in 100 million years. Against a backdrop of such change, why should we give more than a passing thought to the loss of a species? Well, for the past 65 million years, from when the dinosaurs blinked out of existence up until last century, the earth was losing species at a rate of around one species in a million every year. To put this in context for amphibians, that equates to one species going extinct every 143 years. In the past few decades, thanks to changes brought about by one species, the rate of loss has accelerated to some 100 to 1,000 times this background rate.

So how do we know when a species has gone extinct? How can we really be sure that the last individual has drawn its last breath? The authority on all things extant and extinct, the IUCN, declares an animal or plant extinct when "there is no reasonable doubt that the last individual has died. A taxon is presumed extinct when exhaustive surveys in known and/or expected habitat, at appropriate times (diurnal, seasonal, annual), throughout its historic range have failed to record an individual. Surveys should be over a time frame appropriate to the taxon's life cycle and life form". Proving beyond reasonable doubt errs on the side of caution, and it is likely that the 754 species of animals declared extinct since 1500 is an underestimate of the true loss. Occasionally, however, creatures that have been determined beyond reasonable doubt to be extinct can also prove us wrong – but to this, we shall return later.

᪥

How we respond to the loss of another species on our watch reveals much about our own species. In a poignant article, 'Grief for our Lost Species,' Lorna Howarth writes: "Where were the poets, the visionaries and the artists when 'the Goddess of the River' – the Yangtze dolphin – vanished in China, never again to show her ethereal self from the murky waters of her home? Only empty radio static was picked up by the underwater microphones tracking her movements – her playful spirit gone forever, our concern too late to save her. But humanity did not grieve the passing of this evolutionary miracle." The last Yangtzee River Dolphin Qi Qi (pronounced *chee chee*) died of diabetes and old age in 2002 after being in captivity for 22 years – his funeral was broadcast on national television.

Looking back at the roll call of species that have gone extinct in the past century, I am struck by how many of the last known survivors of the species were captured and taken into captivity to live out their final days behind bars or glass. Is it that by taking these last individuals into our care and humanising them with names like Qi Qi, Martha or Benjamin, we are able to more easily mourn their passing, bestowing a shred of dignity to a magnificent animal that no longer is? Or is it that by taking care of these animals we can appease our conscience with the illusion that we did everything in our power to save them? The final breaths of so many species, drawn through bars, are rarely as dignified as one would hope for the last of a kind. So why do we insist on making these creatures live out their last days on a cold concrete floor while in the wild the species slips out of existence? Is it that we simply don't appreciate these animals until after they are gone?

Consider Martha, the last living Passenger Pigeon, named after US First Lady Martha Wilson, wife to President Woodrow. The Passenger Pigeon was once the most abundant bird on earth, darkening skies as millions flocked across North America. It is easy to see how such abundance could be taken for granted as farmers shot them out of the skies in their thousands. But on 1 September, 1914, as Martha drew her last breath aged 29 in the Cincinnati Zoo, the species ceased to exist. After her passing, Martha was sent to the Smithsonian where her body was stuffed and displayed (it has since been removed), but decades passed before a memorial was erected in her honour in the grounds of Cincinnati Zoo. Did it really take this long to appreciate the loss of a bird that once filled the skies? Martha's last days were later lamented with a beautiful ode by bluegrass singer John Herald, appropriately titled, 'Martha: Last of the Passenger Pigeons'.

Oh high above the trees and the reeds like rainbows
They landed soft as moonglow
In greens and reds they fluttered past the windows

Till the hungry came in crowds
With their guns and dozers
And soon the peace was over
God what were they thinking of?

Oh the birds went down
they fell and they faded to the dozens
Til in a Cincinnati Zoo was the last one

Yes all that remained was the last
with a name of Martha
Very proud, very sad, but very wise

Oh as the lines filed by there were few who cared
or could be bothered
how could anyone have treated you harder
and it was all for a dollar or more

Oh on and on til dreams come true
you know a piece of us all goes with you

Oh and surrounded there by some of whom wept around her
in a corner of the cage they found her
she went as soft as she came so shy til the last song
oh the passenger pigeon was gone...

Four years after Martha's passing, on 21 February 1918, in the very same aviary cage in which Martha had died, the last living Carolina Parakeet (North America's only truly indigenous parrot), Incas, drew his last breath. Incas died within a year of his mate, Lady Jane, and some 14 years after the last wild individual was killed in Florida. No efforts were made to breed Incas with Lady Jane, however, as nobody was aware that these were the last living Carolina Parakeets; the parakeet was not officially declared extinct until two decades later, in 1939. The bird was driven to extinction by a number of factors that, like the Passenger Pigeon, included being shot by farmers who considered them to be crop pests. The tendency of the parakeets to immediately flock back to gather around recently wounded and dead members of their flock expedited their demise, as farmers waited with shotguns cocked for them to return. Compassion, it seems, did not serve the parakeets well.

A sadly undignified end also became the last officially living Tasmanian Tiger, or Thylacine (the largest known carnivorous marsupial of modern times, whose scientific name, *Thylacinus cynocephalus*, is Greek for 'dog-headed pouched one') who died in Hobart Zoo on 7 September, 1936 when he was locked out of his sleeping quarters on a freezing night. An article written by a zoo employee by the name of Frank Darby in 1968 talks about how the Thylacine was affectionately named Benjamin. It later transpired that the zoo never had an employee by the name Frank Darby, and the Thylacine was never actually called Benjamin. It is even unclear as to whether Benjamin was male or female (no genitals are visible in video footage of the animal – but male Thylacines had a curious party trick of being able to retract their scrotums into a pouch and out of sight). Regardless, the name Benjamin stuck. So why did this impostor come forward with this story some three decades after Benjamin's death? Was it an attempt by Darby to posthumously bestow a shred of dignity on the last survivor of a unique species? In some respects it may have worked, as Benjamin is now commemorated every year in Australia – since 1966, National Threatened Species Day has been held annually on the day of his (or her) death.

There is a common thread in the deaths of Benjamin, Incas and Martha; in each case, decades passed before the loss of their species was recognised or commemorated. Did this reflect a growing concern in society for life other than our own, or did it reflect the time it took for the cachet of extinction to elevate the perceived value of these species and embed them in the public conscience? I suspect it may be a bit of both. Recently, the Passenger Pigeon, Tasmanian Tiger, Woolly Mammoth and gastric-brooding frog have been in the spotlight because of plans to bring them back from the dead – something that, thanks to advances in genetic technology, is looking like a very real possibility. Although de-extinction, as it is known, is a fascinating concept with undeniable allure, and sounds on the surface like a noble pursuit, these programmes are often fuelled more by the ambitions of the creators than by a genuine ecological, evolutionary or moral rationale for bringing back the animals from the dead. The practice does nothing to address the root causes of extinction, and raises many ethical and philosophical questions. Is an artificially produced gastric-brooding frog or Tasmanian Tiger really the same animal as that which evolved over millions of years within a dynamic ecosystem? How has that ecosystem changed since its disappearance? Just because we can bring something back, does that mean we should? While it is of course not a zero-sum game (that is, the funds invested in de-extinction may not otherwise be directed to conservation), investing millions on bringing back a particular frog, bird or mammal while hundreds of other species, such as the Yangtzee River Dolphin and Golden Toad, are slipping out of existence under our noses still seems, in many ways, perverse.

Most extinctions on our watch could have been avoided had swift action been taken while the creatures were still among us. The Thylacine was hunted out of existence and the Passenger Pigeon and Carolina Parakeet were shot out of the skies. The Dodo, unable to fly to freedom on the island of Mauritius, was clubbed to death by hungry Dutch sailors and set upon by their domesticated animals. The Yangze River Dolphin succumbed to a lethal cocktail of electric fishing, collisions with boats and ships, habitat loss and pollution. It's fair to say that had these threats been curbed in time, each of these species could have probably been saved. Knowledge of what is driving a species to extinction empowers us to take action. We can regulate hunting or establish protected areas to safeguard core habitat for threatened species; we can reduce pollution or control electric fishing. And in recent decades our efforts to curb these threats have grown with our concern about the havoc we are wreaking on the planet.

But in 1989, something happened that challenged the notion that extinction could be avoided with appropriate and timely action. All of a sudden, species across the world were disappearing, in the blink of an eye, from pristine and protected areas. And not just one or two species; hundreds of species that were protected from habitat loss, hunting and collecting were vanishing. Traditional approaches to conservation were, it seemed, not enough. The question loomed large: what *could* be done to save the amphibians?

To find out, I caught up with some of the scientists and conservationists at the forefront of the extinction wave.

∽

Sixty Lake Basin, Sierra Nevada of California, August 2008

As we stare with disbelief at the carcasses, ghost-like in the crystal-clear water, Vance Vredenburg rises to his feet and says with a glint in his eye, "Follow me." He bounds down a rocky trail like a mountain goat as we gulp for breath in his wake. Eventually we reach a pond a quarter of the size of Die-off Lake, and as we approach the edge a frog jumps out from under our feet and splashes into the water. It is a plump Mountain Yellow-legged Frog. Vredenburg skirts the edge of the pool with a large dip-net fishing out one Yellow-legged Frog after the next, plopping each into a white bucket. Their shadows bounce up and down the sides as they make a bid for freedom, and the metal handle rattles with the movement. Satisfied that he has collected enough, Vredenburg walks back round to join us, places the bucket on the ground and sits beside it. He snaps a latex glove onto his right hand before reaching into the bucket and pulling out a frog, his fingers wrapped snugly around its bulbous waist. With concentration that makes the veins on his forehead bulge, he rests the frog against his knee, pulls out a syringe and carefully injects something behind its head, oblivious to a large mosquito feeding on his temple. "It's a pit tag. A kind of barcode," he says, pulling out a scanner to read the frog. I feel as though I am in a James Bond film. "This way, I can track each and every one of the frogs," he adds. "And these ones, they are doing well." Before plopping the frog back into the water he pulls out a cotton bud and runs it across the bulging thighs of the frog. Back in the lab he will be able to test the sample for the presence of the chytrid fungus.

High in the pristine mountain lakes of the Sierra Nevada, Vredenburg is taking an unconventional approach to protecting these Mountain Yellow-legged Frogs from meeting the same fate as those in Die-off Lake. He is bathing them. By immersing them regularly in an anti-fungal bath he is able to clear individual frogs of infection within days. It is a labour-intensive way of keeping the frogs alive, for if he were to stop bathing them the frogs would likely succumb quickly to the fungus. But it is a way of buying time while he and colleagues steer their research to secure a more permanent future for these frogs. As Vredenburg explains, the key is keeping the animals alive long enough to allow them to

TOP RIGHT: Vance Vredenburg swabs the thighs of a Mountain Yellow-legged Frog to test for the presence of the chytrid fungus.
BOTTOM RIGHT: Vredenburg injects a microchip to allow him to track the progress of the frog.

mount an immunological defence to the pathogen. "The long-term survival of the frogs will require changing the dynamics of the disease and how it impacts them," he says, before looking up, "the fungus is here to stay."

✂

With the Mountain Yellow-legged Frog, Vredenburg has had the luxury of a widespread and formerly abundant species to study – the species continues to be a model for testing novel approaches to combating the fungus. But further south in Central America the fungus was bearing down on frogs restricted to tiny patches of forest or dotted along individual streams. In order to save dozens of species from imminent extinction in Panama, scientists opted for a more dramatic approach than anti-fungal baths.

After Karen Lips caught the fungus in action as corpses littered the forest floor in El Copé, she predicted that it would continue to move south and reach El Valle de Anton – in the bowl of an inactive volcano – in central Panama in 2006. Given the chilling accuracy of Lips' previous prediction, scientists were faced with an opportunity and a challenge to save frogs from imminent extinction ahead of the wave. And so, an army of volunteers led by Ron Gagliardo and Joe Mendelson of Zoo Atlanta headed into the jungles of El Valle. They collected frogs in their dozens and kept them in a rented house with piles of rotting fruit in the corners to attract flies for frog food. "It was pretty stinky," confirmed Gagliardo.

The Lemur Leaf Frog, *Hylomantis lemur,* from Panama.

Crowned Treefrog, *Anotheca spinosa*, Panama.

Without permanent accommodations in place, some of the frogs were airlifted to the safety of Atlanta – a journey that caught the attention of the *New York Times*, which published an article entitled "To stem widespread extinction, scientists airlift frogs in carry-on bags." "When you can make predictions with respect to catastrophic population declines and extinctions, we all agreed you have a moral and ethical responsibility to do something about it," Mendelson told the author of the article, adding: "We are going to over-collect hundreds of animals. That flies in the face of all conservation logic."

Meanwhile, a facility was frantically built close by to house the rest of the accumulating Panamanian frogs. The facility soon housed dozens of rare species, some extinct in the wild, with the hope that one day the frogs could be returned to the forest. In the controlled environment of the Panama facility and Zoo Atlanta, infection from the chytrid fungus was kept at bay by keeping the frogs warm. But back in the forest, the fungus waited like a death trap. Although many species of fragile frogs had been snatched from the jaws of extinction, the question loomed: What next? Would the frogs ever be able to return to their natural environment, or would they be consigned to live out their last days in cages, like Benjamin, Martha and Incas?

Two scenarios began to emerge under which the frogs could eventually be returned to the wild; either the fungus would have to be eradicated from the environment, or the frogs would have to be able to live alongside the pathogen. With no feasible way of eradicating the fungus from the environment, attention turned towards finding out what would enable frogs to live with the pathogen. As research began in earnest, the story of the vanishing frogs took an unexpected twist.

CHAPTER 5

LAZARUS FROGS

Cajas National Park, Ecuador, April 2007

I am on a quest with Ecuadorian scientists Luis Coloma and Santiago Ron to find two harlequin frogs that have not been seen for two decades – feared victims of the deadly chytrid fungus that had already swept through southern Ecuador. It is my first search for lost frogs, and I have little idea of what to expect. It feels like an incredible long shot that we will find either, but I am drawn to the challenge and even the slightest chance of seeing a harlequin frog in the wild. Our first target is the Black Cajas Harlequin Frog. It seems a fitting place to start; the frog was named *Atelopus nanay* by Luis Coloma in 2002 to represent the loss of frogs throughout the Andes for, in the native language of Quechua, 'nanay' means sadness. The small black frog, last seen in 1989, is a totem of nostalgia for Ecuador's lost amphibians.

We set off along thinly-marked trails through shaggy windswept grass on the high mountain passes of Cajas National Park. On either side, mountains retreat into the distance and lakes shimmer in the valleys way below – a more majestic and remote setting would be hard to imagine. The thin air whips my flushed cheeks, and my head pounds with each footstep as altitude sickness kicks in. Before embarking on our hike I had inquired about obtaining coco tea to overcome the sickness I knew I would begin to suffer from almost three miles above sea level. "You can't get coco tea here," I was told. "Take this instead," Coloma had said as he handed me a bottle of rum. He seemed serious, and so I stuck it in my bag.

A couple of hours into the hike we establish that everybody thought that somebody else was bringing food, and so instead of lunch we sit and pass round the bottle of rum. Soon I am unsure whether the pounding head and increasing dizziness is a result of the elevation, the rum, or a cocktail of the two. And so I take another swig and keep going. A couple of hours later we realise that our destination is further than we anticipated and we stop to take stock. If we continue we will not make it back by nightfall, and the chances of finding an offer of a bed are slim. The group is reluctant, having come this far, to turn back, but the decision is made to do just that.

The Black Cajas Harlequin Frog, *Atelopus nanay.*

On our return we meet a local woman carrying a large bag of beans on her head, on a walk that will take from sunrise to sunset to sell her beans at market (I am amazed to learn she will only make a couple of dollars for this effort). We offer to give her a lift once we reach our vehicle at the entrance to the Park, and she gladly accepts. The conversation turns to our reason for being out here, and we ask if she has seen a small black frog in these parts. To our surprise, she nods, before convincingly describing the Black Cajas Harlequin Frog. "And they are still there?" asks Ron. "Yes," she replies, "they are still there." We climb into the vehicle and, as the mountains disappear in the rear window, I ponder the possibility that somewhere up there, the small black frog still hops.

❧

Our next target is the Lime-green Harlequin Frog, *Atelopus exiguus,* last seen around the same time as the Cajas Harlequin Frog in moist forest a little further down the mountains. After a good night's rest we make an early start to the forest reserve. At the entrance to the reserve we meet a ranger who raises his eyebrows when we tell him why we are here. "The frogs used to be so abundant that I had to watch my step," he tells us as he looks longingly

OVERLEAF: The sun sets behind a derelict building in southern Ecuador.

Italo looks out over the mountains and lakes of Cajas National Park in southern Ecuador.

into the forest. His tone becomes more solemn as he continues, "but I have walked these trails every day for the past 12 years, and I haven't seen a single one." He fixes us with a forlorn expression and bids us luck on our quest.

I am pitifully unprepared for the thin, humid Andean air, and a relentless wind drives through my clothing as we make our way towards a small stream transecting the forest. How cold can it be on the Equator, I had thought as I packed. As the chill sets in, I lose feeling in my toes as they press against the hard sides of my Wellington boots, and I sense it is going to be a long day. We begin our search by slogging up the stream, its white waters cascading over rocks into swirling pools. I feel the familiar pang of nostalgia at the thought of small green frogs picking their way across rocks on the banks and I regret that I will never witness the spectacle. Using clear plastic trays we scan the water for tadpoles – the tray working like a miniature glass-bottomed boat to allow us to see underwater – but there are no tadpoles to see.

Hours spent searching the stream and banks for frogs begin to drag. The only life visible in the stream is the occasional trout darting for cover. Cold and tired, we make our way back to the ranger's hut where we will spend the night. In the ebbing light, we continue to lift logs and rocks – an impulse that seems deeply embedded in all herpetologists. Walking past a rotting log without turning it is like trying not to scratch an itch. And sometimes – just sometimes – the impulse can pay off. This is one of those times. A cry of delight rings out from Italo, an exceptional young field biologist, ahead of me. Could it be? We rush over. I can barely believe my eyes – a small, bright green toad sits crouched under a rock. The air is charged. The Lime-green Harlequin Frog has, somehow, clung on against all odds.

Italo searches tirelessly over the coming days until a mate is found for the small frog, and the pair is taken back to Quito to form a breeding colony with the hope that the frogs can eventually be released back into the wild. The prospect of the Lime-green Harlequin Frog dotting the stream once more fills me with hope.

The following year, Coloma and Ron return to Cajas National Park and find the Black Cajas Harlequin Frog exactly where the local woman had told us they lived. Over the following two years they collect six females and three juveniles for the captive colony at the University in Quito. They eventually secure a male, and I was thrilled in September 2012 to receive a photograph of a jet-black male harlequin frog clinging to the back of a female in amplexus. They may just have to change the name of the frog to 'Kusikuy', the Quechua word for happiness.

⚕

What did the reappearance of the black and green harlequin frogs in Ecuador mean? Were they isolated cases, or were other species that were thought to have vanished from the forests of Costa Rica, Panama and Australia also poised to make a miraculous reappearance? It was a tantalising prospect. There were, indeed, indications that something more significant than the reappearance of a couple of frogs was happening.

The first indication had come in July 2003, when a young biologist by the name of Justin Yeager was doing a study-abroad programme on poison dart frogs in Costa Rica. Yeager was familiar with the species that had vanished from these forests – and so was sceptical when his guide started to talk to him about a yellow and black frog living in the rainforest. You must be mistaken, Yeager had told the guide who was clearly describing the Variable Harlequin Frog, *Atelopus varius*. Their harlequin frog – the very same species that Alan Pounds had come to Costa Rica to study – had been missing for eight years and was believed extinct because repeated searches had failed to turn up a trace. But although Yeager's curiosity was piqued, he was not able to go and check for himself because of access restrictions to the area, and he asked the guide to provide evidence of the existence of this yellow and black frog. Two days later his scepticism evaporated when the guide appeared holding a pair of Variable Harlequin Frogs.

ABOVE: The Lime-green Harlequin Frog, *Atelopus exiguus*.
LEFT: The Variable Harlequin Frog, *Atelopus varius*.

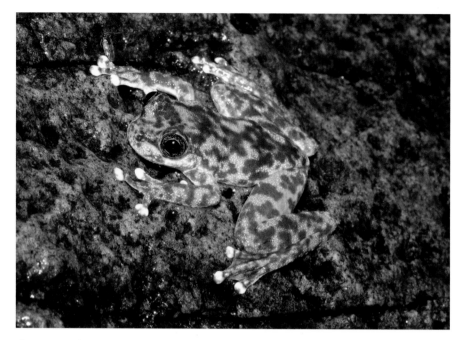

The Armoured Mist Frog, *Litoria lorica*, disappeared for 17 years before being rediscovered in 2008 in north-eastern Queensland, Australia.

Costa Rica, where the story began with the Golden Toad, was poised to become a hotbed of surprise rediscoveries. One rainy day in the spring of 2009 Juan Abarca, a young Costa Rican biologist, was walking through oak forest on the western flanks of Volcán Barva, an area where amphibian populations had crashed in the 1980s (and 12 out of 18 species had not been found in years), when he came upon some small brown toads. Although he initially assumed that they belonged one of the common species from the area, they were too young to identify. He took the toads into captivity to raise them for six months, which was when he realised that they were far from common. Abarca had just rediscovered Holdridge's Toad, a species that had vanished 25 years previously and was declared extinct by the IUCN. Because Holdridge's Toad is the closest living relative to the famed Golden Toad, its rediscovery sent ripples through the amphibian community. Did it mean that there could be a glimmer of hope that Golden Toad survives? "More than a glimmer of hope," replied Alan Pounds when I asked him.

Meanwhile, on the other side of the world, a young scientist by the name of Robert Puschendorf was conducting research of the amphibians of the forests of eastern Australia. Having previously studied in Costa Rica, Puschendorf was drawn to Australia because of the similarities between the two countries in terms of what was happening with amphibians. The similarities were set to continue. In June 2008, Puschendorf and colleagues were crashing through the dry forests of north-eastern Queensland when they came across something that was not supposed to be there; the Armoured Mist Frog. The frog was last seen 17 years previously in rain forest habitat, and was at that time thought to be a rain forest specialist. In the same year, fisheries conservation officer Luke Pearce was conducting research on an endangered species of fish in the Southern Tablelands of New South Wales when, while trying to catch a pygmy perch along a stream, he saw a beautiful olive-green frog with mottled bronze markings broken by yellow stripes. He was looking at the first Yellow-spotted Bell Frog (*Litoria castanea*) to be seen in more than 30 years. He returned the following year to find a 100-strong colony and confirm its identity with amphibian experts. The state environment minister responded emphatically: "I'm advised that finding this frog is as significant a discovery as a Tasmanian Tiger."

⚭

The reappearances of the Variable Harlequin Frog, Holdridge's Toad, Armoured Mist Frog and Yellow-spotted Bell Frog were surprising twists in the story of decline and extinction among amphibians. But what did these reappearances mean against the backdrop of what some were calling earth's sixth mass extinction? Could these Lazarus frogs hold clues to predict the future of these and other amphibians? How were these frogs surviving alongside the fungus that wiped out others around them? And were there more frogs out there concealed from the eyes of the world just waiting to be rediscovered?

It was time to set off in search of answers.

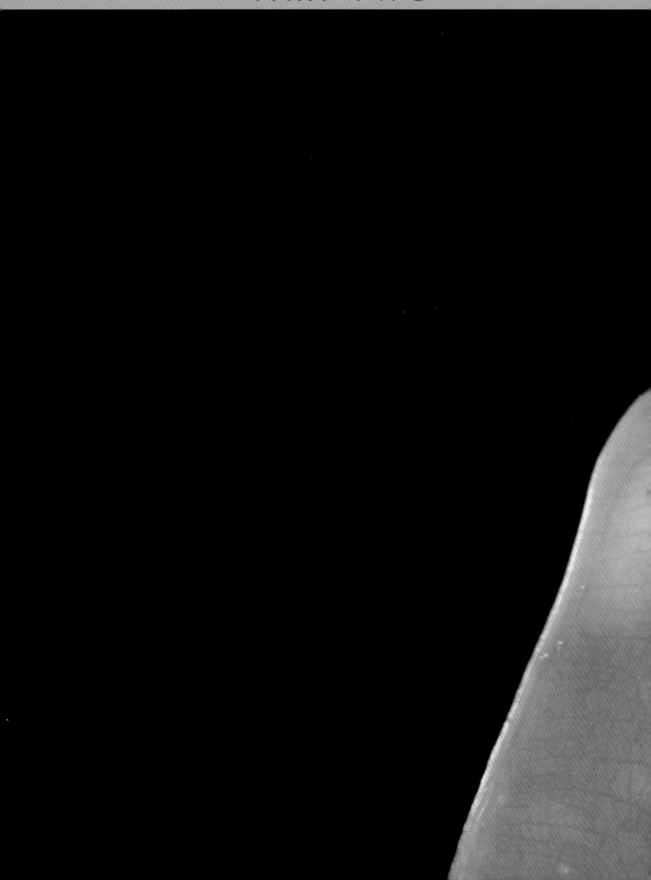

PART TWO

CHAPTER 6

THE SEARCH FOR LOST FROGS

What would happen if you simultaneously dispatched more than 100 researchers in search of dozens of missing frogs across the globe? We were about to find out.

The idea for a search for lost frogs was conceived in February 2010, in a brainstorming meeting between myself and colleagues from the IUCN Amphibian Specialist Group: Claude Gascon, Don Church and James Collins. The discussion turned to ways we could shine the spotlight on amphibians; to raise the profile of these often overlooked creatures and at the same time provide valuable data on the status of amphibians worldwide. It seemed clear that proclamations of apocalyptic scenarios were doing little to motivate people to care about the loss of amphibians. What we needed was to tap into our sense of awe and wonder; to inspire rather than guilt people into action. With the creative juices flowing, we floated the idea of putting out a list of the 'Most Wanted' amphibians to encourage scientists to go in search of creatures that had been lost to science, in the hopes that they would bring home stories of rediscovery and hope.

I was excited by the idea. Over the following weeks and months I set about compiling a list of lost frogs. The task wasn't as straightforward as I first imagined, as it became clear that there was no standard definition of a lost species and opinions on the subject varied wildly. I started with the list of 'possibly extinct' species compiled by the IUCN, and put out a call for nominations from amphibian experts around the world. Nominations began pouring in and, while it proved challenging to determine when exactly a species was last seen, the list began to grow. I was inspired by the positive response from the scientific community.

So what exactly is a lost species? Without any standard definition, we had to come up with some criteria. Ten years without trace was deemed be a good minimum length of time for an amphibian (whose generation times are typically several years) to qualify. As the nominations came in, three main reasons for a frog becoming "lost" became apparent.

First, there were those species that had disappeared as a result of rapid and enigmatic

RIGHT: 'Wanted Alive' poster reproduced from Conservation International's Search for Lost Frogs campaign.

WANTED ALIVE

One rainy evening in May 1989, a lone golden toad appeared at a pool high in a Costa Rican cloud forest. He was the last golden toad ever seen. Join Conservation International in the search for this and other lost amphibians. Countries and dates indicate where and when these "top ten" were last seen alive. **Reward**: Pest control, nutrient cycling and other services provided by amphibians for people worldwide.

Golden toad

Coasta Rica 1989

Gastric brooding frog

Australia 1985

Mesopotamia beaked toad

Colombia 1914

Jackson's climbing salamander

Guatemala 1977

African painted frog

Rwanda 1950

Rio Pescado stubfoot toad

Ecuador 1995

Turkestanian salamander

Turkmenistan 1909

Scarlet harlequin frog

Venezuela 1990

Hula painted frog

Israel 1955

Sambas stream toad

Malaysia/Indonesia 1924

declines – probably disease, climate change or a combination of the two – and, despite repeated searches, had not turned up in many years. The Golden Toad, gastric-brooding frogs and harlequin frogs fell into this category. Rediscovery of any of these species could yield vital clues as to what had led to their decline and what could be done to avert future extinctions.

Second, there were species that had been lost following the destruction of their habitat. The Hula Painted Frog from Israel was a good example; a species whose disappearance coincided with the draining of its marsh habitat. Haitian frogs, such as the La Selle Grass Frog – a species not seen in 25 years less than an hour from the bustling capital of Port-au-Prince – also fell into this category.

Finally, there were species that had gone decades without being seen simply because they lived in such remote, inaccessible or hostile areas that nobody had been to look for them. Species falling into this category included the Borneo Rainbow Toad, last seen 86 years previously in the unexplored mountains of western Sarawak, the African Painted Frog, unseen for 60 years in the remote jungles of the Democratic Republic of Congo, and myriad species in the conflict-riddled jungles of Colombia.

Little by little the list grew to 100 species last seen, for one reason or another, between 15 and 140 years previously. Next, to boost the chances of rediscovery, we offered support for teams of scientists to go in search of these lost frogs. Within weeks more than 30 search teams composed of more than 120 researchers had signed up to set off in search of lost frogs in 21 countries. The idea had turned into the biggest coordinated global search for lost species. At this point, it seemed, we had the makings of a media campaign. When I bumped into Rob McNeil, the media manager at Conservation International, as he was, in his words, "wandering the corridors looking for clever ideas that would be both accessible and would help to tell the bigger conservation story," I ran the idea past him. "I f****ng love it," he said. When I asked him later why it had appealed so quickly he said, "I thought that it seemed like a clever way of communicating both the need for more investment in research into whether these animals were still alive – and therefore more investment in the protection of any remaining habitat – and also a means of helping tell the story of the chytrid fungus and the global amphibian crisis."

And that was that. Within a week I was sitting around a table with the communications team at Conservation International: web developers, writers, graphic designers and media managers, plotting a strategy for engaging the public. "When I suggested the lost frogs campaign to the rest of the communications team at CI the degree to which it was immediately and wholeheartedly jumped on made it pretty clear that it was a compelling idea," Rob said, adding, "By the time that we launched the campaign it had become the central focus of the whole communications team. We were all buoyed and excited about it." First we had to decide on a name for the campaign. *The Search for Lost Amphibians* was briefly discussed before being dismissed; it was not snappy or appealing to the general public. We wanted to reach and engage people who may not even know what an amphibian is. And so it was decided, even though we would be looking for, frogs, toads, newts, salamanders and caecilians, the campaign would simply be called *The Search for Lost Frogs*.

Next up, we needed poster children for the campaign: the top ten Most Wanted. Compiling the top ten was a subjective exercise. Candidates were selected based on their geography, ecology, behaviour, rarity, appearance and the availability of images or illustrations. The idea behind the top ten was to hook the most visual creatures of them all. We needed our charismatic frogs to be our flagships for the campaign, an entry point for people to learn more about the plight of the less colourful or less charismatic creatures.

First, the Golden Toad, *Incilius periglenes*, the poster child of the amphibian extinction crisis, also became a poster child for lost frogs following its dramatic, mysterious and high profile disappearance from the cloud forests of Costa Rica in the late 1980s. Even though 20 other amphibian species disappeared around it, few could match the Golden Toad for film star appeal.

Second, the gastric-brooding frogs, *Rheobatrachus silus* and *Rheobatrachus vitellinus*, frogs last seen in the mid-1980s with a unique and truly bizarre behaviour, embodied a lost opportunity for human medicine. These two were treated as one, and elected to represent the lost frogs of Australia – of which there were dozens. After all, who could resist a frog that gives birth through its mouth?

Third, the Hula Painted Frog, *Discoglossus nigriventer*, was selected for its compelling back-story and symbolic value. This frog from eastern Israel had disappeared some 55 years previously after its home – the Hula Lake – was drained, resulting in the extinction of a unique ecosystem. Although some of the area had been reflooded in response to public pressure, it appeared to be too late for the frog, which became a poignant symbol of extinction in Israel. The story of the Hula Painted Frog was, however, far from over.

Fourth, the Rio Pescado Stubfoot Toad (actually a type of harlequin frog), *Atelopus balios*, from Ecuador, last seen in 1995, was hard to beat in terms of beauty, bearing black dots on a lemon-yellow skin. With harlequin frogs such as the Black Cajas Harlequin Frog and the Lime-green Harlequin Frog turning up in Ecuador after years without being seen, scientists were inspired to consider the possibility that other species believed to be extinct could be hanging on.

Fifth, the Scarlet Harlequin Frog, *Atelopus sorianoi*, in Venezuela looked as though it has been dipped in the same tin of orange paint as the Golden Toad. This frog, with a more slender physique and pointed nose than the Golden Toad, was known only from a single stream, where it was abundant, before its sudden and mysterious disappearance in 1990.

Sixth, the Mesopotamia Beaked Toad, *Rhinella rostrata*, from central Colombia, last seen in 1914 and known from only two individuals, was elected to represent those frogs lost as a result of armed conflict. An artist's watercolour rendition portrayed a toad with a large, pyramid-shaped head that seemed to belong alongside the dinosaurs. A month after the launch of the Search for Lost Frogs I would be hacking my way through the forests of Colombia, hoping to be the first in almost 100 years to uncover the toad.

Seventh on the list was the Sambas Stream Toad, *Ansonia latidisca*, also known as the Borneo Rainbow Toad. This was a tree-climbing multi-coloured toad known only from two individuals seen 86 years previously on the remote and relatively unexplored mountains near Sarawak. With no photos ever taken of the toad, a line drawing provided the only artistic representation.

Eighth, the African Painted Frog, *Callixalus pictus*, was last seen in the Democratic Republic of Congo in 1950 and is represented today only by a black and white illustration. As with many frogs in such remote corners of the world, little is known about the African Painted Frog beyond an initial description, and it is unlikely that anyone has been to look for this frog in more than 50 years. Until now. This frog was elected to represent all those African frogs that have fallen off the radar simply because nobody has been to check whether they are still with us.

Ninth, the first of two tailed amphibians on the list, the Turkestanian Salamander, *Hynobius turkestanicus*, was as rare and elusive as it gets. The salamander was known only from a few individuals collected in 1909, all of which have since been lost, as have all records of the salamander's exact location. The range of the salamander is described as being "between Pamir and Samarkand" – an area which is possibly in Kyrgyzstan, Tajikistan or Uzbekistan. Attempts to map its possible distribution, and hone searches, have been based on assumptions of those conditions most suitable for salamanders along the expedition route of the original collector.

Last on the list was the striking yellow-and-black Jackson's Climbing Salamander, *Bolitoglossa jacksoni*, from Guatemala, described by notable amphibian biologist Dave Wake as "the most beautiful of salamanders". The salamander belonged to a group of web-footed salamanders that inhabit rainforests through Central and South America. When Jackson's Climbing Salamander was discovered in 1975, the only known individual was transported to California for preservation. One more individual was found in the same year and transported to Berkeley where it mysteriously disappeared two weeks later, believed lost or stolen. The species has not been seen since. The reappearance of some other salamanders in Guatemala instills some hope that this salamander may still exist.

⚘

The Search for Lost Frogs launched on August 9, 2010. Over the following weeks and months teams from the Ivory Coast to Indonesia, Brazil to Borneo, and Cameroon to Colombia travelled by plane, car, boat, foot and on horseback in search of cave squeakers, button frogs, puddle frogs, bubble-nest frogs, rainbow toads, scarlet frogs, harlequin frogs, Golden Toads, gastric-brooding frogs, beaked toads and long-headed caecilians, for anything from seven to 32 days straight in the field. An unprecedented coordinated search for lost amphibians was underway.

I had no idea, as we sent out a press release the evening before the launch, whether any outlets would pick it up. And then, late that night, I got a text telling me to check the BBC News website. It seemed almost surreal, but there it was front and centre: "Global hunt begins for 'extinct' species of frogs." The following day the story ran on National Geographic Daily News, Al Jazeera and more than 140 other news outlets. I was gobsmacked, and not altogether prepared for the media whirlwind that ensued. I spent much of that week in a taxi going from one studio to another or with my phone stuck to my ear talking with journalists. People, it seemed, were enthralled. While much of the week was a blur – for reasons that I will reveal in the next chapter – my interview with John Humphrys for Radio 4's *Today* Programme was memorable. I was a little apprehensive about Humphrys' notorious style of grilling interviewees. Early in the interview he asked, sounding incredulous, "Are you suggesting people should go into their backgardens and look for *frogs*??" I thought briefly before responding, "Well, yes, actually," an answer that seemed to satisfy him, and from that point on the interview was one that I enjoyed the most.

The realisation that the eyes of the world were on the campaign was thrilling, but it also tied a small knot around my stomach. One question was repeatedly posed: so how many rediscoveries can we expect? "I think we will be really lucky if half a dozen species turn up," I would reply with a smile, but I genuinely had no idea, and all the while I was thinking, "I will be a happy man as soon as one shows up!" People were drawn to the unpredictability of the campaign, but they also wanted assurances. They wanted to flip to the last page to see how it would end – and so did I. Several media outlets wanted to accompany a search – as long as I could guarantee they would come back with a story. I was walking a fine line between engaging the media and raising false hope. How was I to respond to such requests?

I decided to invite one journalist on our first expedition to Colombia to search for the Mesopotamia Beaked Toad. Lucy Cooke (a writer, filmmaker and now TV presenter) had a demonstrated passion for amphibians and a thirst for adventure. She was willing to accompany us for the whole week rather than dipping in and out for a day as some of the other journalists wanted to do. If we found the toad, after close to 100 years, it would be a big story. If we didn't find the toad, Colombia offered the most promising stage on which to find other stories to tell. Lucy was excited by the prospect of joining us, she understood the risks, and went about securing a commission to write a feature on the expedition for the *Telegraph* magazine, accompanied by my images. With Lucy on board I now just had to hope that we could give her a good story, rediscovery or no rediscovery. And I had to take some nice photos.

⚮

So how exactly do you go about looking for something no bigger than a golf ball that hasn't been seen in decades? First, you need to decide where to start looking. As teams prepared for their respective quests, I became fascinated by the different approaches. Take the meticulous preparation of Michael McFadden and team in their quest to find the Northern Gastric-brooding Frog of Eungella National Park in northern Queensland. Before heading into the field McFadden and team pored over all previous amphibian surveys and reports for the area and gathered all records for the species. They spoke to amphibian biologists that had surveyed parts of Eungella Park, where the frog was last seen in 1985, for their advice on logistics. They knew that previous efforts to locate this species had been prior to the discovery of the chytrid fungus in 1999 – searches had ceased when the species was declared extinct by the IUCN – and this gave them an insight into the possible cause of disappearance that previous search teams didn't have. They were encouraged by the reappearance in the previous three years of two species unseen in Australia for 17 and 30 years (the Armoured Mist Frog and Yellow-spotted Bell Frog respectively); both surviving with the chytrid fungus, in addition to a species – the Eungella Tinker Frog – that had disappeared alongside the gastric-brooding frog only to reappear half a dozen years later. They took advantage of increasingly sophisticated mapping technologies, and set about mapping potentially suitable habitat – mainly lower elevations streams – where they felt the Northern Gastric-brooding Frog could survive alongside the fungus. Their hope was pinned on the fact that in such a large, impenetrable rainforest as Eungella National Park, there were many parts that had never been surveyed for frogs due to inaccessibility. By reaching these remote recesses, they reasoned, they stood a shot at finding the frog.

Once you have figured out where to start your search you need to determine *when* to go. This is just as critical as where – many amphibians have a narrow window of activity that is dictated by the seasons and prevailing weather. In the tropics, where temperature changes little throughout the year, it is rainfall that is usually most important for moisture-dependent amphibians. The rainy season is typically most conducive to amphibian-hunting, and this can mean braving hurricanes, monsoons, flooding and landslides – elements that proved decisive for many of the search teams.

Once you have determined where and when you are going to conduct your search, the next question is *how*. The how depends on the behaviour of the frog, salamander or caecilian you are looking for. Is it active during the day or night; does it live on or under the ground or up trees, in water or on land; does it lay eggs in water, on the forest floor or in bromeliads, or does it skip the tadpole stage altogether? The behaviour of the creature can sometimes be pieced together from published records but, as is often the case with lost species, when no such records exist a little detective work needs to be employed. We often need to make inferences based on what we know about closely related species. Take the Mesopotamia Beaked Toad of Colombia. All we know of this toad is gleaned from two individuals that were collected from an area of forest near Sonsón, Colombia, in 1914. While we can make little in the way of inference about its behaviour from this, we do know that other beaked toads are active during the day and give birth to fully formed toadlets on the forest floor, and we can take our chances that the same applies to the Mesopotamia Beaked Toad. The toad also bears a striking resemblance to a dead leaf in both shape and colour. We can therefore hone our search to the leaf litter on the forest floor during the day.

Most amphibians are active under the cloak of darkness, some are easier to hear than to see, but we would be searching for a long time if we stood still and listened for salamanders, for they do not call. Some amphibians congregate at breeding pools for a few weeks of the year while others lay eggs or deliver young on the forest floor. Aquatic species and tadpoles can be searched for with drag-nets, and ground-dwelling species can be captured in pitfall traps. As they dispatched into the field, search teams prepared to employ the whole gamut of techniques tailored according to what they knew, or could infer, about their target species and the area that they would be scouring.

But even with the most meticulous preparation of where, when and how to search, once in the field the search teams were at the mercy of the elements, and unforeseen challenges started to arise. Take the team led by Jeff Streicher that embarked on a search for Wake's Moss Salamander, last seen 20 years ago in the mountains of southern Guatemala, only to find that the known range of the salamander fell squarely in land owned by suspected drug traffickers. Undeterred, the team hired armed security guards to accompany them at night and scoured nearby bank-owned property. Herpetologists can be a persistent lot.

Next up, you have to hope that your local guides know where they are going, and that you have allocated enough time to make it your destination. Thomas Doherty Bone and team fell at both hurdles as they set out in search of lost caecilians in Cameroon. Doherty Bone tells me after the expedition: "I embarked on an overly ambitious hunt for these animals, with a narrow schedule that still makes my eyes water." He goes on to describe how he travelled on the back of a truck, then a motorbike onto which both he and his equipment were strapped, to a small village where he was "warmly greeted by the village chief who promptly provided food and beer and a roof to sleep under". His quest encountered one challenge after the next, and he describes how attempts to reach their destination of Makumunu were "set back by a problem in communication with local guides, who took the team in the wrong direction to Tinto when the stated destination was Tinta". Rectifying the mistake required crossing the border into Nigeria, without transit visas, or else walking for two days through forest. Neither option was feasible, and the team never made it to Makumunu to search for their lost caecilian.

Then, of course, you have to hope that large Saltwater Crocodiles aren't waiting for you at the top of waterfalls – something Robert Puschendorf and team clearly didn't hope for hard enough when out searching for lost frogs in Australia. "At the top of a waterfall!" he exclaims as he recalls the incident. "Who would have thought, Saltwater Crocodiles could climb steep waterfalls? It made camping and exploring that specific site much more interesting," he says.

And then there is the most universally unpredictable element of all: the weather. In Costa Rica, Adrián García and team had to abandon searches for lost rain frogs because a tropical storm was causing rivers to overflow. Just three days into their search for four lost species in Mexico, Georgina Santos Barrera and her team of five researchers returned frustrated after "several parts of the mountain collapsed" and the police advised them to get out before the road was closed. Spirits dampened but not destroyed, they set off again four weeks later. Santos Barrera reported after day one of the second attempt: "Just to say that we arrived yesterday from the field site in Guerrero. We made an intense effort to find nothing!!!" Returning home empty-handed once more, they speculated that their bad luck could have been related to seasonality and they vowed to return at a different time of year.

Where some teams found challenges, others found opportunity. In Borneo, Indraneil Das and team from the Universiti Malaysia Sarawak were making the most of some changes that had happened since the Borneo Rainbow Toad was last seen 86 years previously: the construction of a golf resort near the summit of the Gunung Penrissen mountain, the least studied mountain massif in western Sarawak. The clearing of the forest had improved access to the area for Das and team, and I could almost feel the glee as Das described driving around in golf carts collecting snakes: "The short grass gave no chance for snakes to hide," he reported triumphantly.

As reports came in thick and fast from the field, I found myself rooting for the scientists from behind my computer screen. Those from Das I found especially evocative, and I could almost imagine clicking on my headlamp and slogging up the cool streams with the search team, scouring the vegetation lining the river for a small toad with slender limbs. I could feel the tingle of excitement as they fished out some tadpoles that could have belonged to the rainbow toad followed by the crushing disappointment as they identified them later as another, less elusive species. I found the unbridled optimism and enthusiasm of many of the searchers intoxicating, and I started to feel a part of something bigger, driven by the passion and the energy of remarkable individuals.

But as reports of landslides, overflowing rivers and unsuccessful searches trickled in, the anxiety of failure also grew. Rather like watching a struggling Andy Murray from the sidelines at Wimbledon, I felt powerless to determine the outcome. What I needed to ease the anxiety was to immerse myself in a quest; to get out there with the search teams, to hack through forest and wade up streams in search of lost species. And so, a month into the campaign, I planned to board a plane to Medellín, Colombia, to meet with a team of scientists and journalist Lucy Cooke in search of the Mesopotamia Beaked Toad. But as the departure date neared, something happened that put my plans on ice. I was unsure whether I could, or should, set off in search of lost frogs.

THE THIN LINE
BETWEEN LIFE AND DEATH

"A little while and I will be gone from among you, whither I cannot tell.
From nowhere we come, into nowhere we go. What is life?
It is a flash of firefly in the night. It is a breath of a buffalo in the wintertime.
It is as the little shadow that runs across the grass and loses itself in the sunset."

CHIEF CROWFOOT

Washington, DC, 10 August 2010

It is the day after the launch of the Search for Lost Frogs and I am in a taxi on my way to the BBC studios in Washington, DC to conduct some interviews, when I receive a phone call that makes my blood run cold. It is my wife, Iciar, calling from Madrid, where she is visiting her family. Her voice is fragile. She had been admitted to hospital the previous week with a sudden fever and joints so painful that she couldn't reach to grab a glass of water from her bedside. She is calling from her hospital bed, and as soon as I hear her voice I know something has happened. I process her words and a coldness creeps up my spine as I realise my world has changed in an instant. "They have found fluid in my lungs, and my... ," she pauses, "... heart."

The following minutes, as I get out of the taxi and walk through big glass doors into the studio, pass in a blur. I feel faint. I go through with the interview, but as soon as I get out of the studio I jump in a taxi home and book a flight to Madrid. I will be at her bedside in five long days.

✤

Madrid, 15 August 2010

On the day that I arrive in Madrid, Iciar is moved into intensive care; the cause of her condition still unknown. I make my way from the airport straight to the hospital and wait on a small plastic chair outside of intensive care to be allowed to see her. I am joined by her mother and father; the worry is worn on the faces, and spoken in the silences and the pacing of her father. Back and forth, back and forth.

"You may come and see her now," a young woman in a blue coat eventually says in a gentle voice in Spanish as she leads me into a small room filled with the sounds of bubbling tubes. Iciar is tucked under crisp blue and white sheets that she promptly pulls up over her head to shield me from her gaunt face. I sit down next to the bed and she clutches my arm; I can feel the panic in her grip. Eventually she lowers the sheets and I kiss her on the forehead. It is hard to find the right words – perhaps there are no right words – and so I hold her tight, close my eyes, and will her to be strong and positive, even if I am struggling to do both.

∂

The next night I spend on the sofa next to Iciar when she is transferred from intensive care to a normal hospital room. I awake early to the sound of her gasping for air, and run for help. Within minutes she has a mask on her face and tubes up her nose and is fighting for breath. Within the hour she is back in intensive care, where she stays. As the days pass she grows weaker still. One complication follows another. She fights sleep because as soon as she lets herself go the fever comes and pulls her back into a dark place. She begs for one day without fever, just one. Every day I silently will the fever to leave her and I beg her to sleep; to rest; but every day, as her eyes close and she slips into sleep, it grips her and wakes her in a panicked sweat. She grows increasingly weak, and every day it is harder for her to summon the conviction that she can pull through.

Iciar's family – all doctors themselves – are naturally as riddled with worry as me as, one by one, suspected causes are ruled out. Malaria and tick-bite fever (we had been in Kenya until the week before she came down with fever) both test negative. A week turns into two, two weeks into three, and still the doctors are no closer to a diagnosis. What is clear is that we need some good news, and we need it soon.

∂

The cold plastic hospital chair outside intensive care becomes a significant part of my journey during the Search For Lost Frogs. I am only allowed to spend a maximum of two hours by Iciar's side a day; the remaining twenty-two hours are spent waiting for those two. From the small plastic chair, where I spend extended periods of time, waiting, I am able to hop on an open WiFi connection that allows me to connect with teams dispatching or returning from searches, field inquiries from the media and arrange logistics for my upcoming expedition to search for the Mesopotamia Beaked Toad in Colombia. But it is becoming increasingly uncertain that I will be able to go to Colombia at all – I know I cannot leave until we have some answers.

All the while, the cruel irony is not lost on me, that here I am convening a global search for lost species whilst facing the increasingly real prospect of losing the most important person in my life.

There are few things that can take my mind from the gnawing worry. But there is something about the Search for Lost Frogs that allows me to lose myself for some of the waiting hours. It is not just the frogs that draw me in and keeps me invested – it is the incredible human spirit that pervades the campaign. The Search for Lost Frogs becomes more and more about those passionate and dedicated individuals who refuse to give up hope, and there is something about their boundless energy, optimism and singular focus that inspires and carries me. In many ways, the Search for Lost Frogs helps to give my waiting hours a structure and a diversion from the testing reality of what is spiralling out of my control.

჻

Three weeks after Iciar was admitted to hospital, and almost two since she went into intensive care, the news arrives. They have a suspected diagnosis. But the doctor is cautious as he tells me, for they are still not sure. By process of elimination they have landed on the possibility that she is suffering an acute attack of a rare autoimmune disease. The only way they can know for sure is to knock out her immune system. If they are right, she could recover; if they are wrong, the consequences don't bear thinking about.

Iciar is moved to a larger hospital outside of Madrid and administered a large dose of steroids, and the results are almost immediate, as if she has been kick-started. Although it is perhaps a false sense of wellbeing, the steroids seem to be working. She is on the road to recovery. And over the coming days, weeks and months she regains her strength, slowly but surely.

Coming within a whisker of death (we have since learned that Iciar was days away from dying had they not treated her when they did) hones both her perspective and mine. The following days, weeks and months are a time of striking clarity and appreciation. The simple fact that she is alive, and we are together, is enough.

With my departure to Colombia nearing I face the painful prospect of leaving Iciar's side after weeks – that feel like months – of knowing nothing else; of leaving the daily routine that we have created for ourselves inside the bubble of our hospital room. Once she is given the green light to return home to be with her parents I know she will be well taken care of by family and so I rip myself from Madrid and head to Colombia. I am going in search of the Mesopotamia Beaked Toad.

CHAPTER 8

IN SEARCH OF THE MESOPOTAMIA
BEAKED TOAD, COLOMBIA

Department of Antioquia, Colombia, 9 September 2010

Few things are as effective at keeping biologists out of unexplored forests bristling with life as chance encounters with gun-toting guerillas, ruthless paramilitary groups and landmines. It is no surprise then that northern Colombia – whose remote forests are a hideout for leftist guerillas, right-wing death squads and a mélange of armed groups in between – harbour many species unseen in decades. Despite the allure of potential discoveries and rediscoveries, it would have taken some serious arm-twisting to convince me to traipse through the forests of Antioquia and Chocó in northwest Colombia only a few years ago. But with the restoration of relative stability to the region, a unique opportunity to search for such lost species as the Mesopotamia Beaked Toad, last seen in 1914, beckons.

⚬

My journey begins in Medellín (pronounced, locally, as *mede´jin*), the capital of the northwestern Department of Antioquia. It is my first time in the city and, although I don't have time for much exploration, I get the feeling of being in a thriving hub. It is a far cry from its reputation as one of the most dangerous cities in the world during the 1980s and 1990s on account of the omnipresence of the Medellín cartel, led by ruthless drug kingpin Pablo Escobar. Since Escobar was gunned down and killed on a rooftop in 1993, Medellín has worked hard to clean up its act, and it would appear on first impressions that the 'city of flowers and eternal spring' has succeeded.

I meet with Lucy Cooke and Alonso Quevedo at the airport to begin our journey into the field. Alonso is President of local conservation group Fundación ProAves and will be our guide over the coming week. Having travelled with the stoic Alonso previously I know I can trust him to navigate us through any turbid political waters we may encounter. Lucy, a journalist, producer and presenter, brings boundless energy and enthusiasm to the team. Having secured a feature with the *Telegraph* magazine, she is here on her own quest: to return home with a story. Such as a lost frog rediscovery, "or a new species," she suggests.

"My life dream is to find a new species." No pressure then.

We clamber into a jeep and drive north. I leave my stomach behind several times on the way to Sonsón, a municipality in eastern Antioquia, as the road curves and twists over undulating terrain like a long rollercoaster. I distract myself from travel-sickness by feasting my eyes on sun-drenched farmhouses and a scrolling patchwork of green and brown fields. The ever-changing landscape is more pastoral than the other areas of Colombia that I have explored, and it is easy to see why some claim Antioquia to be the prettiest region of the country. It also feels culturally distinct. There is a strong demographic and cultural Judeo-Arabic influence here: the name Antioquia itself is believed to have derived from the Turkish Hellenistic city of Antioch on the Orontes. The American historian Everett Hagen also noticed another strong influence when he scanned the phone book in Medellín in the 1950s; 15 per cent of the surnames happened to be Basque – and this rose to a quarter of all surnames among employers. This, he inferred, supported the idea that the

ABOVE: Lucy Cooke meets a glass frog.

OVERLEAF: Pastoral landscape in Sonsón, department of Antioquia.

industrious Basques had contributed to the development of Antioquia relative to other parts of Colombia. The influence of the Basques can also be heard still in the regional dialect of Antioquia.

Despite its picturesque appeal, rich culture and idyllic climate, Antioquia is one of the departments most affected by the Colombian armed conflict, and large tracts of forest are controlled by the notorious Revolutionary Armed Forces of Colombia (more commonly known by its Spanish acronym, FARC). Until only a few years ago the forest home of the Mesopotamia Beaked Toad – our target species – was a stronghold for the rebel group. But how real is the threat they pose to a group of biologists? All too real, according to ProAves biologist Juan Carlos Luna who joined us for part of our search. While conducting research on a rare parrot, Juan ran into a group of guerrillas who opened fire on him. He owes his life, he tells us, to a passing friend who confirmed that he was not paramilitary but a park ranger – only then did the guerillas stop firing. The forests we will be exploring have become safer in recent years as a result of a government crackdown that killed some of the FARC leaders. During our search for the beaked toad, FARC top military commander

Steamy rainforest extends as far as the eye can see as we descend into the Chocó.

Jorge Briceno (better known as Mono Jojoy) was days away from being killed in an army bombing-raid in northern Colombia. The Colombian president, whose approval ratings immediately soared to 88 per cent, said the death of Mono Jojoy was the equivalent of killing Osama Bin Laden (who was still alive at the time).

It is my second visit to Colombia and it is thrilling to be back in one of the most ecologically and geographically diverse nations on earth. Colombia is carved into several distinct regions by three Andean mountain ranges that fan northwards through the country; this corrugated topography creates a rich diversity of landscapes and has provided fertile ground for the evolution of unique animals and plants. Colombia has more than 700 known species of amphibians, a number beaten only by Brazil (seven times the size), and more threatened species of amphibians than any other country in the world.

The diverse geography and ecology of Colombia is mirrored by a people that span the spectrum of human spirit and character. In Colombia I have met some of the warmest and most hospitable people on earth living alongside some of the most ruthless gangs; I have been humbled by enormous generosity and appalled by insatiable greed, and have been stunned by some of the highest inequalities of wealth in the world. Colombia is a land of contrasts; of blurred lines between good and bad. Author Steven Dudley sums it up in his chilling book *Walking Ghosts: Murder and Guerilla Politics in Colombia* when he writes: "I wish there were clear-cut good guys and clear-cut bad guys. But Colombia isn't a story of good guys and bad guys. Colombia is much more than that, which is why it's difficult to ignore. It's raw: humans at their best and worst." From the moment I set foot in the country I was captivated by the sharp contrasts that characterise Colombia. And although I had explored regions from the Sierra Nevada de Santa Marta in the north – the highest coastal mountain formation on earth – to the coffee-growing valleys of the Eje Cafetero and the burgeoning City of Bogota, I had never reached the untamed and remote jungles of Antioquia and Chocó. Until now.

⚬

As we near Sonsón, the conversation turns to the reason we are here: the rare and elusive Mesopotamia Beaked Toad. This outlandish casque-headed creature is known from only two toads found in 1914 near the small town of Mesopotamia, close to where we are headed. Since these two individuals were found, reported searches have turned up empty-handed and, in recent decades, the area has been off-limits because of the armed conflict. The first individual to be collected was donated to the American Museum of Natural History by a man by the name of R. D. O. Johnson and described seven years later by the American biologist Gladwin Noble. In his description, Noble states: "It is noteworthy that [the toad] simulates several species of [harlequin frogs] in general form," a feature that piques my curiosity given my fascination with the elusive and enigmatic harlequin frogs. Because no photos have ever been taken of the Mesopotamia Beaked Toad, our search is guided by an artist's impression of what the species probably looks like.

Once in Sonsón we arrive in the charming town of Argelia in time to have dinner with a Colombian herpetology student by the name Diego Riañoa. I am eager to meet Diego, for he has spent the past four weeks scouting the area and scouring the forests around Sonsón in search of the beaked toad. I hope that Diego will be the bearer of good news. Over a calorie-rich and ambrosial soup of beans and pork in a cosy restaurant, Diego regales us with tales of hiking miles in, and miles out, to search for days on end under lashing rain in forest fragments resembling the original habitat of the toad. It sounds thoroughly miserable, but Diego's smile never falters. My admiration for his tenacity grows with each day he was out there by himself, head buried in the leaf litter searching for a brown toad no longer than his index finger. I am waiting for him to break the good news, but it slowly sinks in that, despite his cheerful demeanour, he has not found the toad.

After dinner we retire to our hotel and plan to regroup the next day to target an unexplored patch of forest. Despite his month of failed searches, Diego remains admirably upbeat. The next morning our search team swells as my very good friend and colleague Don Church and his partner in crime from Global Wildlife Conservation, Wes Sechrest join us. Having shared an office for some five years, and having travelled together throughout Africa, Asia and Latin America, I have likely spent more time with Don than I have with my own wife. A better field biologist and more patient, passionate and positive companion is hard to find, and it is always a pleasure to get into the field with Don.

We drive to a tract of forest at the end of a dirt road, clamber out of the trucks and make our way down a grassy field strewn with rocks towards the soft gurgle of water. When we get to the fringes of the forest we fan out, lifting logs, peering into bromeliads and raking through leaf litter. Spirits are high. We remove boots and roll up trousers to cross a river and reach a steep valley where we cling to thin trunks with one hand as we rake leaf litter with the other. But our spirits fade with the light and all too soon it is time to head back to the vehicles empty handed. Tomorrow we will try again – but for now, it's time for a hearty bean and pork soup

⚶

The next morning we tumble out of the vehicles with renewed vigour at a different, and quite beautiful, patch of forest. We peer into bromeliads and lift crumbling logs as we work our way up the banks of a gentle river. By late morning morale is again sagging; not only have we not found the toad, but we have not found a single amphibian. We are thankful to Don for a perfectly timed moment of comic relief when he loses his footing on a large mossy rock and cartwheels in slow motion to face-plant in the river, emerging spluttering and ashen-faced. We allow him a moment to regain his composure before launching into an unofficial but good-humoured 'who can do the best Don falling in the river replay' contest.

Late in the afternoon, as the sun angles through the low canopy and illuminates slender trunks, I lower onto a mossy rock and take from my back pocket a folded piece of paper. It is the watercolour rendition of the Mesopotamia Beaked Toad. I stare at its strange pyramid-shaped head and will it to appear on the forest floor in front of me. I lift my tired eyes to stare into the leaf litter carpeting the forest floor and allow my imagination to kick in: I see the toad hopping toward my muddied boots in slow motion. I freeze in disbelief as the toad stops, as if in mutual surprise. My blood jumps as I steady myself to reach down,

A watercolour painting of the Mesopotamia Beaked Toad provided the only visual reference for the team during searches for this lost species, last seen in 1914. Illustration courtesy of Paula Andrea Romero Ardilla

quickly but carefully, to cup the creature and run with trembling hands to the rest of the team, calling, "I found it! I have one!" as they clamber to be the first people alive to set eyes upon this mythical creature.

I snap back to reality and to the hours we have spent, backs arched, scraping, turning and lifting leaves and logs and stones. I fold the piece of paper and slide it back into my pocket before hoisting myself to find a new, unturned mound of dead leaves to continue scraping and turning. Each unturned leaf is a tantalising glimpse of possibility; each leaf turned the slow drip of disappointment. Leaf by leaf, hope of finding the Mesopotamia Beaked Toad is ebbing.

The realisation that you are not going to find a lost species seeps in imperceptibly, like cold into tired muscles. Even as spirits wane with the passing hours of a fruitless search, the embers of hope continue to glow deep within, extinguished only when the light of day is sucked from the forest, the last leaf has been turned and the mud has been kicked off the boots. Then, and only then, is the cold truth acknowledged. The search is over.

That moment of realisation comes late in the second day of our search, and while it is not said aloud, it is worn on the faces and bowed heads of the team as we drag ourselves back to our vehicles. The dying light of the day drains the colour from the forest, which is

Alonso Quevedo explains to a young paramilitary soldier why we are studying frogs.

now a foreboding conglomeration of grey and black lines and shapes, a backdrop for the revving whir of nighttime insects.

At dinner the conversation is slow. It is Alonso, a man who speaks only when he has something to say, who breaks a heavy silence: "We have three days left, and two options." He has our attention. "First, we can stay here and keep looking for the Mesopotamia Beaked Toad." Or? "Or," he says with a glint in his eye "we can head to the Chocó. There we can look for the lost Chocó Harlequin Frog – and maybe," he clears his throat as if making an important announcement "… maybe even find new species." I can feel Lucy next to me bouncing up and down in her chair. The allure of the untamed Chocó beckons. And so it is decided, we will leave at 5am sharp the next morning.

⚇

The next morning Don and Wes appear at the trucks looking ashen. Don has been up all night with a stomach bug and Wes, sharing the room, has suffered the consequences. Don is adamant that he will drive, ensuring that he has control over vomit stops, and lodges himself in the driver's seat. Wes, realising he is fighting a losing battle, climbs in beside him and throws us a forlorn look as Don steps on the accelerator and disappears in a cloud of dust.

Within hours we are plunging into the steamy depths of the Chocó, a land whose rugged terrain and year-round drenching (16 to 18 metres of rain fall a year, making it one of the wettest places on earth) prevented even the conquistadores from settling here. Steam rises from thick jungle undulating as far as the eye can see. Warm moisture coats the lungs with every breath and large drops of rain agitate puddles on the rutted road – the main artery connecting Medellín with the Chocó capital of Quibto. Many writers have been inspired by the wild, untamed Chocó. In *One River*, Wade Davis describes the region as "thirty thousand square miles of forgotten rain forest cut off from the Amazon millions of years ago by the rise of the Andean Cordillera". Anthropologist Michael Taussig describes it as "one of the most remote regions of the world," and Simon Romero, writing in the *New York Times*, describes the region as having a "lost-world quality." As we plunge deeper into thick jungle I feel the thrill of venturing into unexplored territory. We are surrounded by the biologically richest forests in the world; a hotbed of species known and unknown. What better place to search for lost and new species?

As we rattle down the muddy road we pass military checkpoints manned by teenagers in camouflage, khakis and black boots, and swinging AK-47 assault rifles from their shoulders like yoga mats. I've seen too many movies to feel completely at ease at the

ault weapons and I am unsure whether to feel reassured
There is a palpable fear of armed groups in the area, a
ving paramilitaries (which account for more deaths than
– but who do not tend to be as threatened by foreigners)

er with the soldiers happens later that night as we are
e same muddy road. It is 1am. A group of teenage soldiers
ness into the white glare of the headlights and waves us
heir demeanor that makes me uneasy. They are laughing
der if they are drunk. We slow to a stop and through my
of the dark forest. One of the young soldiers idles over to
n on the roof and leans into the window. "Que haceis?" he
ver quite cracked how to answer this question – it is hard
e at parties what I do, let alone armed teenage soldiers in
anation that we are looking for frogs is cut short as the
ehicle." As his eyes meet mine my heart jumps. I open my
o the front of the vehicle to put my hands on the bonnet.
eating fast as I listen to the crunch of the soldier's boots
d is going to happen, but I don't like the feeling of being
errogator frisks me before demanding to see my camera.
e back of the camera and scroll through my shots – which
top on one photo – a group shot. "Who is this?" they ask,
as joined the search from Global Wildlife Conservation.
 vehicle with Don and Wes some five minutes behind us
ed around the group to laughs and sneers. They like the
era is thrust back to me and we are instructed to get on
ehicle rolls through without being stopped.
ers with teenagers in camouflage are brief and cordial.
graphing frogs beside a stream, I look up to see Alonso
ith an AK-47. The soldier is focused on something in
Alonso's hands and, as I move closer, I see it is a frog. The soldier is enraptured by Alonso's
descriptions of the frog and why they are important components of the ecosystem.

LEFT: A glass frog, *Hyalinobatrachium ruedai*, from behind.

A young glass frog sits on a thumb.

A beautiful Cordillera Central Treefrog, *Hyloscirtus larinopygion*, in Sonsón.

An Andean Poison Dart Frog, *Ranitomeya opisthomelas*, in the Chocó rainforest.

⚬

Our first stop on the road dissecting the Chocó is a pretty, small town where men are relaxing in the shade of old trees overhanging a central square. Time feels slow, unhurried. We check into a small but comfortable hotel, leave our bags and head straight out to search for frogs. For the rest of the day we wade up rivers, clamber over fallen rocks and slice through vines. Under the cloak of darkness – when the night shift takes over – the forest is replaced by a soundscape of chirps and wheeps. We home in on the calls of glass frogs with translucent bellies and find many of them up the first river (mainly Emerald Glass Frogs, *Espadarana prosoblepon*) – a good sign that the forests are healthy, for these frogs are among the most sensitive to change. The day and night is a blur of frogs of all shapes and sizes. Large Canal Zone Treefrogs, *Hypsiboas rufitelus*, clasp thick stems with toes separated by a shock of red webbing, and small rocket frogs with red thighs skip through the shallows. Masked Treefrogs, *Smilisca phaeota*, peer from behind elephant ear leaves, and Harlequin Poison Dart Frogs, *Oophaga histrionicus*, with yellow splashed on black induce "oohs" and "aahs" from the team, as do red and black Andean Poison Dart Frogs, *Ranitomeya opisthomelas*. A more colourful assortment of amphibians would be hard to imagine.

⚬

As we travel from one stream to the next in search of frogs, thick Chocó forest is broken only by the occasional settlement consisting of a dozen or so modest huts. Whereas indigenous peoples are nonexistent in Antioquia, having been killed or forced to flee during the Spanish colonisation, local communities stayed put in, or fled to, the Chocó region. The indigenous population is outnumbered only by descendants of African slaves that were brought by the colonisers to tap the region's rich natural resources and who then escaped. These AfroColombians carved a life on the banks of rivers that ribbon through the jungle, sharing the territory with indigenous communities in a mutual display of peace, solidarity and friendship, and in harmony with nature.

But in the past decade and a half, this harmony has been ruptured in this the poorest region in Colombia. Both AfroColombian and indigenous communities have been displaced from their homes by guerillas, paramilitary death squads and new armed groups vying for access to land for coca cultivation and gold, and to control smuggling routes to the Pacific. The FARC, who have long funded their efforts through narco-trafficking (Colombia produces an estimated 410 tonnes of cocaine annually – providing 90 per cent of cocaine consumed in the US, and anti-drug raids in southern Colombia have pushed the cocaine

trade into Chocó) are increasingly turning to lucrative gold mining (the product is legal, even if the methods of extracting it are not) in addition to squeezing extortion payments from gold-miners and loggers. The region is an escalating hotbed of massacres and forced displacements in a country that is exceeded only by Sudan and Iraq in sheer numbers of internally displaced people. One in 20 Colombians – around four million – have become displaced since the 1980s.

The armed conflict in Colombia is a double-edged sword for forest conservation. More than half of Colombia is cloaked in forest, and the uncomfortable truth is that, without violent coercion, many of these forests would not be standing today. Developers and investors have been kept out of these forests for the same reasons as the scientists, and some large tracts have been protected through what is called 'gunpoint conservation' by guerillas. The National Liberation Army (which goes by the Spanish acronym ELN), the second largest leftist guerilla group in Colombia after FARC, protects the forest of the San Lucas Mountains in northern Colombia by placing red-and-black signs warning that landmines are present. Liliana Davalos, in a paper entitled "The San Lucas mountain range in Colombia: how much conservation is owed to the violence?" reports that, "although some miners admit that not all the woods where these signs are posted are thoroughly mined, the persons interviewed would not try to make the point by walking into any marked patch." The point being that, mines or no mines, the signs are an effective deterrent to those thinking about exploiting the area.

The forests are protected for the cover they afford guerillas, but also – somewhat surprisingly – for their role in preserving the hydrology of the area. The FARC have excluded virtually all agriculture and hunting from the Serrania de la Macarena since 1995, claiming their motivating force to be the preservation of the wealth and beauty of the forest for future generations. It just so happens that the same forests also screen the FARC national headquarters from air raids. One of the most surprising motivating forces for conservation actions by guerillas, however, is compassion. Some members of the FARC adopt flagship animals that they are willing to protect as a result of empathy. In the San Lucas Mountains the FARC, concerned about the plight of a Spectacled Bear whose partner in captivity had died, responded with plans to build a local zoo. Such empathy for a living creature seems at odds with their notoriously ruthless methods, but these acts of compassion do not embody values that are ingrained within the organisations for, even though the FARC and ELN

A glass frog, *Hyalinobatrachium ruedai*, peers through a leaf.

tout their environmental concerns on their websites, the construction of roads through wilderness areas indicates that economic interests can easily trump the noble conservation agenda that the groups claim to pursue.

It is these economic interests that pose a significant threat to the forests of Colombia – and especially the Chocó. The FARC, because of their strategic position during the coca boom of the 1980s and 90s, was the first politically oriented armed group to profit from illicit crops. As a result they have funded most of their activities through the cultivation of coca for cocaine; revenue from a single hectare of coca exceeds the average per capita income of Colombia. But government programs to eradicate illicit crops may have actually done more harm than good, targeting rural farmers and pushing growers deeper into the forests to evade detection, forcing them to seek new land to make up for lost revenue. As the government strategically focuses its campaign to eradicate illicit drugs from the southern parts of Colombia, many guerilla groups have moved into northern areas such as Chocó, turning increasingly to a licit product to fund their activities: gold.

ABOVE: Mating Emerald Glass Frogs, *Espadarana prosoblepon*, in the Chocó.

TOP LEFT: A glass frog, *Hyalinobatrachium ruedai*.

BOTTOM LEFT: Does this make me look fat? Cope's Vine Snake, *Oxybelis brevirostris*, wearing a fly in the Chocó rainforests.

Colombia is one of the top 15 gold-producing countries in the world, and about half of its bullion is extracted by small-scale miners and illegal prospectors with little regard for the environment. One of the biggest threats to the forest and its inhabitants (people included) is the mercury used to separate gold from the ore. A report by the United Nations lists Colombia as the world's largest mercury polluter per capita from mining. Settlers are lured to gold-mining areas by the prospect of making a quick and easy buck. But because people live on the brink of eviction or violent death, there are few incentives for long-term conservation. When the future is uncertain, a short-term mindset prevails. As Steven Dudley writes in *Walking Ghosts: Murder and Guerilla Politics in Colombia*: "In Colombia there are walking ghosts, people who have crossed death's frontier. They're still alive, but many of them wish they were dead. Living, as it stands, is a burden. They're not suicidal. They're just suffering because their enemies have them cornered." The conflict threatens the very foundations of sustainability, because it makes a future hard to imagine.

Despite the clear implications of the conflict for the future of Colombia's forests, there are surprisingly few published studies on this relationship. My quest for research on the topic leads me to Julia Gorricho, a Colombian native finishing the first year of her PhD at Bristol on conflict and conservation in Colombia. While Gorricho laments the marginalisation of conservation in the face of conflict – short-term human needs always seem to trump the environment – she offers an interesting perspective on the potential for conservation to actually contribute to the peace-building process. Although she cautions that those working in the Peace process would "laugh like monkeys" at the suggestion that conservation could lead to peace, she explains how it can help: "Many times when a conflict is very acute, nature conservation projects are among the few activities that continue. They are perceived as neutral among the different actors." Whereas conflict works to destroy networks, conservation works to maintain them. "If you are with a human rights organisation working in some very violent areas, you can't stay more than two to three days because of your focus on areas very central to the Colombian conflict," she explains, "but if you are working with the turtles or the whales or ecotourism, this is seen as something good for the community. This network of stakeholders prevails under violence."

Gorricho provides an example. La Macarena National Park in the north of the country was Colombia's first national preserve and also home to the FARC headquarters. Because

TOP LEFT: A Green Rain Frog, *Pristimantis viridis*, in the Chocó.
BOTTOM LEFT: A Masked Treefrog, *Smilisca phaeota*, sits on a rock in a stream in the Chocó.

of the FARC presence, services from the State such as education and health, police and military were non-existent in the area a decade and a half ago. But National Park rangers were able to stay for two reasons. Firstly, they were not armed – this is a policy in Colombia so that they can do their work without being perceived as a threat. Secondly, they were able to convince the FARC, the government and the local communities that they were just conserving nature and that this was good for all. They involved the communities, giving food as incentives for conservation in the buffer zone of the park. Conservation became the only activity that was continuing in this high-conflict area. The presence of the rangers, and their relationship with the local communities, enabled the government to get a foothold in the area. "They started doing this consolidation programme [to regain territory from illegal actors] using the National Park rangers as the main actors and conduits to the communities to start building the social presence of the State," Gorricho says. The programme brought the military and police into the area, followed by services such as health and education. While Gorricho is careful to point out that the approach is controversial and has a lot of limitations she says that "it's a good example of how nature conservation could contribute to a broader process of peace-building".

Alonso Quevedo demonstrates the translucent quality of glass frog's skin as he holds one inside a clear bag.

As the armed conflict eases its grip and areas such as Chocó open up to development and investment, new conflict arises between indigenous and AfroColombian landowners, and those hungry for gold and land for cattle ranching or coca. Even though the local communities have legal title to the land, they are vulnerable to intimidation and manipulation by guerilla groups, paramilitaries and developers. "Sometimes you have to take conservation into your own hands," explains Alonso as we bounce down the main artery dissecting the forest. With support from groups including Conservation International, Global Wildlife Conservation and Rainforest Trust (previously World Land Trust-US), ProAves has taken conservation of important tracts of forest into its own hands by acquiring land to establish more than 20 private protected areas in Colombia. I ask Paul Salaman, CEO of Rainforest Trust, who has worked in Colombia for more than 20 years, if he feels that this is a promising mechanism for protecting forest in the Chocó. "Private protected areas are a good way of getting a foothold in the community, and it's good because it's a strictly protected area," he says, "but ultimately, to have the greatest impact over the longer-term you need to build on that with community lands and government lands." Half a million hectares of Chocó forest is owned by a few thousand AfroColombian communities, who only populate five to 10 per cent of that area. "They don't live in the forest. They are very superstitious. They live along the rivers," Salaman explains before adding, "but they are being bribed by gold miners to rip up the entire area." I ask if these communities face the threat of being displaced if they don't comply, to which he responds yes, before adding soberly, "well, they are displaced to Heaven."

I ask Salaman what, in his view, are the most pressing threats to the Chocó, and he doesn't miss a beat before responding: "Gold. Without a doubt. It is unlike anything I have seen in over 20 years of working in Colombia." Reagents for gold exploitation and coca processing constitute one of the most outstanding environmental hazards in the Chocó. But what about a new movement called Oro Verde, or Green Gold – involving a process that uses leaves from a balsa tree to separate gold from ore with minimal leaching of toxic substances into the rivers? "People haven't even heard of it," he replies, adding that there are a couple of pilot projects, but he doesn't hold out much hope for it cleaning up gold-mining in the Chocó. It is not only the mining, he explains, which results in the release of mercury into the rivers, but also the settlement that results alongside gold mines, the opening up of previously inaccessible wilderness areas to hunting and deforestation, that is really threatening the future of the forests.

In an attempt to scale up their impact, Rainforest Trust have joined forces with ProAves and other groups to establish a private protected area called Las Tangaras, which abuts the road linking Medellín with Quibto. This has allowed them a foothold in an important area. They are now working with the University in Quibto to make a Regional Natural Park adjoining Las Tangaras. The advantage of this approach, Salaman explains, is that it doesn't need declaration at the National level; just the regional level. The Chocó Regional Natural Park is 166,000 hectares, Las Tangaras forming the entrance that buffers government land.

Another approach that is being piloted in Chocó is tapping into carbon markets and essentially paying people not to cut down their trees. A project in Urabá (a subregion of the Chocó department), the first of its kind on collective lands, has been developed within the framework called Reduced Emissions through Deforestation and Degradation plus Conservation, or REDD+, by an American anthropologist called Brodie Fergusson. The project was developed after Fergusson had completed research on the impact of forced displacement in the region. As families retuned nearly a decade after being displaced, and with the restoration of relative peace to the area, Fergusson approached the communities about the concept of carbon conservation in 2007, and developed a mechanism to provide income to 800 beneficiaries in the local communities for managing the forests. Community stakeholders receive at least 50 per cent of revenues from carbon credit sales, and the project takes advantage of state-of-the-art laser remote sensing technology so that community patrols can monitor forest biomass and wildlife habitat. In an interview with *Mongabay*, Fergusson proudly declares, "This achievement demonstrates that Afro-descendant and indigenous landholders can play a central role in protecting tropical forests and preventing climate change," adding, "for the first time, forest-dependent communities in the Chocó are generating income from carbon markets while preserving their traditional ways of life." The report indicates that "REDD now offers communities in the Chocó an alternative development model that could allow them to continue using their lands for traditional activities while gaining access to improved health and education, microfinance, and sustainable business opportunities". Both Salaman and Gorricho are positive about the project. Salaman suggests that there are challenges to scaling up this approach to other parts of Colombia, however, indicating that the project is working in a relatively low impact area. "But what happens when you have armed stakeholders who want to mine gold or plant coca or cut trees for cattle pasture?" Because there is no real framework for REDD from the Ministry of the Environment, exporting the model would be challenging. In a country as dynamic as Colombia, there is no 'one-size fits all' solution, and many approaches will need to be adopted to protect the treasure chest of natural resources.

What is clear is that the future of the forests of Chocó and Antioquia depend upon the resolution of conflict whilst protecting the trees that will no longer be safeguarded through violent means. Whatever the strategy, it is also going to be necessary to rebuild a relationship between Colombians and their land – a disconnect that Gorricho explains: "If you are an American, you have to go to Yellowstone and enjoy nature. It is part of being American. The problem in Colombia is that, for many years when I was growing up, you weren't able to go into these areas. You knew the Chocó was there and the Amazon was there, but you couldn't go and see them." Gorricho says that instead of exploring her own country she would go on family holidays to the USA: "It was cheaper and easier to get to Miami than to get to the Chocó." While Colombia appears to the outsider to brim with pride for its diversity of landscapes and ecosystems, Gorricho feels that this is more a discourse to sell the country. "It is not embedded in Colombian agenda or politics," she says. As the armed conflict eases, perhaps it will open a window of opportunity for Colombians to reconnect with their remarkable natural heritage, embedding it not only in politics, but in the hearts and minds of people from Chocó to Bogota and beyond.

༉

Meanwhile, in the streams that weave through the Chocó forests, we are discovering the incredible biological riches that the steamy jungles have to offer. I have never seen so many different kinds of frogs in such a short space of time. The abundance of glass frogs along streams is amazing – we find one of the little green jewels every 20-odd metres up the banks – it's a good sign for the condition of these forests that such sensitive creatures are thriving. But something is nagging at me. Despite our bounty of frogs, I can't ignore the fact that no lost species have turned up. Indeed, none of the lost species across Colombia will turn up throughout the course of the Lost Frogs campaign. Lucy's story is looking precarious, devoid of any headline-grabbing findings, and I start to detect a frantic air as she pieces together the story of the failed search. Until, that is, the story takes a turn.

We are hiking a steep, muddy trail into primary Chocó forest in ponchos that seemed like a good idea as we set out but are starting to feel like a gruelling weight-loss programme. We stop to shed layers – a steady rain bringing welcome relief on burning cheeks – and glug cool water, when Alonso appears holding a maroon toad the size of his thumb with ruby-red eyes. It is the first toad with such red eyes that I have ever seen – and, incredibly, it is the first toad with red eyes that Alonso or any of our Colombian partners have seen. It is, with little doubt, a species unknown to science. The air is electric as we bounce around

Alonso Quevedo holds up a new species of red-eyed toad from the Chocó.

names for this new toad. I sense Lucy's elation and relief, and I feel as though the weight of expectation has been lifted. We photograph and release the toad (to describe the species Alonso and team would need to secure the right research permits to return – at the time of writing, the toad is awaiting formal description and naming) and continue on our frog hunt with renewed urgency and vigour.

We are on a roll, and the positive energy leads to further finds. Later the same day we are picking our way up the banks of a small river when Lucy spots some rocket frogs with bright red thighs skipping in the shallows. At first Alonso believes they may be a new species – sadly for Lucy they are later identified as a previously described rocket frog. As we are studying the beautiful red flashes on the thighs of the tiny frogs, Wes appears from upstream with a red-brown toad the size of a thumbnail, with an elongated and pointed nose. It is beautiful, with nodes of blue strewn down its flank like miniature jewels. Alonso takes the small creature between his thumb and forefinger and holds it close to his eyes as though scrutinising a rare gem. As his eyebrows climb up his forehead, I realise that this may be an unusual find. I wait with baited breath before he eventually announces, "This is a beaked toad – none are known to live in this area – it is likely a new species." In an ironic twist of fate, we have discovered, during our search for our lost beaked toad, an entirely new one.

Our new species finds – a final tally of two – are a thrilling antidote to the disappointment of failing to find the Mesopotamia Beaked Toad and Chocó Harlequin Frog. That we uncovered species new to science in just a few days in the field is testament to how rich and unknown these jungles really are. The beaked toad went on to achieve its own fame, being named one of *Time* magazine's top ten new species of 2010. Its popularity was boosted by an off-the-cuff comparison I made between the appearance of the toad and Montgomery Burns, the nefarious villain in the TV show *The Simpsons*. The comparison was validated by George Meyer, long-time producer and writer for *The Simpsons*, who responded by saying "The toad's imperious profile and squinty eyes indeed look like Monty Burns." And so the Monty Burns Toad was born.

Shortly after its discovery, the future of the maroon toad with ruby eyes looked precarious as its forest home came under the threat of imminent clearing for cattle. In a remarkable display of swift action and nimble negotiation, within weeks Alonso bought, with support from Conservation International and Rainforest Trust, the core habitat of the toad to create Las Tangaras Reserve. A research centre was built, and six months later I returned with Don and company to the centre to train a group of young and enthusiastic

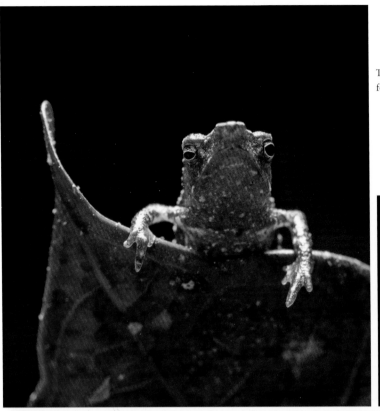

The new species of beaked toad found in the Chocó of Colombia.

Colombian students to search for lost frogs. The centre continues to attract adventure-seeking naturalists and provides revenue for the protection and management of the reserve.

⚭

I feel enormously privileged to have treaded through the Andean forests of Antioquia and the steamy jungles of the Chocó, and to have been part of a search team that uncovered two undescribed species, confirming just how much remains to be known about these forests. As conflict in this area wanes and threats to the forest loom, we are also poised with an incredible opportunity to protect this biological treasure chest through a variety of public and private partnerships and incentive schemes. It would be a travesty not to.

All of Colombia's lost frogs – 22 in all – remain lost, however, last seen between 15 and 100 years ago. On the surface it doesn't look good for these frogs, but I hold out hope. The forest habitat of the Mesopotamian Beaked Toad has been greatly modified since the toad was discovered and last seen 100 years ago; whittled down to fragments that may or may not be sufficient in size to preserve viable populations. But we have received convincing reports of a small toad with a conical head from two local families in the area. I believe that the Mesopotamia Beaked Toad still exists.

And what about the 12 species of harlequin frogs that are missing in Colombia? Throughout the country, as in other parts of Central and South America, a lethal combination of habitat alteration, climate change and disease may have led to the decimation of many populations. But the role of disease in the decline of amphibians in Colombia has not been widely studied, and its interaction with climate change can only be inferred. With a window of stability allowing researchers to enter these forests once more, we have an opportunity to determine the fate of these species.

Finding elusive frogs requires patience and perseverance. People from the local communities of Sonsón have been trained and encouraged to keep watch for the missing Mesopotamia Beaked Toad, as have individuals who expressed interest in other regions to continue searching for lost harlequin frogs. I draw hope from harlequin frogs that have made a comeback in Colombia in recent years. In 2006 the Painted Toad (*Atelopus ebenoides* – a striking jet black harlequin frog with splashes of white and yellow) reappeared after an 11-year absence of sightings in the Boyaca region of central Colombia, and the Santa Marta Harlequin Frog and San Lorenzo Harlequin Frog both reappeared in a newly created reserve in northern Colombia (created by ProAves with support from Conservation International and Rainforest Trust and named El Dorado) after 14 years without trace. I am

127

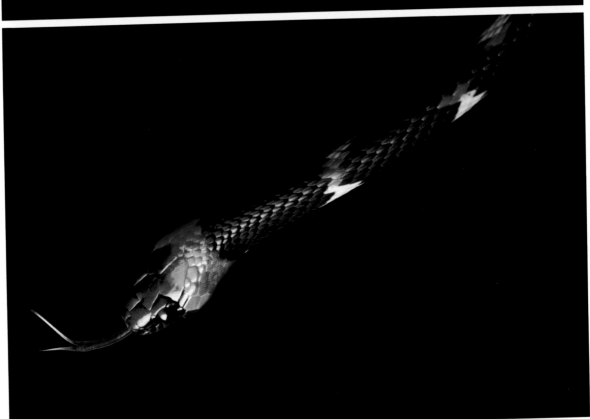

not ready just yet to write off the Mesopotamia Beaked Toad and the lost harlequin frogs of Colombia. Although Colombia tops the world for threatened amphibian species, it also boats an incredible array of known and undiscovered frogs, and offers an opportunity to preserve these species and the forests that they call home.

⚬

My journey in search of lost frogs is off to an auspicious start. With the steamy jungles of Antioquia and the Chocó behind me, I start to plan my search for lost frogs in a country with a very different suite of challenges and opportunities, substituting lush rainforest for fragments of forest clinging onto brown hillsides as dry as a bone. My next expedition will be to Haiti, but in the meantime I return to Washington, DC, to check in on the status of other search teams.

TOP LEFT: A pit viper, *Botrhocophias punctatus*, in the Chocó.
BOTTOM LEFT: A snake from the genus *Dispas*.

CHAPTER 9

LOST AND FOUND

As team after team went in search of lost frogs, with unbridled optimism and infectious enthusiasm, the words of 19th-century naturalist John Burroughs came to mind: "You must have the bird in your heart before you can find it in the bush." But even having the frog in your heart does not guarantee you will find it – as many teams discovered after days and weeks of fruitless searches. The disappointment was palpable in their reports – but many expressed a reinforced drive to find their lost species, ending with "we will return". With the bitter ache of disappointment at not finding the Mesopotamia Beaked Toad still fresh, I was impressed by this display of dogged optimism and commitment. But as report after report came in documenting failed searches, I began to grow concerned that the drive and passion of the search teams might not be enough to bring any of the frogs back. As the weeks rolled by and lost frogs remained lost, the question weighed on my mind: What if not a single lost frog reappeared?

It was a bright morning in early September – a month into the campaign – when things changed. As I opened my laptop, the subject line of an email from N'Goran Kouame in the Ivory Coast caught my attention. N'Goran had been providing regular reports on the progress of their search – which for weeks had proven unsuccessful in finding the Mount Nimba Reed Frog (*Hyperolius nimbae*), last seen 43 years previously, and the Ivory Coast Toad (*Amietophrynus danielae*) last seen 33 years previously. The subject of this email struck a very different tone: "*Hyperolius nimbae* found!" I anxiously clicked on it: "Yes, it is fantastic. *Hyperolius nimbae* has been found after 43 years! I am sending you this news from a Cybercafé in Danané." After a description of how the team of young biologists homed in on the metallic click of the toad to find one male (of which they captured footage taken with a small video camera), the excitement jumped out of the screen as N'Goran concluded: "Yes, it is *Hyperolius nimbae*!" The find validated the importance of a global priority site for conservation, and presented a second chance at saving this rare species. My immediate reaction was first to contact N'Goran with hearty congratulations, then to share the news with my colleagues. The elation – and relief – was palpable in every response.

Africa was about to produce another surprise find, delivered to me through an email from Jos Kielgast, a young amphibian biologist from the Natural History Museum of

Denmark, after he saw the Search for Lost Frogs in the news. Kielgast – who had been elected to the board of the Danish herpetological society when he was nine years old ("They thought it was funny, I guess, to have someone so young," he says) – recounts his discovery in the forests of the Democratic Republic of Congo. "I was not looking for this species in particular," he says, "in fact I thought it was new to science when I initially found it in Salonga National park [DRC's largest national park]. I went there from Kinshasa by a Cessna plane, which took me to a tiny village in the forest. I then hiked 36km to the campsite of some primatologists where I would work for the next month." At the end of the trek into remote jungle, Kielgast's efforts were rewarded when he found the Omaniundu Reed Frog (*Hyperolius sarkuruensis*), a stunning frog of brown mottled with an almost fluorescent green. The frog had not been recorded since 1979.

As we prepared to announce the two findings to the world, another curious report came in, this time from a young amphibian biologist called Sean Rovito. Rovito had been exploring the caves of Mexico in search of the Cave Splayfoot Salamander, and wrote of his expedition: "I began by talking to the people of Durango, in Hidalgo Province, near the only known locality of the Cave Splayfoot Salamander (*Chiropterotriton mosaueri*). I knew that no one had seen the salamander since its discovery in 1941, and that the location of the cave

Mount Nimba Reed Frog, *Hyperolius nimbae*, rediscovered after 43 years in a swampy field in Danipleu, an Ivorian village near the Liberian border.

it had come from was not known precisely, so my expectations were quite low." Some of the locals told Rovito that they obtained their water from a nearby cave, but indicated that they had entered the cave many times and had never seen salamanders. Undeterred, Rovito asked them to show him to the cave. "We went just before sundown," Rovito continues, "the cave was on a steep slope covered with pine and oak trees, with lots of limestone and agave plants all around. No sooner had I entered than I saw a large adult salamander with a very long tail atop a rock on the cave floor."

Rovito had seen many salamanders before, but this one was different. He knew in that instant that it was the Cave Splayfoot Salamander. "It was exhilarating to be the first to see a species that had been seen only once, and so long ago." Rovito continues, "after excitedly telling my companions from the town, I reentered the cave and found another species, *Chiropterotriton magnipes* (the Bogfoot Splayfoot Salamander), crawling upside down on the cave ceiling. This species was only known from a handful of sites, all rather far away from where I was, and was certainly one of the most unusual amphibians I had ever seen with its giant feet and nearly translucent skin." The salamander, although more recently seen than the cave splayfoot, happened to be on the IUCN's list of "possibly extinct" species. In this one cave Rovito had confirmed the existence of two unique salamander species feared to be extinct. He later said of the experience: "I feel tremendously lucky not only to have found these magnificent salamanders, but also to know that both of these species persist in the wild after so many years. The people from the town were also excited to know that the salamander still existed on their land, and invited me to stay for a delicious dinner while we talked about salamanders and other animals and plants they had seen near their town. It was one of the most exciting days I have had in five years of working with the tropical salamanders."

On 22 September a press release went out: 'Making a Splash – 'Extinct' Amphibians Rediscovered After Decades Lost to Science.' The release generated 65 articles in 15 countries in outlets including the BBC, CNN, *National Geographic* and *The Guardian* – and was seen by more than 300 million viewers. People, it seemed, were hooked. Why exactly they cared is something I will come back to later. In the meantime, back to the searches.

TOP LEFT: The Omaniundu Reed Frog, *Hyperolius sankuruensis*, rediscovered in the Democratic Republic of Congo after 31 years.

BELOW LEFT: Cave Splayfoot Salamander, *Chiropterotriton mosaueri*, last seen in 1941, the year it was discovered, was rediscovered in the caves of Durango, Mexico.

CHAPTER 10

LOST FROGS IN THE LAND
OF THE LIVING DEAD, HAITI

Massif de la Selle, Haiti, October 2010

A sadness echoes through the brown hillsides of Haiti, ricocheting off craggy limestone outcrops once cloaked in verdant forest. Where the delicate whistle of the La Selle Grass Frog once rose from moist leaf litter under a canopy of tree ferns, wind now whips dust into spiraling clouds and scatters it into the air around me. As I scour the grassy slopes of the Massif de la Selle, the site where the La Selle Grass Frog was last seen a quarter of a century ago, the frog starts to feel like a poignant symbol of a Haiti past.

Haiti, a land where the line between myth and reality is blurred and the walking dead are accepted as a part of life, has fascinated me since I stepped foot on its parched soil in early 2007. The country does not want for stories of loss; the name is synonymous with misfortune and suffering. But what about stories of hope? To uncover hope in Haiti, one must dig a little deeper, past layers of sadness to a place where dew drips from splendid orchids and a gentle mist rolls through forest, carrying a story on a symphony of calls for whoever will listen. There are few more compelling backdrops against which to search for lost frogs than in the hidden forest fragments that cling to rugged limestone mountains in this misunderstood country.

∝

Port-au-Prince to Massif de la Hotte, Haiti, February 2007

I emerge into the bright sunlight from Port-au-Prince airport to be accosted by a scurry of uniformed men waving passes in my face and trying to wrestle my bags from my hands. I tighten my grip and let them know in my sternest voice that I am OK as I scramble to get my bearings. Beads of sweat roll from my forehead amid the claustrophobic scrum. It is with relief that through the crowds I spot Philippe Bayard, who shepherds me to the air-conditioned sanctity of his car. We drive among people swarming the road, past piles of rubbish being consumed by pigs, to the hotel where I will spend the night. Less than two

Hillsides stripped of vegetation north of Port-au-Prince, Haiti.

hours from Miami, I have entered a different world.

Early the next morning it takes an age to navigate the choked streets of Port-au-Prince, but eventually we leave the city behind and start our journey along the southern Tiberon Peninsula towards the Massif de la Hotte. As the road hugs the coastline, I try to imagine the lives of the people inhabiting small wooden huts scattered along the beach. The setting is picture-postcard; palm trees leaning lazily over calm waters lapping warm sands. But I can't help wondering what the same scene means to someone who wakes up each day to the caustic gnaw of hunger; who stares out to endless sea wondering if today it will provide enough protein to feed their family. The picture-postcard image is an illusionary escape for those who spend most of their lives behind computer screens and under the fluorescent glow of office lights, but it is also the stage for a story of unimaginable hardship and suffering. I feel a wave of guilt as I meet the stares of people through the window of our vehicle; guilty for the glass that separates my world from theirs. The poverty is more acute than any I have witnessed before. We scroll past fishermen and farmers eking out a living from the sea and barren land. Where forest once hummed with life, chiselled torsos glisten in the midday sun as men hack at brown dust, attempting to plant on impossibly steep slopes before the soil is baked or washed away. I stare at mountains that recede in ridges

Children catch fish off a picture-postcard beach in southern Haiti.

mirroring the angular backs of cadaverous cows, and struggle to picture the rich forest that once cloaked and protected the undulating earth.

As Port-au-Prince disappears further behind us and the slopes of the Massif de la Hotte loom closer, children wave from the doorways of huts. I roll down the window to feel the breeze and begin to relax as the gulf between our worlds, for brief moments, dissolves. I put my camera away and simply enjoy these fleeting moments when I feel a welcome guest to their world. But as we pass one denuded hillside after another, I can't help but wonder if I am going to find what I am here for.

⁊

I am in Haiti to find forest. More specifically, I am here to find the forest that contains the richest concentration of critically endangered frogs in the world. My burning desire to visit Haiti was ignited by a study published in 2005 revealing those species whose entire global range has been whittled down to a single site. In terms of extinction risk, these sites and species were the tip of the iceberg – lose the site, lose the species – and, in response, a consortium of several dozen conservation groups formed the Alliance for Zero Extinction, to promote the protection of these critical areas. While more than 500 sites made the list, one site came out top for sheer numbers of unique species. That site, with a staggering 13 critically endangered frogs (this is now 15) found nowhere else in the world, was the Massif de la Hotte in southwest Haiti. The Massif de la Selle, which rises to the south of Port-au-Prince, also made the list on account of the unique La Selle Grass Frog. But the study also revealed something curious; around half of the species occurring in these two areas had not been seen in more than a decade and a half. In a country changing so quickly, how could we be sure these frogs were still there? I wanted to find out if they were.

The sudden spotlight on the Massif de la Hotte caught the international conservation community with its pants down, so to speak. Nobody was doing anything in Haiti to protect the dwindling forests, and few people even realised there was any forest left. But there were a couple of people with their sights firmly fixed on protecting the country's remaining forest. Chris Rimmer, at the time with the Cornell Ornithological Institute, was studying Bicknell's Thrush, a bird that summers in the northeast USA but winters in Haiti and the Dominican Republic. Philippe Bayard, President of local NGO Société Audubon Haiti, was aggressively promoting the importance of conservation from within Haiti. But conservation was eclipsed by more pressing concerns, of which the country had many. With the formation of the Alliance for Zero Extinction they saw an opportunity to bring in the international conservation community – and that included me.

It was with a pang of responsibility, having been involved in the study that highlighted

Pine forests of the Massif de la Selle, rising south of Port-au-Prince.

the importance of the Massif de la Hotte, and with more than an inkling of curiosity, that I booked my flight to join Chris and Philippe on a quest to find Haiti's remnant forests.

⚬

One question loomed large in my mind as I worked on the study that revealed the Massif de la Hotte to be the richest in unique species in the world. *Why*? The reason that Haiti – and the Massif de la Hotte in particular – bursts at the seams with unique and threatened species is revealed by unpeeling the rich history of the country.

Let's start with its location. Haiti occupies one-third of the island of Hispaniola in the Caribbean; the remaining two-thirds are claimed by the Dominican Republic. The Caribbean Islands as a whole are a hotspot of species diversity and endemism – that is, they contain a lot of unique animals and plants. Islands in general provide ideal conditions for the formation of new species. Rather like the Galapagos, the Caribbean islands have been referred to as a 'theatre of evolution' for lizards and other creatures, many of which happen to be very small (the islands of the Caribbean boast the world's smallest bird, the tiny Bee Hummingbird, which is little bigger than, yup, you've guessed it, a bee, the smallest snake, and some of the world's smallest frogs).

The Caribbean islands are a theatre of evolution for lizards and other species, such as this unidentified Anolis lizard from the Massif de la Hotte.

Hispaniola Giant Treefrog, *Oseopilus vastus*, an endangered species on the Massif de la Selle.

The island of Hispaniola, the second largest island in the Caribbean after Cuba, formed some nine million years ago when three lumps of rock came together. Two of these lumps were formerly attached to Cuba and Puerto Rico, a history visible today through species shared by two of the islands. Perhaps the most bizarre of these species, found only on Hispaniola and Cuba, are the solenodons, giant, venomous shrews that look like they belongs in the era of the dinosaurs. The Cuban Solenodon, incidentally, disappeared in 1890 and was long presumed extinct until it made a surprise reappearance in 1974 (since then, sightings have been few and far between).

After Hispaniola formed, sea levels and climate continued to yo-yo for several million years, and mountains were repeatedly joined and isolated by either sea or dry, inhospitable terrain. What this meant was that the forested slopes of mountain ranges such as the Massif de la Hotte and Massif de la Selle became refuges for species adapted to wet, cool conditions. Over time these creased slopes became species factories. Once sea levels and the climate stabilised, a verdant island bursting with unique lifeforms was left.

And then the Europeans arrived.

Upon setting foot on Hispaniola for the first time in 1492, Christopher Columbus was struck by its exuberance and promptly named the island La Isla Española because it

The cloudforests of the Massif de la Hotte were a refuge for species adapted to cool, wet conditions during climatic fluctuations.

reminded him of Spain. "There, in that high and mountainous land, is the land of God," he proclaimed as the lush mountains receded from view for the final time in 1504. He was clearly enamoured by the island, which attracted Spanish and then French colonisers. The latter established a stronghold in the western part of Hispaniola to the point where, in the late 17th century, the Spanish formally ceded this portion to the French. The island was in this way divided into two nations: the eastern two-thirds were called Santo Domingo (later to become – and hereafter referred to as – the Dominican Republic) and the western third Saint-Domingue (which later became Haiti after the Taino word for 'land of mountains'). And so an imaginary line divided the landscapes, the ecosystems and the species – including humans – producing very different futures depending upon which side of the line you fell, a line which is visible today through the windows of an airplane, brown on one side and green on the other.

After Hispaniola's indigenous Taino people were obliterated, the conquistadors on both sides of the line shipped over boat-loads of slaves from West Africa. Although both the Dominican Republic and Haiti imported African slaves, Haiti did so to a much greater extent. So much so that, by the end of the 18th century, there were at least 500,000 black slaves in Haiti compared to only 30,000 whites. With a proliferation of slave labour and untapped natural capital, Haiti quickly prospered, coining the nickname, 'The Jewel of the Antilles.' In the 1750s the country provided as much as half of the Gross National Product of France, and could boast the title of richest colony in the world, supporting the production of more exportable wealth annually than all of continental North America. Forest-cloaked mountains alive with the chatter of birds and frogs fed lush valleys, and sugar, coffee, cocoa, tobacco and cotton abounded. Times were good!

But this burst of prosperity opened Haiti to exploitation, and came at the expense of the country's environmental capital of forests and soils. Cheques were being written for an account that was fast running into the red. Times were about to change.

In the 1790s the revolution that was taking hold in France spread across the ocean as the country's colonial slaves also began to revolt. In 1804 Haiti became the world's first sovereign black republic. From this point forward a sinister dance of greed, corruption and environmental devastation plunged the Haitian masses into some of the most acute misery of any people in the world. In order to achieve France's diplomatic recognition, the young nation of Haiti had to pay a crippling sum to its former coloniser. It was not just foreign powers that exploited Haiti, but also its neighbours and its own rulers. A string of dictators raped and pillaged Haiti for all it was worth – the country did not have a freely elected President until 1990, when Jean-Bertrand Aristide was elected – then ousted – then reinstated. Oh, and then ousted again.

The Hispaniola Yellow Treefrog, *Osteopilus pulchrilineatus*, an endangered species in the Massif de la Hotte.

To the east of the line, meanwhile, the Dominican Republic benefitted from a relatively stable political system. The country also enjoyed a more fortunate geography, for the northeast tradewinds blew in the Dominican Republic's favour, bringing rains that fell on Hispaniola's highest mountains on the Dominican side and formed rivers that mainly flowed eastwards, away from Haiti. The Dominican side had broad valleys, plains and plateaus and much thicker soils, making some areas, such as the Cibao Valley in the north of the country, some of the richest agricultural areas in the world. As a result, much of the environment of the Dominican Republic was spared, and the country still has some 40 per cent forest cover and 118 protected areas.

Across the imaginary line in Haiti, a combination of a large human population and low rainfall drove the loss of forests and soil fertility, exacerbating challenges to agriculture presented by a rugged limestone topography and semiarid climate. The changes were both rapid and dramatic. In 1925 Haiti boasted 60 per cent of its original forest cover; it now clings on to less than two per cent. The loss of trees has predictably led to desertification, severe erosion in the mountains, and periodic but catastrophic flooding. Haiti has been dragged to the precipice that overlooks ecological collapse. Where once stood bubbling theatres of evolution now stand clumps of trees amid an expanding sea of barren, infertile soil. Almost all of the remaining broadleaf forest on Haiti is restricted to remote and inaccessible areas high on the rugged limestone slopes of the Massif de la Hotte and, to a lesser extent, the Massif de la Selle.

It is in these remote forests that some of the most imperilled frogs in the world are found. Fifty species of frog are known from Haiti and a staggering 46 of these at risk of extinction; no other country in the world comes close to this level of threat. The Massif de la Hotte and Massif de la Selle are the last refuge for many of these species – a quarter of all frog species known from the island of Hispaniola occur only in the Massif de la Hotte. If, that is, the frogs and their forest home were still there.

&

"First I would head to Castillon on the northwestern flank of the Massif de la Hotte," Dr. Blair Hedges, the authority on Haitian frogs, had urged as I prepared for my first expedition. Hedges had discovered and described a good portion of the frog species on Haiti and was the only person to have recorded many of these. It would be three years before I would meet him in person, but in the lead-up to this first expedition he was invaluable in honing my mission. "This was one of the best spots in the Caribbean for frogs," he continued, "but that was in 1990. Hopefully things won't have changed too much…" His parting words ring in my ears and loop around my stomach in a tightening knot as we traverse the Tiburon Peninsula toward the Massif de la Hotte. I can't help but feel that, in the past 17 years, things may have changed.

We spend a long first day clinging on with white knuckles as we barrel along roads strewn with potholes, as if our momentum will carry us over the top, dodging people as they run through the traffic. People everywhere. Vehicles come at us on our side of the road, swerving out of our path at the last minute. The ride, while hair-raising, is a chance to soak in the different landscapes and learn more about Haiti from my traveling companions Chris Rimmer and Philippe Bayard. Chris hails from the northeast USA but has been drawn to Haiti by Bicknell's Thrush. He is, on account of his concern for the future of Haiti's forests, largely responsible for me being here. Philippe is a Haitian businessman who dabbles in everything from renting aircraft to printing the National Currency. Closely cropped grey hair and a commanding voice lend him a distinguished air. He talks passionately – sometimes angrily – about the state of Haiti's environment. Philippe is President of the Societe Audubon Haiti, or SAH, one of few active environmental organisations in Haiti, and is clearly driven to change the status quo.

As the light is waning we roll into Jeremie, a bustling but rundown town on the northern coast of the Tiburon Peninsula. We eat well and turn in for a good night's rest; the next day we will wake early to start our ascent into craggy mountains that pierce billowing clouds; the Massif de la Hotte.

We make an early start and enjoy the golden morning light and cool air as we set off. The road winds up the foothills of the Massif de La Hotte, past small villages and long stretches of brown hillsides. Where is the forest? I stare through my dust-speckled window at thin smoke plumes rising like incense from hillsides as smooth as a swimmer's chest. Children carrying sticks on their heads watch us pass from the roadside. The occasional mound of earth covers smouldering branches slowly forming charcoal – the country's primary source of fuel. Eventually we reach a small gathering of huts by the side of the road and the car grinds to a halt. We clamber out to stretch stiff limbs and are quickly surrounded by people. The entire village, it seems, with nothing else to do has come to watch us. Empty market stalls line the road and I catch the faint whiff of charred corn on the cob. "Welcome to Castillon," says our driver. "Are you sure….?" My voice trails off as we spread a map on the bonnet: it looks like we are indeed in Castillon. I walk to the road edge and scan the landscape: smouldering, smooth hillsides roll as far as the eye can see.

"Let's walk," announces Philippe as he sets off along a trail leading from the road. We scurry after him in a line like eager ducklings.

An ethereal mist envelops us as soon as we set off along the trail and a slight breeze carries the sound of chanting. The source of the chanting is unclear, but it is both beautiful and haunting. When the mist lifts momentarily I see that it is the song of women as they clear and burn vegetation below us. We pass some pockets of vegetation clinging to steep ravines, but they deserve only a cursory exploration for they are little more than poignant reminders of forest past, now too small and too isolated to offer any kind of refuge for threatened species. Any species inhabiting these fragments are likely to be what are referred to as "living dead," serving out a sentence while the last trees around them are slashed and burned.

We walk for two hours, becoming disoriented at times in the thick mist, before a

Children playing in the Ravine du Sud.

shared sense of hopelessness peters us to a halt. It is hard to imagine that this place was ever anything other than barren hillsides. "Let's head back," says Philippe. Nobody argues. We walk, heads bowed, back to the car.

Things, it would appear, have changed.

⚶

Back at the car we spread the map on the bonnet; the only antidote for our wilting spirits is to plan our next approach to the Massif de la Hotte and launch a renewed quest to find forest. Having approached from the northwest, we will approach it tomorrow from the south. It is a longer and bumpier drive that includes a river crossing, but it offers our best chance at setting foot in cloud forest. We cut across the Tiburon Peninsula, reaching the southern coastal city of Les Cayes – birthplace of the great ornithologist and artist John James Audubon – in the pale light of evening. It is our last point of civilisation and so we find a basic but comfortable hotel to spend the night before embarking on the rough ride towards Caye Michel, a small settlement in the foothills of the Massif.

The following morning is cool as we set off from Les Cayes, and a deep blue sky is broken by cloud that hugs the angular outline of the mountains ahead of us. I learn that the Michel, after whom Caye Michel (our destination town) is named, was killed driving across the Ravine Du Sud, at the point in the river that we are on our way to traverse. It is now the dry season, however, and while the river is wide, it is an easy crossing as it barely tickles the underside of the car. Once through the river we start our slow ascent on rocky 'roads'. Several hours, 1,000 metres higher, and six punctures later we roll into Caye Michel. As we are down to our last tyres, one of the vehicles promptly turns around to make the journey back to Les Cayes to get spares. "And what if they get a puncture on the way?" I dare to ask. The response is a wide-eyed shrug that indicates that bridge will be crossed as and when needed. Sometimes, in Haiti, it is better not to ask.

Within minutes of arrival we are surrounded by the entire population of Caye Michel. I start to wonder if Haitians everywhere are simply sitting around waiting for us to show up. They clamber to be hired as cooks and porters, and soon the bartering begins – a loud and impassioned exchange in Creole between Erwin (our driver and guide) and the locals. As it escalates I timidly inquire "Ummmm … is everything OK?" "We need to be careful in choosing who we hire as porters," Chris explains, "last time, all the porters were from one family. The next week their homes were burned down. We need to make sure we avoid creating jealousy." I let them get on with it.

Caye Michel is a scattering of buildings, many derelict and decaying, on the fringe of Macaya Biosphere Reserve, a 5,500 hectare reserve that protects some of the last forest on Haiti. From here I am treated to the sight of limestone forest hugging rugged slopes and lining deep ravines, transitioning to pine and cloud forest higher up the mountain. The knot in my stomach loosens and a surge of excitement wells at the prospect of hiking in.

⚘

"It has straps …" I offer as one of the porters grabs a large backpack and swings it onto his head. "Or I guess you can also carry it like that ..." He is already out of earshot, bounding between craggy limestone outcrops towards the ravine, and so I hurry after him and join the train. We walk through fragmented forest and rowed fields before the path rises steeply up the deep crease of the ravine. I feel as though my heart is going to pump through my ribs as we make the steep climb to the 2,200 metre Pic le Siel. Soon, we are walking on a carpet of brown needles, and a welcome mist rolls through the pine trees to cool flushed cheeks. We slowly transition from pine forest into cloud forest as ferns and trees dripping with bromeliads loom out of the mist. I imagine a hundred tiny frogs folded in the leaves of the bromeliads; this is the Massif de la Hotte I had imagined. It is perfect frog habitat. Soon we enter a small clearing on Pic le Ciel, drop our bags, stretch and breath in the cool humid air. It feels a million miles from the scorched fields below and even further from the claustrophobic Port-au-Prince. This is a Haiti we rarely hear about; a Haiti that few Haitians and fewer outsiders have seen or heard or felt. I sit on a tree stump and quench my thirst with a long glug of cool water.

Refreshed, I start to turn logs and peel apart bromeliads in the search for frogs. I am surprised by how many frogs I find, considering it is the dry season. Most of the frogs in Haiti – and all of the frogs I find that day on the Massif de la Hotte – belong to a group called the rain frogs (genus *Eleutherodactylus*). The rain frogs skip the tadpole stage, instead laying eggs on the forest floor and in bromeliads, that will hatch directly into froglets. This works well in the limestone slopes of the Massifs of Haiti, where standing water is scarce.

My first find, barely the size of my fingernail, is a brown Tuck-wheep Frog. The frog was first described as far back as 1923 and named for its call. It may be small and brown, but I am excited to have found my first Haitian frog. Although I uncover many frogs, the more elusive species – the Ventriloqual Frog, Crowned Frog, Mozart's Land Frog and Glandular Land Frog – evade me, as does the wonderful Green Spiny Frog. To really search properly for these frogs I would have to plan a return visit in the rainy season, and ideally with the person who knows these frogs the best, Dr. Blair Hedges. Two days later, as the Massif de la Hotte disappears in our rear view mirror, I know deep down that I will return. I have frogs to find.

৯

"We're going to Haiti in January, put it in the diary." It is 2010, three years after my first trip and my boss Claude Gascon has rallied some of the higher-ups at Conservation International including Olivier Langrand, head of the Centre for Conservation and Government and Russ Mittermeier, the President, for a visit to see if and how we can engage in Haiti. Planning for our visit is in full swing when I turn on my computer on the morning of 13 January to a news headline that makes the hairs on my neck stand on end: "Haiti devastated by massive earthquake." I grab my phone – my first instinct is to call Philippe Bayard – but the lines are dead. A couple of days pass before I hear that he and his family are OK. I struggle to comprehend the scale of the tragedy and what it means to Haiti, but Philippe urges us not to cancel our visit. And so, some 16 weeks after the earthquake, I return to Haiti.

৯

Port-au-Prince, Haiti, May 2010

Blue pools dotting the Miami landscape disappear behind us, replaced less than two hours later by blue tents dotting the Port-au-Prince landscape as our plane descends. Driving from the airport is like touring a movie set, the scenes at once familiar and surreal. Piles of rubble entomb bodies waiting to be uncovered; men perch precariously on slabs of concrete, tapping them with small hammers in a futile bid to break them into chunks small enough to move – it is like trying to move a haystack with a spoon. "They cannot afford to have their homes removed. So they try to do it themselves," Philippe explains when he sees my look of disbelief.

I am amongst the carnage but strangely removed. It takes some two hours to cross a city choked with SUVs bearing the logos of international humanitarian and AID groups. We make it out to the Massif de la Hotte for a night, and then to Massif de la Selle for a night, and after a flurry of meetings and engagements Claude, Russ and Olivier depart. I stay on for several days, which I spend in tent cities photographing and videoing conditions for a humanitarian watchdog. It is one of the toughest few days I have spent on any assignment.

147

Walking through a claustrophobic, hot alleyway weaving among closely packed tents I feel the brush of a young boy's hand as he – no older than six years old – reaches up to grab mine. I feel touched by the innocent and friendly gesture, and wonder if he wants to show me where he lives. And so I allow him to guide me. He leads me to a large tent, inside of which a woman is applying makeup to another, towel-clad, woman. The boy cranes his neck to look at me with big dark eyes and says, "Here are the pretty bitches for you," before turning and running off into the maze. He has brought me to the local whorehouse.

My four days in tent cities flit between the surreal and the harrowing. Gruesome stories of unimaginable loss send chills up my spine. Every person has a story to tell, and they are eager to share, as if opening up may unburden them of their suffering. Tear-stained eyes burn into mine as horrific stories of loss are relived. Like the pull of a slow, deep, river, the emotional force of these days in the tent cities drags me into a dark place. As children sing for me, their innocence and vulnerability makes the inhumanity of the situation all the harder to swallow. I ask people about their hopes for the future, and the response is ubiquitous: it's in God's hands. People cannot afford to hope, or to imagine a brighter future. It is something that has struck me repeatedly in Haiti – people appear so worn down that they have all but given up, placing the responsibility of their future into the hands of a higher being.

On my way back to the airport a message scrawled in spray paint on a corrugated metal fence catches my eye. It says: "We can change". It is simple but significant; a recognition that Haiti needs to change from within. It is somewhat paradoxical that, with the earthquake, a window of opportunity has opened for Haiti to change. The eyes of the world are on the country, willing the rebuilding of a better Haiti. There is also a recognition that now is the time to not only rebuild the lives of the Haitian people, but to repair the damage done to Haiti's environment. Without a healthy environment the country will continue its bitter spiral into self-destruction. "Now is the time," urges Philippe, "we need to get the protection and restoration of Haiti's forests on the agenda."

In order to do that we would have to show people what they have to be proud of and to plant the seeds for rebuilding a brighter future. It was also time to show the world that there is more to Haiti than misery, suffering and bad luck. It was time to hold up symbols of hope.

TOP LEFT: A girl sits in a tent city for those displaced by the January 2010 earthquake.

BELOW LEFT: Children and adults go about their business close by a vast city of tents.

CLOCKWISE FROM LEFT:

A disabled girl looks despondent as she opens a bag of crackers in a camp in Port-au-Prince.

An old face on a young girl in a tent city in Port-au-Prince.

A young boy smiles despite the conditions in a tent city in Port-au-Prince, just months after the January 2010 earthquake.

⚂

Massif de la Hotte and Massif de la Selle, Haiti, October 2010

Less than six months after my visit to the tent cities, and two months into the Search for Lost Frogs, I finally join Blair Hedges and a SWAT team of naturalists, photographers and videographers to return to the Massifs de la Hotte and de la Selle in search of lost frogs. We planned our trip for bang in the middle of hurricane season; risky from a logistical standpoint but ideal for finding frogs that favor the rains. I had wrestled with the sensitivity of the timing; Haiti was still reeling from the earthquake and we were going to look for frogs. The enthusiasm of our Haitian partners tipped the scales for me; their desire to present a side of Haiti other than misery and suffering. We needed to shine a spotlight on the importance of conservation in Haiti and we needed to do it now, by highlighting and celebrating Haiti's hidden treasures. The timing was right to hold up the frogs as totems of optimism and hope. Now, we just needed to find those frogs.

⚂

On the Massif de la Hotte we are going in search of six frogs last seen two decades previously; the Ventriloqual Frog, Mozart's Land Frog, the Macaya Breast-spot Frog, La Hotte Glanded Frog, Macaya Burrowing Frog and Hispaniola Crowned Frog. On the Massif de la Selle, a less remote and far more degraded mountain, we will be searching for the La Selle Grass Frog, last seen 25 years previously. The La Selle Grass Frog is a diminutive animal that once hopped and chirped from dew-soaked blades of grass in the mountains rising from Port-au-Prince, but has evaded repeated searches, and is feared extinct by Blair. "Now that's a lost frog," he says, his voice tinged with the weariness of someone who has spent long nights crouched with a headlamp searching without success. I admire his tenacity – the fact that the frog is on our target list is a sign that he isn't ready to give up.

The lost frogs of Haiti share a behaviour that would determine how we look for them; they skip the tadpole stage. Skipping the tadpole stage means that the frogs lay eggs in bromeliads or on the forest floor that hatch directly into froglets, and because they do not need water to breed, they do not congregate at water bodies during breeding season. Therefore, they are dispersed throughout the forest, and our best chance at finding them is going to be homing in on their calls. Identifying a frog from its call requires, naturally, knowledge of its call. Luckily, we have Dr. Blair Hedges, a walking encyclopedia of the frog calls of Haiti. Blair is an eminent biologist at Penn State University; he is a tall, slender man with an articulate and gentle manner. I am intrigued as to how he can recognise a call that he has not heard in some two decades. "I was listening to them on the plane over," he says as if it is the most normal thing in the world, holding up a recorder upon which he has diligently recorded and labeled every Haitian frog he has ever heard. I can't help but imagine the reactions of the other people on the plane if they were to learn that their neighbour was listening to the chirps, tucks and weeps of frogs.

Blair is responsible for naming many of the frogs of Haiti, including most of those on our wanted list. Meticulous by nature, he puts a lot of thought into the names. "Yeeeah," he says, "I really prefer scientific names that have a meaning, rather than patronyms after your best friend or spouse. Although every now and then I will name one after someone." As we rattle in the back of our jeep towards familiar angular peaks of the Massif de la Hotte, I ask him about a couple of names that piqued my curiosity. First the Mozart's Land Frog – I assume that the frog is not capable of composing complex symphonies from an early age? "When I discovered the frog in the 1980s, I recorded its call," he explains. "When I got back to the lab, I made an audiospectogram, and the pattern that came out looked exactly like musical notes!" He sounds incredulous, as if seeing the notes for the first time. And the Ventriloqual Frog – I can only assume it can throw its call? "Well … hopefully you will find out," he replies as he fixes me with a wry smile. Only three individuals of this critically endangered species have ever been collected, all in 1991 and all by Blair. "That would be a good find," he muses, before echoing, "definitely a good find," as if posing himself a challenge.

It is exciting to be on our way to search for frogs in the Massif de la Hotte, with perhaps the most qualified team imaginable stuffed into three vehicles. In addition to Blair the team consists of Miguel Landestoy, a naturalist and photographer from the Dominican Republic with keen eyes and fast hands; Jurgen Hoppe, a videographer from the Dominican Republic with the unenviable task of lugging around multiple kilos of equipment after the frog hunters; Joel Timyan, hailing from the USA but with 20 years of work in Haiti under his belt, Joel knows more about Haitian plants and conservation than just about anyone; Claudio Contreras, a very talented photographer and fellow Associate of the International League of Conservation Photographers; and the enthusiastic and energetic Carlos Manuel Rivera, who has come to collect frogs to try to breed them at Philadelphia Zoo.

Organising the logistics of carting such a motley crew to the remote reaches of Haiti in hurricane season would be enough to give most people heart palpitations. The potential for things to go wrong is huge. But behind Blair's mild manner and soothing drawl lies an astounding attention to detail, as itineraries are drawn out well in advance, even down to toilet breaks. In the weeks leading up to the expedition Blair had circulated comprehensive itineraries and backup plans. With contingencies for the contingency plans, I feel at ease in good hands.

In order to reach Caye Michel we have to cross the infamous river, Ravine du Sud, which this time looks swollen and strong. It takes about 20 minutes of deliberation, involving a lot of staring, head-scratching and lively discussion, to make the call that we are going to attempt to drive through. We have barely entered the water when I feel the tug of the river trying to dislodge the wheels of the car from its rocky foothold. As water starts spouting through the doorframe, my stomach turns. Needless to say, I am here to tell the tale and so I will save you the suspense – we make it across. "Let's just hope it doesn't rain and trap us on this side!" Blair jokes, before his expression changes and he adds, looking at me now, "but seriously, how flexible is your schedule for getting home?"

One puncture and several bumpy hours later we roll into Caye Michel, by which time the sun has already fallen behind the Massif de la Hotte. The building we stayed in three and a half years ago has decayed to the point that it is no longer habitable, and so we are

Mozart's Land Frog, *Eleutherodactylus amadeus*, a critically endangered species found on the Massif de la Hotte, Haiti and last seen in 1991.

ushered into the garden of a local resident to pitch our tents on a concrete slab outside their hut before being served generous helpings of brown mushroom rice and goat meat. We eat in a dimly lit room consumed by a large table. I eat standing, cowering sheepishly to avoid banging my head on low rafters. We polish off the food like lions around a fresh kill, but our minds are on the chirps and wheeps that are filling the deep night air. And so, with stomachs full, we click on our headlamps and go in search of frogs.

Caye Michel, at around 1,000 metres above sea level, is ideally situated for finding frogs, for a curious bulge in the number of species happens at around this elevation, where the lowlands meet the mountains. Dark patches of forest in the fringes of the Macaya Biosphere Reserve offer the promise of frogs, and we walk with our ears to the night. "Shhhh!" says Blair as he raises his right hand. We stop and stand in silence before a *whee-whee-whee-whee-whee-whee-wheeep* pierces the dark, rising in tone at the end as if asking a question to the night. "That's it!" he says, already bounding towards the source of the sound. As we idle beside him he whispers "The Ventriloqual Frog. It's the Ventriloqual Frog!" He explains that it is the only frog known from here with an unmistakeable seven-note call. It is likely that our presence will deter him from calling again and so we click off our headlamps to stand in the cool darkness and wait. I knock my head back and enjoy the night air, breathing in deeply to soak in the rich sounds and smells.

And then again: *Whee-whee-whee-whee-whee-whee-wheeep*. It seems to be coming from an overgrown and crumbling wall some 20 feet in front of us. We click on our lights, inch closer, turn off our lights and then wait again. Inch by inch we home in on the call, lights swinging and clicking on and off like half a dozen lighthouses. Five adults trying to find a brown frog little bigger than a peanut that can throw its call – in the dark. At this point I can confirm that this frog can indeed throw its call. Each time we home in on what appears to be the source, it moves. A long hour of this and slowly, one by one, we peel off, blaspheming, to go in search of something that doesn't have voice-throwing capabilities. I am an early retiree, with a lower threshold for breaking through thorny bushes than Miguel, who sticks it out another hour before emerging from the thorny tangle of vegetation empty-handed, scratched and crestfallen.

Later in the night we again hear *whee-whee-whee-whee-whee-whee-wheeep*, this time emanating from a large, succulent plant some ten feet high with fleshy tubular leaves fringed by rows of clothes-ripping, blood-spilling thorns. We move into position, surrounding the plant, and for the next hour conduct a stop motion dance, slowly moving after each call into this large thorny plant, unhooking spines from clothes and flesh after each movement. And

Macaya Burrowing Frog, *Eleutherodactylus parapelates*, a critically endangered species from the Massif de la Hotte. Last seen 1996.

again it is an exercise in futility, as if the frogs are laughing at us from above, and we give up on our search.

We are drawn to a largely dry riverbed by the chuckle of Hispaniola Treefrogs coming from a small pool. I crouch to observe and photograph some of the frogs, oblivious to the drama that is unfolding as the team moves upstream. Blair has been stopped in his tracks by a call he does not recognise – something that doesn't happen very often. Diving to his knees, he starts to dig frantically, and he does not surface until he has in his hand the prize – a large frog. The species? He is unsure. Further inspection reveals it to be a Macaya Burrowing Frog, last seen in 1996 and never before found in this area. It is a striking creature, with eyes like black pearls and flashes of brilliant orange and black on the thigh.

∂

The next morning Blair and Miguel go off to scour the forests as I stay back with Claudio to photograph frogs. When they return, it is clear from their faces that they are pleased with themselves. Miguel pulls out a small clear plastic bag and proudly presents to us the elusive Ventriloqual Frog. It is a small yellow-brown frog with a dark band across the top of its back, its beauty magnified by its rarity and the effort taken to capture it. I

marvel at the frog, only the fourth individual of this species ever recorded. I am excited to capture it on camera, for it is in photographs that I believe the real beauty of these small frogs is revealed; details too small for the eye are recorded crisp and sharp; colours barely discernible become brilliant.

Later the same day, Miguel finds another hidden gem: it is a small reddish-brown frog with a row of tubercules on the crest of its head – the Crowned Frog, last seen in 1991 and, like the Ventriloqual Frog, known from fewer than 10 individuals. I study the frog, which has a body slightly flattened in an adaptation that allows it to squeeze between the leaves of bromeliads and orchids, before photographing it.

After lunch we prepare for our hike up the mountain to Pic le Ciel, to retrace our steps of three and a half years ago. We pack our tents, plenty of water and enough trail mix to see us through the next couple of days and set off on the heart-pumping hike up the mountain. I am encouraged by the state of the forest, which seems to have changed relatively little since my last visit. I find an old tree that I photographed on my previous trip and am heartened to find it still dripping with bromeliads. Other than a couple of brief stops to hydrate and lift some logs in search of frogs, we make the ascent in one vigorous burst and set up camp in the clearing at Pic le Ciel. Within an hour the light of the day is replaced by a darkness illuminated by sound. The night is owned by the frogs and, with a click of our headlamps the frog-hunting begins in earnest. We don't have to go far to find them; our tents become unlikely frog magnets. Clear plastic bags fill with frogs that range in size from a little larger than a grain of rice to the size of a golf ball and in colour from reddish brown to mottled green. It is an impressive haul, totalling 12 species, with three notable finds; the first records of three species unrecorded for close to two decades. I am thrilled to lay eyes on a live Mozart's Land Frog, a reddish-brown creature with slender limbs, and comforted in the knowledge that the frog still contributes to the symphony that echoes through the forest. Barely larger than a grain of rice, a small Macaya Breast-spot Frog is perhaps the smallest frog I have ever seen: this frog has also not been seen for two decades. But perhaps my favourite is the critically endangered La Hotte Glanded Frog, a mottled brown and beige frog with striking sapphire eyes. It is the only frog here with such

TOP LEFT: Ventriloqual frog, *Eleutherodactylus dolomedes*, a critically endangered species in Macaya Biosphere Reserve on the Massif de la Hotte, Haiti. Only known from a few individuals and last seen in 1991.

BELOW LEFT: La Hotte Glanded Frog, *Eleutherodactylus glandulifer*, a critically endangered species on the Massif de la Hotte. Last seen 1991.

blue eyes, and I struggle to find an evolutionary explanation for their colour and intensity. Perhaps the ladies just like blue eyes.

In the morning I crawl out my tent and feel the dewy grass between my toes. I breathe in the cool damp air and remind myself that I am in Haiti. We pack our tents and start to make our way down the mountain, but not before the heavens open and raindrops the size of frogs career from the sky. Head bowed, I try to ignore the cool trickle of water down my back and imagine being back at camp with a cup of steaming hot chocolate. The riverbed that was dry only the day before is now a torrent of thrashing brown water – and my thoughts turn to our river crossing planned for the next day. Luckily, by the time we have to cross the level has subsided enough for a safe crossing. Without a generous blanket of forest to feed the rivers, the fluctuations in levels are dramatic, rising quickly as rain gushes off naked hillsides and subsiding quickly afterwards.

With the Massif de la Hotte behind us, we make our final stop in Haiti: the Massif de la Selle, home of the lost La Selle Grass Frog. It is a short ascent from Port-au-Prince to an auberge nestled in pine forest in a picturesque spot called Furcy. We spend the day and

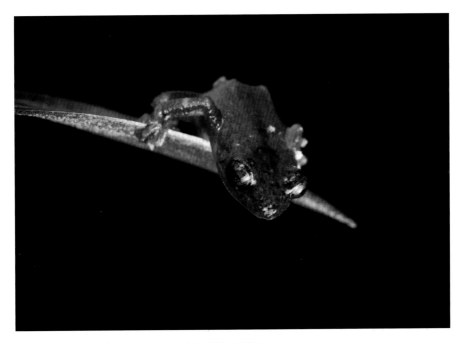

LEFT: Blair Hedges collects frogs on the Massif de la Hotte.

ABOVE: Hispaniola Crowned Frog, *Eleutherodactylus corona*, a critically endangered species from the Massif de la Hotte, Haiti. Last seen 1991.

Blair Hedges puts up his tent up at Tete Boeuf, a remote peak in the Massif de la Hotte.

Loading the helicopter at Tete Boeuf.

Joel Timyan meaures the atmospheric pressure at Tete Boeuf, a remote peak of the Massif de la Hotte, to see whether the helicopter will be able to land to pick us up.

night scouring the forest and hillsides of grass and, while we find a beautiful Hispaniola Giant Treefrog that looks like lichen with legs, we neither see nor hear the La Selle Grass Frog. With heavy heads bowed as we scuff boots through grass, it feels as though we may be looking for a frog that no longer exists. I like to believe that some day the La Selle Grass Frog may prove us wrong but for now, it eludes us.

⚵

Our expedition to the Massifs de la Hotte and de la Selle recorded 24 species of frogs – about half of those known from the country, including six species that had not been seen in close to two decades. A little over a year later I returned to the Massif de la Hotte with Blair and team to helicopter into some remote and unexplored mountain peaks. Over the course of several such expeditions Blair collected 20 frog species unknown to science. These are now awaiting description (including three of the world's smallest frogs, all measuring less than 12mm fully grown) and confirm that, despite the massive and widespread desecration of the environment, Haiti still has wildlife to cherish and protect. Remote cloud forests still echo with the calls of frogs, and the fabric of the Massif de la Hotte has yet to be unravelled to the point of no return. But it is close – and some, including Blair, are preparing for impending ecological collapse.

"I could hold all the biodiversity of Haiti, frozen in time, in one room," Blair says proudly as he leans back in his office chair, arms behind his head, when I speak to him over Skype some three years after our first expedition to the Massif de la Hotte. "I could keep 50,000 species of everything, bacteria and fungi included. That has never been done," he says with a grin. "People have cryobanked a mammal here, a frog there, but nobody has ever cryobanked the whole biodiversity of a country." Blair's dream of being the first to do so with Haiti is ambitious, but is it possible? He has already frozen the cells of a thousand animals representing between 80 and 100 species, animals that could be used to bring back the species. "It wouldn't be expensive to do," he says about the frozen zoo, "all I would need would be five or six tanks of nitrogen, and they cost just 200 bucks a year. And if the power goes off, it doesn't matter. The tanks sit there in the dark and still work. The hardest thing of course," he adds, "would be to actually go up into the mountains and collect 50,000 species."

Cryobanking is a very last resort for Haiti's species, under a somewhat apocalyptic scenario of everything going extinct in the wild. A second-to-last resort is the captive breeding of live animals as a safety net. At Philadelphia Zoo, Carlos Martinez Rivera has established a breeding programme for ten of Haiti's critically endangered frog species. It is admirable that the zoo has elected to focus on small, brown, but highly threatened frogs, and they have had some breeding success. But with such efforts to keep Haiti's frogs in glass tanks and frozen in vats of nitrogen, what is the prognosis for keeping Haiti's frogs alive within their forest homes?

There is no simple answer to the question. But there is most clearly a need to change the relationship between people and the environment; to provide incentives for people to keep the forests standing for future generations. We are currently working with local and international partners to establish a Trust Fund that will find and support the protection and management of some of the last remaining patches of forest in Haiti. In 2011, the year after the Search for Lost Frogs expedition to the Massif de la Hotte, I helped co-found a programme called Frame of Mind to connect young people in Haiti with their natural and cultural worlds through photography and visual storytelling. It has been one of my most rewarding experiences to date. With three workshops in the Massifs de la Selle and Massif de la Hotte, a photo exhibit and book launch in Haiti under its belt, the programme has proven to be a powerful way of connecting young people with their environment, and their

ABOVE: Red-eyed Mottled Frog. A new species of frog, genus *Eleutherodactylus*, from Morne Pangnol, a remote mountaintop in the Massif de la Hotte.

RIGHT: Female Pangnol Weeping Frog, a new species of *Eleutherodactylus* frog in a bromeliad on Morne Pangnol.

images and stories have been an effective conduit for delivering an important message to parents and peers. When we took participants to meet the Environment Minister for the region I got goose bumps as Lovely, a slight twelve-year old, stood up and asked, "What is your reforestation policy for Parc La Visite?" Working with Haiti's youth, who are too often marginalised or 'treated as animals' in the words of Nicole Simeon from local partner Panos Caribbean, has inspired me and infused a renewed sense of optimism for the future of Haiti's forests and their inhabitants. I hope, through Frame of Mind, to help more of Haiti's youth to see the natural wonders that are on their doorstep through new eyes, and to give them a voice. It is, after all, their future.

LEFT: Macaya Breast-spot Frog, *Eleutherodactylus thorectes*, a critically endangered species found only in the Massif de la Hotte and rediscovered after 19 years without being recorded.

ABOVE: La Hotte Landfrog, *Eleutherodactylus bakeri*, another critically endangered species found only on the Massif de la Hotte and rediscovered after 19 years.

CHAPTER 11

LOST! AMPHIBIANS OF INDIA

Delhi, India, November 2010

"Wait here," my driver, Pease Mohammed, says to me as he darts from his taxi and across four lanes of a busy road, avoiding honking cars and tuk-tuks like the hero of the video game, 'Frogger', and disappears up some steps into a small flat. As I sit in the taxi, parked at the side of the road, wondering where he has gone and when he may be coming back, I have the first chance to soak in the fact that I have arrived in Delhi. As my senses adapt to the chaos and cacophony of vehicles and people miraculously avoiding one another on the street, my driver reappears dancing across the road toward me with something balanced in each hand. He signals for me to open my door, hands me a cup of milky tea and proudly holds out a plate containing six slices of white bread smothered with butter. I am touched. After a slice of bread I feel as though I have had my weekly intake of butter, but despite my polite declination of more, the plate is thrust towards me with a "please?" This is repeated until I have consumed all six slices washed down with my milky tea. Tea and bread all gone, my host delightedly dances back across the road to return the crockery to his home.

Once back in the driver's seat, Pease talks to me about all the great things he can take me to see while he weaves through traffic. Eventually we arrive at my destination, the University of Delhi, where I am greeted by my good friend Dr Sathyan Das Biju. I am here to deliver a keynote address at the inauguration of Lost! Amphibians of India, a unique national campaign inspired by the Search for Lost Frogs and spearheaded by the brilliant Biju. With the global Search for Lost Frogs well underway, Biju had seen an opportunity to elevate the profile of Indian amphibians on the global stage. The incorrigibly competitive Biju also set his sights on involving more people and pulling off more rediscoveries in this national campaign than in the entire global campaign. "It will put Indian amphibians on the map," he tells me with a vigorous shake of his head, and I welcome his friendly rivalry.

RIGHT: Dr S. D. Biju during a field trip to Colombia with the author to fulfill his dream of seeing a glass frog – here he is holding two.

Even before the launch, he is off to a good start, having compiled a list of 50 lost Indian amphibians last seen between 14 and 170 years previously.

The scale of the Lost! Amphibians of India campaign was nothing less than I expected from Biju who is, alongside Dr. Blair Hedges, one of the most prolific amphibian systematists (people who describe species) I know. "How many species has he described again?" Biju would probe occasionally about Blair, throwing his head back with a smile, as though revelling in the competition. Biju has to date described well over 50 amphibian species, and is shooting for 100. But he was a late arrival to amphibian research – starting his career some three decades earlier by studying plants, before coming to the screeching realisation that "plants are very boring", and promptly switching his attention to a group that he had come to appreciate more during his fieldwork – amphibians. "I saw frogs of different shapes, sizes and colours and heard their varied calls. I was increasingly drawn to frogs," he says, continuing, "What eventually captured my fascination and laid the foundation for a switch to frogs was photography. The pictures of frogs I took revealed such diversity and beauty that easily escaped the casual eye. That was it." With a burning desire to know the names of these frogs, which he often found to be unknown, he snagged a second PhD (as you do) and for the past two decades has devoted every waking minute to cataloguing and promoting the frogs of India. "Since then, there has been no turning back," he says, "and I continue with frogs with undiminished passion. I explored the Western Ghats for nearly 10 years; I spent all monsoons in the jungles seeking out known and unknown amphibians."

In 2001, Biju published his first findings in an article entitled: 'Discovery of over 150 new species of frogs.' But it was in 2003 that he made the discovery of a lifetime, a one in a million find: he described a purple frog that belongs to an entirely new family, and whose closest relatives live in the Seychelles. The bizarre Purple Frog spends eleven months of the year sixteen feet underground, runs and squeals like a tiny, angry pig, and has tadpoles that cling onto the side of rock faces in streams. The discovery would make the career of any aspiring systematist, but Biju is as committed today as ever to preventing the nameless extinction of India's amphibians. "I told my wife that in five years I will be a good husband. In the meantime, I have work to do," he says. Dry statements roll off Biju's tongue as his

TOP LEFT: The Dehradun Stream Frog, *Amolops chakrataensis*, was only known from the original description of a single specimen in 1985. The frog was rediscovered after 25 years by a team of graduate students from Delhi University.

BELOW LEFT: The Purple Frog, *Nasikabatrachus sahyadrensis*, a frog belonging to an entirely new family discovered by Biju.

expression flits between a scowl and a half-grin, making it difficult to gauge if he is deadly serious or joking. I suspect the truth lies somewhere in between.

When I arrive at the University of Delhi I am impressed with the preparations for the event, with beautiful banners stretched out across the University campus. I wonder if the meticulous preparations have worn the nerves of Biju thin. "Of course I have been up all night," Biju declares, his head shaking vigorously from side to side as we make our way to the auditorium to prepare for the presentations. With less than an hour to kick-off, a failure of the projector sparks an edgy Biju to explode at the audio-visual technician. "This is a *disaster*!" he splutters at the cowering technician "Please. Sir. You must fix this. It is simply not acceptable. You are quite useless." The technician cannot fix it, and after avoiding the wrath of Biju, he scuttles out the room as the auditorium begins to fill. More than 100 people gather, including government officials and notable scientists rarely seen in the same room together. Guests of honour are seated at a table the length of the stage, facing the audience. Before proceedings can begin, a series of introductions and acknowledgements are made, and each of the guests of honour is presented with a gift. The ceremony takes the best part of an hour, after which the table is removed and presentations begin. It is an honour to be a part of such a celebrated event. I present on the Search for Lost Frogs to provide some global context, before speaking about the importance of India, and specifically the Western Ghats, for amphibians. All in all, it is a wonderful inauguration for a groundbreaking initiative.

After the event Biju is visibly more relaxed and attentions turn to the next day, when we embark on a field trip to Kerala. I am on my way to the Western Ghats.

⚘

We fly into the bustling town of Tivandram and cram into two vehicles to embark on a drive to Parambikulam Tiger Reserve. Despite the name, I am told not to hold out much hope of seeing a Tiger. Nobody is quite sure how long the journey will take, and Biju does not appreciate being asked: "I am not a tour guide!" he barks as we shrivel like naughty children in the back. The traffic on the roads gradually thins and the landscape becomes more rural, and I sit back and enjoy the ride through the province of Kerala.

⚘

What makes the Western Ghats – a mountain range that runs parallel to India's western coast from Gujarat to Kerala – so special? For one, the region is astoundingly rich from a biological perspective, and home to more than half of India's 325 known species of

170

The Anamalai Dot-frog, *Ramanella anamalaiensis*, rediscovered after 73 years. This narrow-mouthed frog is named after the Anamalai Hills in the southern Western Ghats where it was discovered (and last seen) in 1937 and the appearance of yellow spots on its upper side and scattered white spots on its underside. The original specimen was lost and there was no confirmed information on the species until its rediscovery.

amphibian. A remarkable 32 species of frogs in the Western Ghats have not been recorded since their original description between 19 and 170 years ago. According to the *Economist*, whose article 'Frog Hunters of the Western Ghats' graced the front cover of the Christmas 2011 edition: "Kerala's rainforests are thinly populated. Only the very determined, with a clear purpose and considerable resilience, venture into them. Among those are Sathyabhama Das Biju, an amphibian researcher at Delhi University, his students and his growing band of followers." The article, needless to say, was a proud moment for Biju.

As with many biological hotspots of the world, the Western Ghats is also very threatened, and the unique forests in this region are suffering rapid degradation. Only 1.5 per cent of the original forests remain, and dozens of frogs in the region are threatened with extinction, with several species thought to be extinct already. The Lost! Amphibians of India Campaign is a bid to reveal just the extent of these losses and to put on the map a smaller group of creatures living in the land of the Tiger. I am excited to be plunging through the Western Ghats to witness these unique forests firsthand.

☙

After several hours, and after stopping for lunch much to the chagrin of Biju ("You would never survive in the field!" he barks, his moustache visibly twitching with rage, as we ask timidly if there are plans to stop for lunch) we arrive at a small wooden lodge in the heart of the tiger reserve and on the edge of a beautiful lake. We unpack our gear and melt into our serene surroundings. Biju relaxes visibly and starts to joke, pretending to throw others into the lake before adding, "I am just kidding," just in case there is any doubt. The last thing I am expecting, as I wander into the kitchen, is to discover a lost frog. But, as I lift the lid of a small plastic bin, something rockets off the sides and ricochets like a pinball inside the bin. Out of instinct I dive to cup my hand around the small frog before hurrying to show my find to Biju: it is, after all, my first Indian frog. His eyes almost pop out of his head as he pulls me aside and whispers, his moustache twitching with delight, "Do you know when that frog was last seen?" I shake my head, unaware of what I am holding in my

The Elegant Tropical Frog, *Micrixalus elegans*, was known only from the original description based on a collection in 1937. The original specimen was subsequently lost and the species evaded detection until it was rediscovered in 2011.

The Silent Valley Tropical Frog, *Micrixalus thampii,* was not recorded for 30 years before its rediscovery in a rubbish bin in a field station in Silent Vallery on a fieldtrip following the launch of the LAI campaign in Delhi. The team later observed several more individuals adjacent to a streambed under leaf litter, in closed forest cover within the Kunthi River watershed.

hand. "Thirty years ago," he says, before repeating, "Thirty years. Oh my god, you have just found a lost frog!" The Silent Valley Tropical Frog, it would turn out, had indeed not been recorded for 30 years. I had just discovered a lost frog in a rubbish bin. And I had left my camera at home.

Naturally, leaving the camera at home means that our eyes feast on some incredible sights during our two days in the reserve. In the evening we go for a drive and come eye-to-eye with elephants, and out of the darkness catch the eye-shine of a passing Tiger. It all feels rather surreal and wondrous. The presence of such incredible creatures lurking in the shadows lends these forests an air of mystique. And without my camera close by I am able to absorb it and savour the moment without constantly mentally composing shots. It is in many ways refreshing and liberating to store the memories gathered during my two days in the Western Ghats in my head rather than in my memory cards.

The Chalazodes Bubble-nest Frog, *Raorchestes chalazodes*, last seen in 1874 before being rediscovered 136 years later by Dr. Biju and team. This striking fluorescent green frog with ash-blue thighs and black and golden pupils (highly unusual traits among amphibians) leads a secretive life, presumably inside reeds during the day. It is thought that the species does not have a free-swimming tadpole stage, but completes development inside the egg.

❧

Following the launch of the Lost! Amphibians of India campaign, hundreds of scientists and citizens headed out in search of elusive frogs from the jungles of the Western Ghats to the mountains of northeast India. Within weeks, five rediscoveries were announced, including my Silent Valley Tropical Frog and the striking Chalazodes Bubble-nest Frog, a fluorescent green frog with yellow eyes and cat-like vertical black pupils that, until it was rediscovered by Biju, had not been seen since 1874. "I have never seen a frog with such brilliant colours in my 25 years of research," Biju said, before adding, "Our hunt has just begun. And it is a good start."

It was indeed off to a good start, and as a frog wearing a crown hit the front pages of the *Economist*, Indian amphibians were in the limelight. But it was about to get better.

At the time of writing Biju and colleagues are preparing to publish the tally of the Lost! Amphibians of India campaign in a scientific journal; a staggering 36 frog species last seen between 15 and 137 years previously were rediscovered by an army of researchers and citizen scientists. It is an unprecedented quarry of lost species from a single country, and a testament to how little explored many of these forests are. It provides reason for hope in a region where forests are rapidly dwindling.

The Lost! Amphibians of India campaign caught the imaginations of the public in India and internationally to raise the profile of frogs in the land of the Tiger. Biju used the campaign as a platform to promote the conservation of the threatened forests of the Western Ghats, saying that this is "not only a last chance to save some of the planet's most endangered wildlife, but it will also focus attention on remote, rural communities in India and how they depend on the integrity of the environment for its provision of natural resources". Biju had managed to promote amphibians as flagships for conservation, and he continues to push tirelessly for the development of a network of protected areas to safeguard these forests and the species that call them home.

The amphibians of India are fortunate that Biju has elected to channel his brilliance and his ambitions to studying them – and, in recent years, to promoting their protection. Even though he grew up surrounded by nature, and spent years studying and cataloguing dozens of species, it is only in recent years that he has recognised the importance of preserving the world he took for granted. "Frogs I observed in one season were gone on my next visit, or their habitat had shrunk drastically. This trend started to worry me, and this concern continues to grow," he says. I ask whether frogs and caecilians will ever receive equal billing to the charismatic Tigers in people's hearts and minds. He fixes me with a look as though I had just announced my intention to urinate on his floor, and says, "Please don't talk to me any more about Tigers," and walks off.

CHAPTER 12

MOST WANTED STILL LOST

The first phase of the Search for Lost Frogs campaign officially ran between August 2010 and February 2011, a period during which more than 30 search teams were deployed in search of lost species. During this time I went in search of lost frogs in Colombia, Haiti and India, and in between my own searches for lost frogs I liaised with teams in the field and helped to develop half a dozen press releases to communicate newsworthy findings to the media.

Two months into the campaign, however, despite a number of rediscoveries and potential new species discoveries, none of the top ten Most Wanted species had turned up. Searches for the Golden Toad in Costa Rica, Jackson's Climbing Salamander in Guatemala, Scarlet Harlequin Frog in Venezuela, African Painted Frog in the Democratic Republic of Congo (DRC), gastric-brooding frogs in Australia, Hula Painted Frog in Israel and Rainbow Toad of Borneo had all been unsuccessful, as had our mission to find the Mesopotamia Beaked Toad in Colombia. I will admit that I was disappointed; I had hoped for at least one of the top ten species to be rediscovered, and was concerned that these, the poster children for the campaign, were no longer with us.

Then I received an email from Santiago Ron in late October, soon after returning home from Haiti, informing me that after 15 years without trace, they had found a Rio Pescado Stubfoot Toad, *Atelopus balios*, during a night-time search along a stretch of stream in southern Ecuador. The team was led to the stream by a family of local peasants that gave convincing accounts of sightings of the frog – reinforcing the importance of seeking local knowledge when looking for lost species. Ron sent a photograph of the beautiful frog – with black dots on delicate yellow skin – and a video captured on a mobile phone of the moment the frog was discovered on a leaf on the banks of the river. Having spent many days searching for harlequin frogs in Ecuador I was thrilled to receive the news that one

TOP RIGHT: The Rio Pescado Stubfoot Toad, *Atelopus balios*, was the first of the top ten Most Wanted amphibians to be rediscovered, after 15 years, in Ecuador.

BELOW RIGHT: The Borneo Rainbow Toad, *Ansonia latidisca*, was rediscovered after 87 years without a trace in the mountains of western Sarawak.

more species feared to have become extinct had bounced back. The frog appeared to be surviving in just one stretch of stream on farmland – habitat that we hope to help Ron and team set aside as a private reserve to protect this fragile creature and facilitate research on the species.

The Search for Lost Frogs campaign wrapped up with a final press release in February 2011 that announced the rediscovery of the Rio Pescado Stubfoot Toad and the first five rediscoveries in India, bringing the tally to some 15 rediscoveries and two potential new species discoveries. In all, the Search for Lost Frogs had resulted in more than 650 news articles in 20 countries (most articles appearing in the USA, Australia, Germany and the UK, closely followed by Brazil), attracting more than a billion potential viewers. The announcement of the rediscoveries in Haiti, entitled "Mozart, Ventriloqual Frogs sound a note of hope and warning for Haiti's recovery," released on the anniversary of the earthquake, was picked up by journalists hungry for stories of hope from Haiti, generating 120 articles in 20 countries and more than 200 million potential viewers. The frog rediscoveries proved to be an effective vehicle for delivering a more complex message about the state of Haiti's environment and the repercussions for its people. This encapsulated the communication strategy behind the Search for Lost Frogs; the search and subsequent rediscoveries were a hook for delivering more nuanced messages about the state of our world (habitat loss and the chytrid fungus were touched upon in more than 220 articles and the message that

Scarlet Harlequin Frog, *Atelopus sorianoi*, from Venezuela, last seen in 1990.

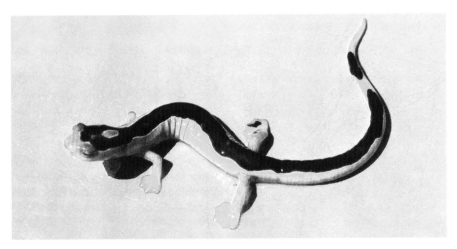

Jackson's Climbing Salamander, *Bolitoglossa jacksoni*, from Guatemala, last seen in 1977.

amphibians are indicators of ecosystem health was present in more than 280 articles); the lost frogs were symbols for bigger issues that touch each of us.

Although the communications campaign had drawn to a close, the Search for Lost Frogs continued in hearts, minds and imaginations around the world. Dr Indraneil Das and team were not done with their attempts to rediscover the Borneo Rainbow Toad, *Ansonia latidisca*, and continued to launch expeditions to the mountains of western Sarawak. Their dogged determination, amazingly, paid off. In early July 2011, Das emailed me with the news – they had rediscovered up a tree the first Borneo Rainbow Toad to be seen in 87 years, and captured the first ever photos of the beautiful green, yellow and red creature with spindly limbs. It was a phenomenal rediscovery and a testament to the persistence and unbridled optimism of Das and his team of students. Curiously, the team had found the toad at a couple of hundred metres higher elevation from where it was previously known to exist. Although we can speculate that the toad has moved upwards in response to a changing climate, we cannot know for sure that this is what has happened. The image of the toad captivated the imagination of the public, spreading far and wide on the Internet, and the tally of top ten lost frogs found was doubled. Das uncovered more toads and initiated a research programme to determine their status and possible threats to their survival.

The rediscovery of the Borneo Rainbow Toad created a stir five months after the end of the Lost Frogs campaign, but the most intriguing story about one of the top ten Most Wanted frogs was about to get even more interesting. The story unfolds in a place that is rarely associated with frogs; to find out more, I would have to head to Israel.

CHAPTER 13

IN SEARCH OF THE
HULA PAINTED FROG, ISRAEL

Tel Aviv, Israel, January 2013

"So you are going to a place that is not in Israel, with someone you have never met?" The surly woman at Israeli immigration stares at me, unflinching, as she delivers this summary of her interrogation. "Well, now that's not exactly what I said …" I begin, explaining again that the Hula Valley really is in Israel even if she has never heard of it, and while I have never met my travel companion, we have exchanged many emails, and he is waiting for me in arrivals. And he's one of the leading amphibian biologists in Israel, in case that helps? It doesn't. Eyes glazing over, she turns to her colleague to ask if he has ever heard of the Hula Valley. "The where?" he mutters without moving his lips. Would it help my case to suggest she Google it? Probably not. "And what will you be doing in this supposed Hula Valley?" she asks. Here we go. "Well, I'm looking for a frog, actually …" I taper off as I watch her eyebrows creep further up her forehead. We stand in silence, locked in eye combat, for a very long minute before she grunts, reluctantly thumps a stamp onto a piece of paper, slides it into my passport and thrusts it towards me. Welcome to Israel.

Still reeling slightly from the surprise interrogation, I breathe deeply once I make it through immigration and into arrivals, where I am greeted by Dr. Sarig Gafny. Sarig, as I explained to the disinterested immigration officer, is one of the leading amphibian biologists in Israel. He helped plan the logistics of my expedition to look for the Hula Painted Frog and offered, in a dazzling display of hospitality and generosity, to devote three days to helping me in my quest. His serious and forthright demeanour is at first a little intimidating, but I soon relax into his company during many hours spent in the car and in the field. He is proud to show me his country and its amphibians, and his eyes light up when I mention that I would like to eat some good hummus. "I will take you to eat the best hummus," he says, relishing the challenge almost as much as the quest to find an elusive frog.

I learn that Sarig's interest in amphibians did not, like mine, stem from a childhood fascination, but from an experience that came during his undergraduate degree. As a child

Grass tussocks in the Hula Nature Reserve.

he had little interest in them. "We do not have many amphibians" he explains – seven species, to be precise, the same as the United Kingdom. He was, however, interested in fresh water and trained as a water specialist. During an evening expedition with his professor, he came across a Syrian Spadefoot Toad, and it fascinated him. He was intrigued by the way it only appeared above ground on rainy nights, "That's fifteen to twenty nights a year, OK?" he says. "On those nights, they eat enough to survive and to produce thousands of eggs by eating snails whole – shell and all," he imitates a toad stuffing a snail into its mouth before adding "OK?" as if checking that I am keeping up with him. He was also drawn to the fact that little was known about the toad, and much of what he tells me about its habits has been discovered by him. It is clear the Syrian Spadefoot Toad is close to his heart – but not as close as another, altogether more elusive frog. The Hula Painted Frog.

Sarig takes me for a dinner of hummus and kabobs: the food is delicious but he is quick to assure me that we will find better hummus, before turning in for the night. We set off early the following morning to make the three-hour drive to the Hula Valley. I feel the prickling excitement of finally being here, for nestled in the Hula Valley is the Hula Nature Reserve, home of the Hula Painted Frog. But my excitement is tempered by the anxiety of disappointment. I know how it feels to travel this far to not find what I am looking for, and I know I am facing long odds of finding this frog. We soon leave the Tel Aviv suburbs behind and scroll through a rolling, pastoral landscape. I remark that it is greener than I expected. "Well, it is the rainy season," Sarig tells me – I had timed my trip to coincide with the rains in early January. "In a couple of months this will be a blaze of wildflowers. And then in the summer it will be dry as a bone. But now it is green. It is a nice time to come. OK?"

As we arrive at the reserve a fine mist rises from a wetland bristling with reeds and tussocks of grass. Cranes and pelicans wade and swim in the shallows while cormorants stretch their wings to warm in the morning sun. The occasional kingfisher flits onto a branch before swooping out of sight. As we climb out of the car and breathe the clean, cool air, I scan the reserve and imagine Hula Painted Frogs hidden in the reeds.

It is a long way to travel for a frog. But the Hula Painted Frog has a particularly compelling story that has elevated it to somewhat iconic status – a story that propelled it onto the list of top ten Most Wanted frogs. It is an attractive frog, splashed with hints of ochre and olive-grey, transitioning to a charcoal-black belly speckled with little white spots. Long fingers and a fold across the neck make it look unusual, and its primitive rounded tongue is not used to catch prey – again unusual for a frog.

The Hula Painted Frog was discovered in 1940 when two adults were collected from the eastern shores of Lake Hula and described three years later by Professor Heinrich Mendelssohn from Tel Aviv University and Professor Steinitz from the University of Jerusalem. The three-year gap between discovery and publication was because Mendelssohn, apparently, didn't like to write. An agreement was struck between the authors that the larger frog would go to Jerusalem, and the smaller animal would go to Tel Aviv. It was an amicable and fair arrangement. Until, while the frogs were being housed in an aquarium for observation, the larger of the frogs – in a somewhat defiant gesture – promptly ate the smaller one. The larger individual still went to Jerusalem as agreed, but because the smaller frog happened to be in its stomach, it went with it. Tel Aviv University seethed, accusing Jerusalem of stealing their frog. It was a source of animosity that is evident to this day. Two tadpoles that had also been collected in 1940 were lost in the 1948 war, leaving just one adult frog in a jar of formaldehyde in Jerusalem.

Not to worry, thought scientists at Tel Aviv, we will just go out and collect another frog. But the next year, despite extensive searches, no frogs could be found. Nor the year after. The area was scoured every year for the next seven years, but the Hula Painted Frog had disappeared. The scientists had all but given up hope when, some 15 years after the first two Hula Painted Frogs were found, a third individual turned up. The find added insult to injury for Tel Aviv University, however, when the frog was gifted to Jerusalem. Jerusalem:

2, Tel Aviv: 0. Not to worry, thought Tel Aviv, if the frog is back, we will just go and collect another. But it wasn't to be; the frog was not seen again. In 1996, fifty-six years since its discovery and more than 40 years since the last sighting, and with no habitat left, the declaration was made by the International Union for the Conservation of Nature (IUCN): the Hula Painted Frog was extinct. It was the first amphibian to be declared as such.

The nail in the coffin of the Hula Painted Frog was the destruction of its home, Lake Hula. Lake Hula was one of the oldest documented lakes in the world and one of the few large freshwater habitats in the Near East. The shallow pear-shaped lake fringed by swampy meadows and dense papyrus stands extended over 12 square km in the Hula Valley. The lake and surrounding swamp provided fertile hunting and fishing grounds for tens of thousands of years, and a thriving ecosystem was home to many unique species. But it was also seen as a breeding ground for malaria, which was so rife in Israel that slaves imported from Sudan were selected as carriers of the rare genetic disease sickle-cell anaemia; carriers of this disease happen to have a natural resistance to malaria. And so in an attempt to control the malaria, against the warnings of scientists, in 1951 a large volcanic plug was cracked and Lake Hula was drained like a giant bathtub. By 1958, only three square km of marshland remained.

The draining of the lake was initially hailed a success, but slowly the costs started to reveal themselves. First, the water table lowered by several metres. Exposed soil blew away in heavy dust storms and dry peat ignited, starting underground fires that smoldered for the next four decades causing the ground to literally sink. Without the marsh to act as a filter, water quality declined in surrounding water bodies. Add to this the near extinction of an entire ecosystem and its unique wildlife and you have what some may call an unmitigated disaster. The repercussions of the draining were not lost on an Israeli public, whose growing concern about the ecological and economic costs led to the last three square km being set aside as the Hula Nature Reserve in 1964. Pressure continued and in the 1980s a restoration project was set in motion with the aim of restoring wildlife habitat and developing ecotourism in the area.

Despite the positive steps, for many of the species that called this area home, it appeared to be too little too late. The results of hasty biological surveys in the 1950s were collated and published in 1992, revealing that more than 100 species had not been recorded in the Hula Valley since the draining. Some of these, such as the Hula Painted Frog, were

OVERLEAF: Cormorants and other water birds in Hula Nature Reserve, Israel.

found nowhere else. Extensive surveys in the 1980s and 90s failed to turn up any of the frogs and, as parts of the Hula Valley were finally being reflooded in the mid-1990s, the death knell was sounded as the Hula Painted Frog was finally declared extinct. The frog swiftly became a poignant symbol of irrevocable loss; of the consequences of our careless actions. But it also became a symbol, to some, of more than this. In *Trillions and Trillions of Heartbeats*, a series of poems lamenting the loss of twenty-three animal species by Meg Hamill, a short poem dedicated to the Hula Painted Frog entitled, 'Palestinian Painted Frog or Israel Painted Frog' included the following passage: "Frog your posthumous name change by the Israeli government has been referred to as another attempt by Zionists to erase any vestige of the name 'Palestine' from human memory. And now frog you are becoming a symbol. Your name pops up in pro-Palestine arguments all over the world." The Hula Painted Frog was unwittingly representing the conflict between people, and was becoming a household name – even if that name changed depending on the household.

As the 20th century turned, so did the story of the Hula Painted Frog. "The story takes place some time in mid April, mid-morning on a sunny day [in the year 2000] at the Aammiq wetlands, south-east Lebanon," writes Colin Beale, scientific officer at the time for the Lebanese Nature Preservation Agency, A Rocha Lebanon, in a report. "I was carrying out a butterfly survey along the avenue of trees with a visitor to the project, when a frog sitting in shallow water (half in/half out) in the ditch nearby caught our attention... We both had a very good view of the frog through binoculars and in good light at a distance of approximately three metres. Having some experience of frogs of the genus *Discoglossus* [the painted frogs] from Portugal I was confident that the individual we were watching was a member of this genera. Unfortunately neither of us was aware of the significance of such a record at the time and made no attempts to handle it, or take special notes of the circumstances. That said, however, I do remember it quite well, as it was the first (and subsequently seems to be only!) time I'd seen one at Aammiq and it stuck in my mind at the time."

No painted frogs had ever been found in Lebanon, and only one was known from the Near East; it was, of course, the Hula Painted Frog. In response to the sighting, an expedition was launched in April 2004 into Lebanon to hunt for the frog, led by François Tron (scientific officer for A Rocha France) and Rémi Duguet (a French amphibian specialist). Their sights firmly set on a monumental rediscovery, they first identified suitable water bodies to target by going out in the early morning, when the low sun slanted and glanced off water, so that they could see ponds like mirrors scattered across the landscape. They searched for adult frogs at night by listening for calls and scouring the banks of ponds with headlamps, and fished for tadpoles by day with pond nets and dragnets. Tired and dejected, the team came home empty-handed, but they did report an unidentified frog call heard several times at three sites. Given that nobody knew what the call of the Hula Painted Frog sounded like, it was impossible to make any positive identification – plus, the call was not recorded. Another shred of evidence came in the form of reports from locals of a fourth species of frog – one more than was known from the area. A bounty of fifty dollars was swiftly offered to anyone who brought forth the mystery species. Their money was safe; nobody brought any frogs.

Not quite ready to hang up their pond nets, the team launched a second expedition in search of the frog the following year to the Bekaa Valley in South East Lebanon. The expedition consisted of ten people, including five experienced herpetologists of three nationalities, and more than 80 hours were spent in the field scouring 76 sites. The expedition, an international partnership between A Rocha, the American University of Beirut and the Université du Liban, again scoured ponds by day and night and again a bounty was offered to anyone who could produce a Hula Painted Frog. One of the areas surveyed flowed directly onto the Hula Valley, and hopes were high for finding the elusive frog.

But once again the expedition team returned home unsuccessful. In their final expedition report the team offered several conclusions, but did not dismiss the possibility that the painted frog was still there. "Not finding the species after two years of intensive field work does not mean the species does not occur in Lebanon," they wrote optimistically. So did Beale see the Hula Painted Frog that sunny April morning in Lebanon – the first sighting of the species in forty-five years and the first ever in Lebanon? Despite a convincing observation report and circumstantial evidence of a mystery frog, with no live animals, no photos and no recordings, we are left with nothing more than anecdotes. The frog remained, as far as the world's scientists were concerned, extinct.

☙

The Hula Painted Frog, although lost, was not forgotten. When the call for nominations for the top ten Most Wanted lost frogs was put out in the Spring of 2010, Yehuda Werner of the Hebrew University of Jerusalem responded immediately to nominate the frog for the list. With such an intriguing back-story, it was a strong candidate, and the grainy black and white photo of the frog was added to the poster of the ten globally Most Wanted frogs.

The frog, last seen in 1955, the year Elvis hit the TV screens, was back in the limelight, and the curiosity of Israeli amphibian biologists and wardens at the Hula Nature Reserve was piqued. So much so that in late November 2010 Yoram Malka, a warden who had been patrolling the Hula Nature Reserve for 15 years, turned to Sarig Gafny and said, "You know, I believe the frog is here. I believe it is looking at us and laughing." Sarig, who over his 30-year career had spent weeks, months and years searching for the Painted Frog in both Israel and Lebanon (while he was posted there during his army service he always carried a pond net in his backpack to scour ponds during his breaks) replied, "Bring to me a frog with a black belly with small white dots, and then I will believe that the Hula Painted Frog exists." Still strangely confident, Yoram responded: "I will. Just give me a year and I will bring you the frog."

Fast forward to 15 November, 2011, a year minus one week to the day that Yoram had turned to Sarig with his bold promise. Sarig was teaching at Tel Aviv University, feeling somewhat unwell with fever and looking forward to finishing up and getting home to rest. Done lecturing, he returned to his office to find 15 missed calls on his phone, all from Yoram. "I called him back immediately," Sarig says as he recalls the incident with nervous excitement, "but I had no idea what he was calling about." A breathless Yoram answered the phone. "I found the frog!" he told Sarig. Sarig sat down, tried to remain calm and validate Yoram's unlikely claim. First he asked, "Does it have a black belly with white spots?" "Yes, it does." "Take a photo and send it to me," replied Sarig, his heart now beating fast. Within minutes, a photo of the frog appeared in his inbox. He opened the image, dropped whatever he was holding, grabbed his car keys, ran outside and drove two and a half hours to the Hula Nature Reserve.

"I got stuck behind trucks and tractors," Sarig sounds exasperated as he relives the exhilaration and frustration of the drive – one of the longest two and a half hours he has spent behind the wheel. When he arrived, Yoram was waiting for him with the frog. "When I saw it, I was sure it was the Hula Painted Frog," he says, "but I wanted to be 100 per cent sure before announcing it. I told Yoram I would return early the next morning with the original description of the frog, and we would go through it, trait by trait, to be absolutely sure. But in the meantime, I told him, don't breathe a word to anyone." Late that evening Sarig dusted off the original paper in which Mendelssohn described the frog – Sarig hands me the paper, personally signed by Mendelssohn – and prepared for the big day ahead.

LEFT: Sarig Gafny stands at the spot that the first Hula Painted Frogs were discovered in 1940.

Despite the vow of silence, within hours of the find I received an email from Erez Erlichman, wildlife reporter from *Ynet news*: "Great news from Israel! The Hula Painted Frog (*Discoglossus nigriventer*), that was last seen in 1955 was found today in the Hula Nature Reserve. I'm going to see her/him tomorrow! It's still a secret!" Early the next morning an excited and anxious Sarig arrived at the reserve to a throng of reporters and TV cameras. Remaining calm, Sarig and Yoram pulled themselves to a quiet place and diligently worked through the description. As they reached the last defining characteristic of the frog, a surge of adrenaline pulsed through Sarig, for he now knew he was looking at the first Hula Painted Frog to have been seen in 55 years, and only the fourth individual ever found. He could hardly believe his eyes. "I never thought I would see it in my lifetime," he tells me, before continuing with a pang of visible longing, "I only wish Mendelssohn could have been here to see it."

The following day, and again the following week, the Hula Painted Frog made the headlines on Israel national TV. I watch the replays with Sarig, huddled in front of his computer screen. A giddy Yoram – a tall, slender man in his early 40s – re-plays the moment for the camera: "I was driving to find some pelicans with transmitters and I took a different route. I saw something jump towards me. It was a little unusual, a little darker than anything I knew, so I thought it was worth investigating." He goes on to explain how he captured the frog: "I place my hand over her, and she tries to escape. My heart is beating. My head is telling me it is the Hula Painted Frog, that it isn't, that it is. I am in internal conflict. I run to take the book with an illustration of the frog on its back and, as soon as I see it I know it is it!" Enjoying his theatrical moment in the spotlight, he continues; "It seems to me as though, as much as I looked for her, she looked for me. I knew that some day I would find her. This was the time for me to discover the frog and for her to discover me." Sarig interprets for me, pausing the report to interpret the narration: "Amphibian freaks used to sit on the edge of the water and tell the legend of the Hula Painted Frog and how they hoped it would reappear." I look at his face for a sign that he is joking before asking if the reporter really just referred to amphibian freaks, or if he made that up? "Nope. He said amphibian freaks," he responds, face straight as a die, and presses play on the video.

The rediscovery of the Hula Painted Frog is big news in Israel and beyond, not just with amphibian freaks, and Yoram is clearly relishing his moment in the limelight. In an interview with Cryptozoology Online (a website dedicated to the study of things hard to find) he enthuses "It's very exciting; to me it's like finding the Dead Sea Scrolls of nature conservation in Israel." The reappearance of the Hula Painted Frog was hailed as the icing on the cake of a conservation success story for the Hula Valley – and the frog was swiftly promoted from a poignant symbol of extinction to a symbol of resilience. Over the coming weeks Yoram searched intensively to find more frogs. Two weeks after his initial find he uncovered another – a female frog, slightly smaller than the first male. Over the next few months a total of 11 Hula Painted Frogs were found, all within an area of 1.25 hectares.

As the news rolled in, I grew increasingly eager to see the frog with my own eyes, and to stand in the spot where the events of November 2011 had unfolded. And so I started planning my visit for early January 2013, at which time the frogs should be active. As my trip neared, however, and the rains arrived, I received the rather unsettling news that no Hula Painted Frogs had turned up – none since the end of the previous rainy season. Perhaps it should not be surprising that a frog known for its disappearing act had failed to show this season. Working with wildlife – and especially frogs – is uncertain and fraught with chance, and so I decided I would take my chances.

⚇

Arriving at the Hula Nature Reserve, Sarig and I head straight to the ranger's station to meet with Yoram who, we have been assured, will be waiting for us. I am excited to meet him and receive a personal re-enactment of the rediscovery. It is with gut-wrenching disappointment that I learn that he is not here – and it is clear that Sarig is confused and angry. We are escorted by a reserve biologist, Yfat, to the area where the frog was rediscovered. I feel privileged to be allowed access to this area that is closed to the public, but the feeling is short-lived. We skirt the shore of the wetland before arriving at a grassy strip fringed by water on the right and an impenetrable tangle of reeds and brambles to the left. The car stops and Sarig climbs out to show me the spot where the frog was rediscovered. Almost all of the individuals were found in the tangle of reeds and brambles and so, without further ado, we clamber in.

As I begin raking the leaf litter and rotting logs in search of the frog, a discussion between Sarig and the park biologist becomes increasingly heated. Given that my Hebrew is limited to "hello," "please," and "thank you," I cannot follow their discussion, although I can confirm that hello, please and thank you do not feature prominently. Being British, I shrink from conflict like papier mâché from water, and keep my head buried in the reeds as the battle unfolds above. Abruptly, less than 20 minutes into the search, Sarig announces that it is time to leave. My stomach sinks; my quest to see the Hula Painted Frog is over before it really started.

As we drive out of the reserve a quiet Sarig turns to me and asks pointedly: "Disappointed?" "A little," I reply, downplaying my crushing disappointment for fear of sounding ungrateful. "Well I am," he spits, "more than a little disappointed. Not disappointed that we didn't find the frog. I am disappointed that we didn't even have the chance." His anger stays with him as he drives, occasionally bubbling up. "This is what I am up against," he says, "the Nature and Parks Authority (the NPA, who manages the reserve and dishes out permits for research) want the information about the frog, but they won't let me go near it." There are so many questions surrounding the frog that Sarig is eager to answer. Where has it spent the past fifty-five years? How many frogs are there and are their numbers increasing, stable or declining? Where does it breed? Does it call – and, if so, what does it sound like? The frog is as enigmatic in life as it was in its disappearance. But what I didn't expect was for Yoram to be just as elusive: I would not get to meet him once during my five days in Israel despite numerous attempts to contact him. It transpires that the NPA did not want me to go and look for the frog in the first place, and it becomes clear that there was likely never any intention for me to meet and accompany Yoram into the reserve.

I am not sure what to make of all this, but it seems that the rediscovery of the frog has driven a crowbar into the differences between the government agency and the scientific community. In order to understand the frog further and to manage the reserve to increase its chances of survival, it will be necessary to find middle ground. The rediscovery also seems to have rubbed salt in the wound between the universities in Jerusalem and Tel Aviv. The first hint of continued animosity came immediately following the rediscovery, when I read with surprise a post online by Yehudah Werner from Jerusalem. Werner, who had eagerly promoted the inclusion of the frog on the top ten list of lost frogs, now dismissed its rediscovery as insignificant. When I question his change of heart he responds, "The Parks Authority courted popularity by releasing all [the frogs], maybe except putting one in Tel Aviv University, who could not stand the species being only at Hebrew University of Jerusalem." Sarig offers his perspective on Werner's change of heart: "Well, it's obvious. He didn't find it now, did he?" before turning to me with a twinkle in his eye and saying, with deep satisfaction, "and now Tel Aviv will have its frog."

❧

Sarig makes up for the disappointment at the Hula Nature Reserve with the best meal of our trip at a restaurant close by; a full plate of warm hummus drizzled with olive oil, pine nuts and garbanzo beans. As I dip the fresh, warm pitta into the delicious mix Sarig poses a rhetorical question, "Want to see a blue treefrog?" I reply that I didn't realise that there were blue treefrogs in Israel, which as far as I knew was home to just one treefrog called the Lemon-yellow Treefrog. "There aren't," he replies cryptically, before elaborating; "well, there aren't supposed to be. I had not seen one in all my 55 years." Until the previous year that was, when someone turned up at his office holding a frog that he had come across in a forest in eastern Israel. "Well, I wondered if it was a new species, of course," he explains, "but then we ran some genetic tests and it turned out to be a Lemon-yellow Treefrog. Only it was blue! OK?" As we enter his office the following morning, he pulls the lid off a small aquarium decorated with leaves and a small frog clambers onto his hand. It is delicate and beautiful – and most definitely sky-blue. I am excited to photograph him. "I want to return him to the wild," Sarig explains, "as soon as I am able to return him to where he came from." I am happy to have seen him before he returns, and for a moment I forget the awful disappointment at the Hula Nature Reserve.

Of Israel's seven species of amphibians, five are frogs: the Hula Painted Frog, the Lemon-yellow Treefrog, the Levantine Frog (a small brown spotted frog that we happened upon in the Hula Nature Reserve), the Green Toad and the Syrian Spadefoot Toad. The

A rare blue Lemon-yellow Treefrog, *Hyla savignyi*.

remaining two are tailed amphibians – the Banded Newt, and a salamander that I had been aching to see in the wild for close to three decades, ever since I was nine years old and my grandparents presented to me, as my first pet, a beautiful Fire Salamander (so-named because it was believed to live in fire as it would appear, naturally, out of logs that had been set ablaze). My Fire Salamander lived in an aquarium in my bedroom for most of the year, spending the winter months hibernating in a margarine tub in our fridge, testing my family's patience. She was my introduction to the exotic world of salamanders, and through her I developed a deep affinity for this particular species, but I had never had the chance to see one in the wild.

Sarig offers to try and help me find a Fire Salamander, adding that nothing is guaranteed. We pull into Tel Dan reserve, where he tells me he saw one when he was 11; this was 44 years ago, which doesn't inspire confidence that we will find one today. It is mid-morning, sunny and warm and while I recognise that our chances are close to zero, I am eager to stroll through salamander habitat. Tel Dan reserve, formed in the 1970s after conservationists prevented the diversion of the Dan River, is truly beautiful. Water from the Dan River – the largest of three tributaries of the Jordan river fed by melting snow from the Hermon mountains – bubbles among stepping stones and through quiet forest carpeted with freshly fallen yellow leaves. The reserve prides itself on being the home of the beautiful Fire Salamander, and a sign by the side of the road instructs cars entering and leaving to slow down and avoid crushing salamanders under their wheels. The measures have been effective, as road casualties have dropped dramatically. One casualty two months earlier made national news when tadpoles were recovered from a critically injured female. I am again struck by the interest in, and concern for, amphibians in Israel. I learn that plans for a restaurant at the reserve were pulled because it would mean cars would have to drive in and out at night when salamanders were crossing the road. To hear stories such as this – where the welfare of the animals is put above a quick profit – is heartening.

As we walk through the reserve I eye the leaves by the side of the trail, willing a salamander to appear. Although no salamanders materialise, it feels intoxicating to be wandering through their home. As we are leaving the reserve one of the rangers invites us to come back in a couple of days to accompany them on their early morning patrol. If it is raining, he says, the chances are very good. And so, on my penultimate day in Israel, I wake at 5am to hear the encouraging swish of wet tyres on tarmac. It is still dark when Sarig picks me up, and we arrive at Tel Dan Reserve soon after sunrise. As the rain tumbles down, we each grab an umbrella and follow the ranger into the forest. My heart is pounding with the silent promise of seeing a salamander. And then there she is, sitting elegantly on the leaf litter some three feet from the trail; about the length of my hand with lemon-yellow spots blazed on a deep black background. Within three minutes we see as many salamanders; it is a magical and surreal scene. In the Holy Land I feel what I can only describe as being close to a religious experience. As I watch the salamanders pad across the carpet of leaf-litter and the rain patters around us, I am transported back to the moors of Scotland, and that tingling excitement of discovery that I felt as a child thirty years ago. And then I remind myself; if it were not for the Hula Painted Frog I would not be here. I owe this moment to it.

⚬

The focus of my five days in Israel was on the amphibians, but it was impossible to ignore the long history of struggle of the peoples of this region. As we drove through an alley of eucalyptus near Syria, Sarig told me that they were planted so that, during the Six-Day War of 1967, the Syrians wouldn't be able to shoot the Israelis as, "They would shoot at everything that moved". Three doors down from my hotel was a bar called Mike's Place where, on April 2003 two British Muslims approached with bombs strapped to their chests. One exploded, killing three civilians and injuring fifty. At the time a film crew from the US was filming a documentary on the bar; the documentary took a turn to become the chilling *Blues by the Beach*. On our second day, driving through the town of Tiberias on the shores of the sea of Galilea, we were stopped while a bomb squad detonated a suspicious object in front of us. The sight of the bomb-detonating machine sent a chill up my spine, but Sarig didn't bat an eyelid. "It is all we know," he said with a shrug. "It's not nearly as bad as it used to be. We get on with our lives. We enjoy ourselves," he explained, "but always, in the back of your mind, you are alert." I try hard to imagine living like this but I don't think, until you have, you can truly comprehend what it is to live in fear.

Against this backdrop of human struggle, I find it all the more surprising that wildlife and the environment get such a high billing in the daily lives of people. Bridges are constructed over roads for animals to safely pass, people care when salamander tadpoles are saved from a dying mother, and the rediscovery of the Hula Painted Frog is celebrated nationwide. I am surprised when my taxi driver, upon learning that I am here to find a frog, responds unprompted and with pride, "Ah yes, there was a frog that was found last year after many years." I ask Sarig about this apparent awareness of, and concern for, nature. "Well many people here see the value of conservation. But it's not always a priority. There are times when, of course, the urgent needs of humans come first. For me too, OK?" As

we talk about relations within the region, I ask about how this impacts conservation and science, and he indicates that there are collaborations, and that he is willing and ready to collaborate with Palestinian scientists, "even if I have to do 90 per cent of the work and share the credit," he says, implying that this is what he expects. "I am prepared to do that," he concludes nobly. It seems that science and conservation have their own politics and rivalries that are independent of those of broader society. In that respect, it is perhaps no different from anywhere else in the world. Regardless of the bickering rivalries and strong opinions, I can't shrug the feeling of a deeply woven appreciation for nature in Israel. Many animals and wild flowers are protected – and people seem to respect that. Perhaps it is the small size of the country that makes people feel closer to their nature. Perhaps this invokes a sense of ownership and pride in their rare animals and plants. Whatever the reason, I can't help but feel we could all learn something from Israel.

☙

On my last evening, Erez Erlich – a wildlife journalist for *Ynet news* who broke the news of the rediscovery of the Hula Painted Frog – offers to arrange a meeting for me with a man by the name of Harel Cohen. He seems eager to connect us, and so I meet him at a café in downtown Tel Aviv. Harel greets me with a friendly smile, and we chat briefly before he starts to recount his story.

"It was a cold sunny morning on the 4 October, 2009," he begins, "and I was visiting the Hula Nature Reserve with my family; my wife Ella and my three children. It was not my first time in the reserve – we sometimes go there to enjoy nature. We set out for a tour when, just a few steps before a wooden bridge, I saw something on the road. It took my attention. I took a few steps closer and realised it was alive. I asked my family to stand still, and I moved towards it. It was a large frog, about this big," he holds his hands about the length of my iPhone apart. "It was a chilly day, and it seemed to be enjoying the sun. As I started to take photographs my family walked away, wondering why I was so interested in this frog. I don't normally stop to take photos of frogs. But it seemed very interesting to me – the colours, the pattern. It was not a regular frog. I saw that the toes were long, and I could see the dark belly with the white spots." He opens the pictures on his phone and shows them to me across the table, pointing to the long toes. It is, unmistakably, a Hula Painted Frog. "And then I forgot about it," he says. "Until last year, when I saw on *Ynet news* that Yoram Malka

LEFT: A Near-eastern Fire Salamander, *Salamandra infraimmaculata*, in Tel Dan Reserve.

had found a rare frog, and I saw the picture. I rushed to my computer, opened my photos and put them side-by-side. They were the same."

Harel left a comment on the *Ynet news* article celebrating the year anniversary of the rediscovery, indicating he had seen the very same frog in 2009. But he left only his first name, and no contact information. Erez was exasperated, desperate to track him down and confirm his story. He first called the Hula Nature Reserve – it turned out that Harel had called them, but had not responded to a follow-up email. They were, however, able to supply his full name. With that, Erez checked the Israel yellow pages and found between 40 and 50 Harel Cohens. "And so I started at the beginning of the list and called each one," he says. "I spent two days calling people. I had some interesting conversations," he continues, laughing, "when I told them why I was calling, people were interested in the story of the frog." It proved to be an interesting, if somewhat unconventional, public awareness campaign. After around fifteen calls, Erez struck gold when he reached the wife of the right Harel Cohen.

Harel tells me of his subsequent email exchange with Yoram: "Why didn't you pick it up?" Yoram had asked. "Well, this is not a place you are supposed to pick up animals!" Harel had replied, a man clearly with a deep respect for nature and the rules of the reserve. Of the realisation that he had found the Hula Painted Frog he says, "I knew there was something special about it, but I didn't know it was this special. It's quite exciting. It's something." His expression becomes more serious as he leans toward me and quietly says, "Erez told me I am the fourth person in history, and the first civilian, to have found this frog. Is it true?" I pause to think about this before responding, "I believe that is true, yes." A wide smile spreads across his face as he sits back in his chair, his eyes glinting.

The Hula Painted Frog has different meanings to different people. To some it is a symbol of hope; to others a symbol of the conflict between environmental and economic interests and the triumph of the former, and to others still it is a symbol of the divisions between and within societies in conflict. Everyone has his own Hula Painted Frog story. But it occurs to me that Harel's story is different, and there is something very pure and genuine woven into the story that stems from a deep respect and appreciation for nature. It is not about seeking recognition or credit for his find. But as I listen to him animatedly recount the story, I am convinced that he will carry this story with him for the rest of his life; that he will sit with his grandchildren and hold up his photos as he recounts that crisp October morning when his attention was grabbed by the special frog with the unusual pattern and long toes; of how, in that moment, he became the fourth person in history and the first

A Hula Painted Frog – the first individual to be seen and photographed in over 50 years.

civilian to find, and the first person to ever capture a colour photograph of, the beautiful, remarkable and elusive Hula Painted Frog. And nobody can take that away from him.

♂

During my time with Sarig he had repeatedly alluded to a new discovery about the Hula Painted Frog, adding, "but I can't say more until it is published". Five months after my trip to Israel, he published with colleagues a paper indicating that the Hula Painted Frog is not, according to their analysis, a disc-tongued frog of the genus *Discoglossus* as believed. It is, instead, the only living representative of the fossil genus *Latonia* – a genus of frogs that was thought to have died out 100,000 years ago. The fact that the frog is the last living representative of an extinct group places even more importance on its protection, and makes its rediscovery all the more significant.

The story of the Hula Painted Frog – a living fossil relic – had taken another turn. Something tells me that it will not be the last.

IN SEARCH OF THE VARIABLE
HARLEQUIN FROG, COSTA RICA

Osa Peninsula, Costa Rica, May 2013

I am face-to-face with one of the most delicately colourful creatures I have ever seen. If a master sculptor and painter conspired to create something impossibly beautiful, they would be hard-pushed to top this. Slender limbs stem from a delicate body that is granular lime-green on top and creamy white underneath, flanked by a slate-blue panel lined with half a dozen cream-coloured ribs. But it is the eyes that command my attention. Perfectly rounded, tomato-red and rimmed with the same deep black as in its vertical pupils, they look like shiny porcelain orbs so fragile that they could shatter. The Red-eyed Treefrog is an icon of Costa Rica, and may be one of the most photographed frogs in the world; but it is for good reason. As my headlamp illuminates the fragile creature I need to remind myself that I am seeing this, not on the screen or on the page, but for the first time in the flesh. It is a rich welcome to my first time on Costa Rican soil.

⚘

Just three decades ago Costa Rica was losing its forests at a rate unmatched by any other nation on earth, reducing tree cover to just one-fifth of the country's land area. But, in a miraculous turnaround fuelled by smart incentives for forest protection and an impressive network of protected areas, forest now cloaks around a half of the country, ranking Costa Rica fifth in the world (and first in the Americas) in the 2012 Environmental Performance Index and pushing it to first place on the Happy Planet Index twice in four years. It is, by all accounts, the greenest and happiest place in the world; a shining example of how to live a good life that doesn't cost the earth. Upon discovering that the country had oil, the government swiftly placed a moratorium on its exploitation – it draws ninety-five per cent of its energy from renewable sources and boasts an ecological footprint per person that is one-quarter that of the USA. And if that weren't enough, in 2012 Costa Rica became the first

RIGHT: Red-eyed Treefrogs, *Agalychnis calidryas,* in the Osa Peninsula – top pair in amplexus..

Piro Biological Station in the Osa Peninsula.

country on the American continent to ban recreational hunting after a photograph posted by a hunter on Facebook resulted in a public backlash.

Costa Rica boasts some 200 species of amphibians – not bad for a country two-thirds the size of Scotland (Scotland boasts six native amphibian species) – including beauties such as the Red-eyed Treefrog, poison dart frogs, glass frogs and harlequin frogs. But the country's amphibians are also infamous; for it was in the pristine and protected forests of Costa Rica that the rapid and mysterious disappearance of frogs and toads in the late 1980s raised the alarm among conservationists and the public alike, and heralded the onset of the sixth mass extinction. The Golden Toad has since become a poster child for the extinction crisis. While I won't retell the tale of the Golden Toad, I will expand upon the story of another frog that disappeared alongside this toad – a disappearance perhaps even more dramatic. It is the story of a frog that vanished not only from the pristine cloud forests of Monteverde, but also from across the Pacific and Atlantic slopes of the Cordilleras de Tilaran mountain range and south into western Panama.

The Variable Harlequin Frog – or *Atelopus varius* – is so-called because it displays a remarkable variety of colour forms; from lemon yellow to orange to fiery red mottled on black. Three decades ago the frog existed as more than 100 populations from northern Costa Rica south into Panama, and where it occurred it was extremely abundant; one survey in the early 1980s found 751 adult Variable Harlequin Frogs along a 200 metre stretch of river. When Dr. Alan Pounds arrived in Costa Rica to study the curious arm-waving breeding behaviour of the frog in 1982, he was disappointed by their failure to breed that season. Little did he know that only a few years later the frog would have disappeared entirely from streams throughout its range. A census conducted in Monteverde between 1990 and 1992 found precisely zero individuals. By 1996 experts had concluded that all populations of the frog, all the way from northern Costa Rica to Panama, had been completely wiped out.

But this was not the end of the story of the Variable Harlequin Frog. In 2003 a budding young herpetologist called Justin Yeager was doing his study abroad programme near Quepos, a town on the Pacific coast of Costa Rica just south of San Jose. Yeager was focused on studying poison dart frogs in the area, but one day his guide talked of yellow and black frogs in the forest. Yeager dismissed the claims, well aware that the Variable Harlequin Frog – the only frog in these forests to match the description – had been declared extinct. He was told he could not get permission to visit the stream in which the frogs lived as it required traversing private property, but his jaw dropped when the guide appeared the next day holding two yellow and black frogs, for he knew instantly what he was looking at. Yeager was not granted access to visit the streamside home of the frogs on that trip, but subsequent expeditions confirmed the presence of between 60 and 95 Variable Harlequin Frogs along a single remote stretch of riverbank. For reasons that were unclear, these frogs had survived while others around them had been wiped out. Several years later, a second population was discovered about 100 miles southeast in a site called Las Alturas, at the foothills of the Talamanca Mountains – this is the only confirmed breeding population of the species in Costa Rica, and the frog is now classified as critically endangered. Following its re-appearance the Variable Harlequin Frog became a poignant symbol of hope for all those frogs that had disappeared from the forests and streams of Costa Rica and beyond.

The re-appearance of the Variable Harlequin Frog captured the imagination of many people – including me, while its rediscovery nurtured in me a deep fascination for the harlequin frogs. Whether it was their striking and beautiful colouration, their elegant gait, their rarity, or their enigmatic air that drew me in I am not sure, but I suspect it was a combination of these qualities. Not long after learning about the miraculous reappearance of the Variable Harlequin Frog I embarked on my own search for lost harlequin frogs in the high Andes of Ecuador. It was with the harlequin frogs that I began my journey in search of lost frogs, and it was fitting to end my search with them. And so I began planning an expedition to Costa Rica on a quest to find and photograph the elusive and beautiful Variable Harlequin Frog.

OVERLEAF: Volcanic sands of the Osa Peninsula near Iguana Lodge.

❧

My quest for the Variable Harlequin Frog did not get off to a promising start. I read on a website devoted to harlequin frogs, that, "humans almost never see the extremely rare *A. varius*" – and seeing one with my own eyes was starting to feel like a pipe dream. While I was all too familiar with the challenges of locating very rare frogs, I had never come up against such secrecy shrouding the whereabouts of a species. I kicked off my quest by contacting several notable herpetologists in Costa Rica to inquire about the possibility of visiting one of the two known populations of the frog. More than a dozen emails were either met with radio silence or an apologetic acknowledgement that they couldn't help. A couple replied, "Let me know if you succeed – I would love to see this frog!" I could understand why the whereabouts of the frog were shrouded in secrecy; if collectors knew where to find these valuable animals they would be gone within days, and it is for this reason that I will be vague about locations – but what was surprising to me was that even many eminent scientists in Costa Rica were in the dark.

My breakthrough came, by chance, in a bar in Washington, DC (where I live), when I ran into an old friend and colleague, Sarah Wyatt. Sarah had spent a year in Costa Rica working with the group ProCAT (a non-profit organisation dedicated to research and conservation of cultural and natural richness in Latin America) and so I told her about my quest, and that trying to visit this particular frog was like trying to gain access to Fort Knox. Before I could utter the name of the frog she cut in, "*Atelopus varius*?" It clicked that we had, just a couple of years previously, supported Sarah and colleagues to conduct research on this very frog. "I *may* just be able to help," she said with a wry smile.

Sarah connected me with a colleague at ProCAT, also another ex-colleague and friend of mine from Conservation International, Jan Schipper, and the wheels were set in motion for arranging a visit to Las Alturas, and a shot at seeing the frog. "There are some obstacles to overcome," Jan cautioned, "but I think we can make this work." I was starting to feel a glimmer of hope, and that glimmer was all I needed to book my flight to Costa Rica.

❧

I arrive into San Jose still awaiting the final confirmation on the logistics of my trip to Las Alturas, and make my way southwest to one of the wildest regions in Costa Rica, to take advantage of the rare opportunity to spend some time in what *National Geographic* magazine has referred to as, "the most biologically intense place on earth", the Osa Peninsula.

The Osa Peninsula is a 430,000-acre block of land that juts into the Pacific from south-

Golfo Dulce Poison Dart Frog, *Phyllobates vittatus*, in the Osa Peninsula. One of the most toxic frogs in the world.

west Costa Rica, close to the border with Panama. As Roy Toft and Trond Larsen write in their beautiful book *Osa*, with "an embarassment of riches, the Osa seems to call for superlatives at every turn. Within Central America, for example, it contains the largest swathe of lowland rainforest on the Pacific Coast and the most expansive mangrove wetlands; the tallest tree, a 77 metre kapok; the healthiest population of scarlet macaws … and it boasts more species of trees and plants than any forest occurring north of Panama." Add to that the fact that the Osa Peninsula accounts for more than half of all species that live in Costa Rica (and four per cent of the world's species of plants and animals), but occupies just three per cent of the country's total land area, and you have a hotspot within a hotspot of biological riches. Because it is drenched in rainfall much of the year – some six metres annually – the Osa also offers a mouthwatering array of frogs including some, such as the Golfo Dulce Poison Dart Frog, that live nowhere else on earth. At this low elevation, the frogs of the Osa have been spared the devastating impact of the chytrid fungus, which thrives in cooler climes, making it a true haven for frog-lovers.

⚬

My Cessna plane lands on a small strip in Puerto Jimenez, the largest town on the southern tip of the Osa Peninsula. As I step onto the hot tarmac I am welcomed by the moist kiss

CLOCKWISE FROM RIGHT

Green and Black Poison Dart Frog, *Dendrobates auratus*, in the Osa Peninsula.

A Reticulated Glass Frog *Hyalinobatrachium valerioi* poses for the camera on a banana leaf.

Reticulated Glass Frog backlit against a leaf in the Osa Peninsula.

of tropical air. I spend the first days in the Osa getting accustomed to the heat – and a humidity that dampens the bedsheets – at the idyllic Iguana Lodge, where lush forest meets roaring sea. Days and nights are filled with the crashing of waves as they pound charcoal-grey volcanic sands that stretch for mile upon deserted mile, absorbing the heat of the tropical sun like exposed metal and burning bare skin on contact. The sound of the waves is joined occasionally by the screech of Scarlet Macaws as they pass overhead, ruby red flashes against a sapphire sky, or by the rumble and crack of thunder followed by the clatter of raindrops on iron roofs. Once in a while the sound of thrashing branches overhead signals the arrival of White-faced Monkeys in search of fruit, sending Jesus Christ Lizards skittering into the undergrowth on lanky hind legs. On some mornings howler monkeys deliver a guttural wake-up call that would rouse the dead; if I didn't know better I would think that they were in the room with me.

After dark a whole new soundscape takes over, as male Red-eyed Treefrogs court females with melodic whoops from large leaves overhanging an old fountain, producing gelatinous egg masses to develop and plop tadpoles into the waters below. It is in the grounds of the lodge, by this old fountain, that I cast my headlamp on my first ever Red-eyed Treefrog in the wild, and savour my rich introduction to the Osa Peninsula and to Costa Rica.

From Iguana Lodge I move on to spend a few days in the nearby Piro Biological Research Station, a well-equipped outpost in a forest clearing operated by Osa Conservation. I arrive to find spider monkeys cavorting in the trees next to the main station. Manuel Sanchez,

A glass frog guards eggs laid on a nearby leaf.

an employee of Osa Conservation who grew up wandering these forests, welcomes me with a tantalising question: "What would you like to see?" I reply that I would love to see the Golfo Dulce Poison Dart Frog, *Phyllobates vittatus*, an endangered, beautiful and highly toxic frog that lives here and only here. And also on my list, since he is asking, are the Green-and-black Poison Dart Frog, *Dendrobates auratus* and the Gliding Treefrog, *Agalychnis spurrelli*. Manuel smiles at my optimism, for the Gliding Treefrog only appears after heavy rains and on a full moon – and replies "Well, OK, we will see. First things first. This afternoon, we will try to find the Golfo Dulce Poison Dart Frog."

Unlike most frogs, the poison dart frogs are active during the day; being toxic, they can afford to be so bold. But they do tend to prefer the cooler hours, and so we wait until the heat of the day subsides before heading out along a well-kept trail through the forest, past large buttress roots that snake into the leaf litter and past Halloween Crabs with bright red pincers scuttling across the forest floor. "We have been looking for the poison dart frogs these past days," Manuel tells me as we walk, "but we didn't find them. We could hear them, but they were calling from holes in the ground so we couldn't see them. It is not easy. Hopefully we will have better luck today."

We walk until the forest is turning grey in the draining light. And then Manuel stops and cocks his head. "You hear that?" he says as he turns to me. I tilt my ear towards the forest and listen. And then I hear it, a faint, repeated whistle. "That's the Golfo Dulce Poison Dart Frog," he says with a wide grin, before turning and making his way into the dense understory of the forest and towards the sound. I follow, squeezing through tangled vines and trying to resist the urge to grasp palm trunks adorned with long, black spines. As we move closer, the frog stops calling. "This is what they do," explains Marcelo, a passionate and knowledgeable Costa Rican herpetologist who has accompanied us for the search. "This is why they are so hard to find. They stop calling as soon as you get close." We stand in silence, hoping that the frog will call again. Sweat stings my eyes. After some minutes the frog calls once more and Manuel moves stealthily towards it, before announcing in a loud whisper, "I see it!" I pick my way to see the tiny frog bouncing from leaf to leaf across the forest floor.

I swing my camera bag off my back and assemble my equipment to face the next challenge: photographing something the size of my fingernail that won't stop moving, and which is dangerously toxic to the touch. With the assistance of Manuel and Marcelo, who direct the frog and stop it from disappearing down a hole using leaves and a ziplock bag, I lay on the forest floor and position myself to photograph it. In the dark understory I

Northern Cat-eyed Snake, *Leptodeira septentrionalis*.

position two flashes with diffusers to soften the light on either side of the frog to bring out the detail. Up close I can see and appreciate the beauty of the frog; two red stripes the length of the body and flashes of aqua blue are set off against a black background. The frog refuses to sit still, and as I writhe on the ground to find the right angle a large ant decides to sink its large mandibles into the tender flesh on the underside of my arm. Several failed attempts and many expletives later I get the shot I'm looking for – my record of a frog I may only see once in my life. I sit up, stretch my back, rub my arm and watch the frog hop into the darkness. As we make our way back to the station I feel a wave of grubby contentment. My first endangered Costa Rican frog.

ॐ

With the Golfo Dulce Poison Dart Frog under my belt, I turn my attention to the other species of poison dart frog that lives in these forests; the Green-and-black Poison Dart Frog. It is a frog that I am eager to see, for I used to keep this very species in a glass terrarium in my living room when I was 11 years old. But I have yet to encounter one in the wild. And so we set off early the next morning to scour the forest floor for the miniature jewel. A couple of hours pass with no success, and my eyes are growing tired, when it appears – a small

bright green and black frog skipping across a carpet of dead leaves.

I excitedly assemble my camera and flashes and lie down to compose the shot, when the unthinkable happens. My camera fails. My stomach lurches. The LCD screen on the back won't go on, and all of the buttons have stopped working. I reboot the camera, but it is dead. I ask Manuel if we can collect the frog to photograph back at the station, where I have an old backup camera, and so he gently guides it into a clear plastic bag filled with air to make our way back to the station. All the way I feel a pit in my stomach as I envision the shots I will no longer be able to get without my full-frame camera.

Back at the station I tell myself to pull it together – to stop being such a brat and to look on the bright side; at least I have a backup camera that works. I proceed to photograph the small Green-and-black Poison Dart Frog, and I'm guessing you would not be able to tell with which camera the pictures were taken.

⚘

"Watch out for the Fer-de-lance," Guido, our herpetologist guide warns as we wade up the Rio Piro with our headlamps illuminating overhanging leaves. These deadly and aggressive snakes like to hang out on the riverbanks – and you don't really want to be bitten by one out here.

While poison dart frogs decorate the forest floor during the day, it is at nighttime that the forests of the Osa Peninsula really kick into gear. This is when many creatures, and most frogs, are active. One of our first finds on the leaves overhanging the river is a mass of clear jelly filled with writhing tadpoles and a nearby male glass frog cautiously guarding the mound from predators such as Cat-eyed Snakes. Further up the river we find Cat-eyed Snakes, Tree Boas, and under low-hanging branches the orange eye shine of a caiman gleams back at us. A striking Black-and-white Striped Paca – a small mammal – picks its way along the banks and disappears into the undergrowth. We find Red-eyed Treefrogs poised elegantly on branches and a large Milky Frog, with bubbling creamy brown skin, clinging to a trunk. We make our way to a small swamp in which Tungara Frogs in a breeding frenzy fill the air with their whooping calls and decorate the water with white foam nests. Delicate Hourglass Frogs clamber among blades of grass in the shallows, peeping to attract prospective mates. But it is still relatively dry, and there is no sign of the

LEFT: A male Hourglass Frog, *Dendropsophus ebraccatus*, calls to a female on a blade of grass below in the Osa Peninsula.

Gliding Treefrog. Every time I mention my burning desire to see this frog I am reminded: "They only come out on the full moon, and after heavy rains. You have to be very lucky."

☙

On my last day at Piro I am woken early by the clatter of rain on tin. Heavy rain falls the entire day, and as I shelter at the field station my mind turns to the swamp that must be slowly filling with water. I feel excited, but also apprehensive because, if the heavy rain continues, it will be hard to look for frogs and almost impossible to photograph them. But as darkness falls the rain subsides, and we grab our headlamps and hop into a car to go and hunt frogs. We pull in at the side of the road some 20 metres from the swamp, and as I open the car door I am met with a wall of sound as groans, quacks and whistles merge indistinguishably to fill the humid night air at a volume that would compete with the loudest of nightclubs. I stare at Manuel and Marcelo in disbelief.

Entering the swamp we find a mating frenzy of frogs of all shapes and sizes. Enormous Milk Frogs lie in the shallows inflating vocal sacs on either side of the head like bubblegum; tiny Hourglass Frogs peep to one other on blades of grass and Red-eyed Treefrogs clamber

ABOVE: Mating Milk Frogs, *Phrynohyas venulosa*, in the Osa Peninsula.
TOP LEFT: Hourglass Frog, *Dendropsophus ebraccatus*.
BELOW LEFT: Granular Glass Frog, *Cochranella granulosa*, in the Osa Peninsula.

among overhanging branches. The hormones are in overdrive after the first big rains of the season, and the expression 'explosive breeding' – the term given to those frogs that appear *en masse* to reproduce – takes on a whole new meaning. From the middle of the swamp the noise is almost deafening. I don't know where to look or photograph, as frogs clamber and clamour all around me.

Manuel calls to me above the din: "Come and see this." He is standing by a tree at the fringe of the swamp and so I wade over and follow the line of his pointing finger. And then I see it, its yellow webbed feet splayed on a large leaf: a beautiful green frog with magenta eyes. It is a Gliding Treefrog. I crane my neck to look at the moon. It is not entirely full, but it is close enough, and I count my lucky stars that the Gliding Treefrogs chose to descend to the swamp on this, my last night in the Osa.

⚘

I feel a pang of nerves as I leave the Osa Peninsula to embark on the final leg of my journey in Costa Rica – and indeed the final leg of my journey in search of lost frogs. I am off to Las Alturas in search of the Variable Harlequin Frog.

I board a small boat at the end of a small pier, and watch the Osa Peninsula recede behind me as I ferry across the tranquil waters of Golfo Dulce to the town of Golfito on the Costa Rican mainland. In Golfito I rent a car, and receive a phone call with directions to my destination from ProCAT biologist Jose Gonzales. "It is raining a lot however; it may be hard to find the frog," he says. I feel the same disappointment as in Colombia when I realised we were not going to find the Mesopotamia Beaked Toad, and in Israel when the search for the Hula Painted Frog was coming to a close. "Not again," I think as I start to drive, the rain pattering heavily on the windscreen.

I drive south towards the Panamanian border before veering northeast on a very steep, curving road into the mountains and towards Las Alturas. Although I imagine spectacular scenery, the rain occludes the view for most of the drive. Road signs are conspicuous by their absence and I get used to hanging out my window asking for directions. After some three hours' driving, in the final vestiges of light, I turn into a dirt road – at the end of which, apparently, is my destination. I am by this point feeling far from urban civilisation.

I eventually reach the large gates of a private reserve. "Quien?" the man guarding the

TOP RIGHT: An Hourglass Frog, *Dendropsophus ebraccatus*, on a blade of grass in the Osa Peninsula.
BELOW RIGHT: Male Olive Treefrogs, *Scinax elaeochroa*, fighting for a mate in the Osa Peninsula.

Mating Milk Frogs, *Phrynohyas venulosa*, with vocal sac inflated.

gate says when I tell him I am here on the invitation of Jose Gonzales. "Here we go," I think. He looks at me sceptically while I muddle my way through my rationale for being here and why he should let me in. As I slowly dig myself deeper into a confusing story, a woman appears. I hear the man mutter something to her, and she nods. It is enough, apparently, to grant me access, and the man reluctantly hoists open the gate.

Inside the gate, I feel as though I have entered a lost world. Mist rises from a rocky road meandering through verdant forest from which jut large, lime-green tree ferns. In the pastel evening light it looks ethereal. I eventually reach a small settlement at the end of the road, and feel as though I have stepped 50 years back in time as I scan the local grocer's and make out a painted sign above a barn door illuminated by a tungsten bulb that reads 'Cinema'. A young man by the name Diego appears and leads me to a small hut and my bed for the night. A wooden box with an incandescent bulb dries mammal scats by the front door, and field guides, boots, headlamps and posters of wildlife decorate the wooden hut, betraying the recent presence of field biologists. I leave my bags and head to the hut next door to eat a dinner of rice and beans under the dim orange glow of a bare bulb, before retiring for the night, hoping that the rain clears the next day.

⚛

I wake early with nervous energy. Today is the day. Within the coming hours I will either feel the thrill of seeing with my own eyes the Variable Harlequin Frog, or I will feel the bitter pang of disappointment.

Although I am not hungry I wash down a breakfast of rice, salty cheese and scrambled eggs with a steaming coffee. As I eat I ponder the arrangements for the day. Diego's accent was thick, and communication had been difficult. Most of my attempts in Spanish were met with "no intiendo" – and as a result I had no real clue what to do next. He did, however, say something about the river and a man called Clemente. As I am lost in thought I look up from my eggs to see an elderly man with leathery skin and kind eyes leaning against the doorway. He talks to me in Spanish laced with a thick accent, and I again struggle to understand, but when he says "el rio," it clicks. "Eres Celemente?" I ask, and he nods. "Diece minutos?" I respond before wolfing down the remained of my breakfast to go and get ready.

In ten minutes I return to find Clemente and Diego waiting outside the hut. They lead me to Diego's car and I climb into the back for the short drive to the river. The morning is cool and, while it is not raining, a thick blanket of cloud obscures the early sun. "A dry morning!" I say cheerfully, in the hopes that positive thinking will boost our chances: "Perhaps we will find the frog?!" Diego's eyes meet mine in the rearview mirror and he shakes his head slowly. "It's too cold. The frogs only come out when it's warmer than this."

The car shudders to a halt and Clemente and I bundle out. "Buenas suerte," Diego calls as he drives off, clearly not holding out much hope. I follow Clemente through a dense thicket to the banks of a river some twenty feet wide. As we make our way up the rocky bank I quickly abandon any illusions of keeping my socks dry as I plunge my hiking boots into the cool water. We clamber over mossy rocks as slick as black ice and I struggle to maintain my footing. At one point my feet disappear from under me; I manage to save my camera gear from plunging into the water by throwing out my hand to break the fall. Where the banks of the river become too difficult or too deep to navigate, we cut our way into the fringing forest through a tangle of vines and trees to re-emerge further upstream.

We come upon a branch ringed with orange tape with some numbers marked on it. It can only mean one thing. "Does this indicate a harlequin frog sighting?" I ask Clemente. He nods as he cranes his neck into the rock crevices, concluding in Spanish, "but it is not out today. Too cold." I stare towards the sky and will the weak morning sun to pierce the blanket of cloud.

We continue to pick our way up the riverbank and come upon another orange ribbon.

I crouch to peer into tiny caves formed under tangled mossy roots, allowing my eyes to become accustomed to the dark. It is unbearably tantalising to know that the Variable Harlequin Frogs are here, but invisible.

I stop to take a moment to sit on a rock and listen to the gurgle of water, imagining a small yellow and black frog perched in front of me, stretching its spindly limbs as it scales the mossy rock. I feel at once calmed by my surroundings but desperate for the appearance of the apparition. The air is heavy, as though rain is imminent. Sensing the window of opportunity closing, I hoist myself off the rock and continue to pick my way behind Clemente up the river, watching water pour out of holes in his rubber boots like a watering can.

What happens next is difficult to describe, so allow me to use an analogy.

When I was twelve years old, I visited Paris for the first time. A budding young painter, I was mildly obsessed with van Gogh, and copies of many of his paintings including his famous self-portrait against a blue swirling background adorned my bedroom wall. Once

LEFT: Gliding Treefrog, *Agalychnis spurrelli*, with mushrooms, found on the last night in the Osa Peninsula.
ABOVE: Gliding Treefrogs, *Agalychnis spurrelli*, mating.

in Paris I made a beeline to the Musee D'Orsay, home to many of van Gogh's more famous works. Despite the familiarity of his 1889 self-portrait – but more likely because of it – the moment I set eyes on the original painting was a profound, almost reverential, experience. I was face-to-face with something eminently familiar, but seeing it for the first time. I remember the feeling vividly as I imagined van Gogh himself, over a century previously, laying down each individual brush stroke that now undulated from the canvas in a delicate interplay of light and shadow. It was a feeling of being in the presence of greatness; of experiencing something far bigger than myself that was at once humbling and inspiring.

What happens next evokes similar feelings of reverence. For in front of me is something that has grown in my imagination to mythical status. A small delicate frog decorated with flame-orange and black stretches her long slender limbs as she scales a rock by the side of the river. It takes a moment for my brain to register that it not a figment of my aching desire for this sight to be real. In front of me is a Variable Harlequin Frog; the culmination of millions of years of evolution, a survivor of one of the worst mass-mortalities in recent history. I am once again humbled and inspired as I study her gently granular skin and her lime-green eyes meet mine.

I swing my camera bag onto a rock, giddy with the excitement of capturing this moment. I take some time to photograph the beautiful frog, appreciating her beauty and delicacy with every click, before packing my camera bag and bidding her farewell. As we walk up the river, I feel a drop of rain, and I cast one last look back at her. As I watch her sitting there, the heavens open, and as large raindrops plop into the river around me, I struggle to comprehend that, after my journey in search of lost frogs, here I am face-to-face with an icon of hope. I am in the presence of the Variable Harlequin Frog.

⚛

Within hours of seeing the Variable Harlequin Frog I am driving north, through persistent and at times torrential rain, toward San Jose. As mist rises from verdant forest on mountains that soar either side of the road, 'Here Comes the Sun', by the Beatles comes on the radio and I am transported to the curving roads of northwest Scotland. I feel a wave of deep contentment. I have seen the Variable Harlequin Frog, and I am going home.

LEFT: Variable Harlequin Frog, *Atelopus varius*, a critically endangered species that was feared extinct before being rediscovered in 2003.

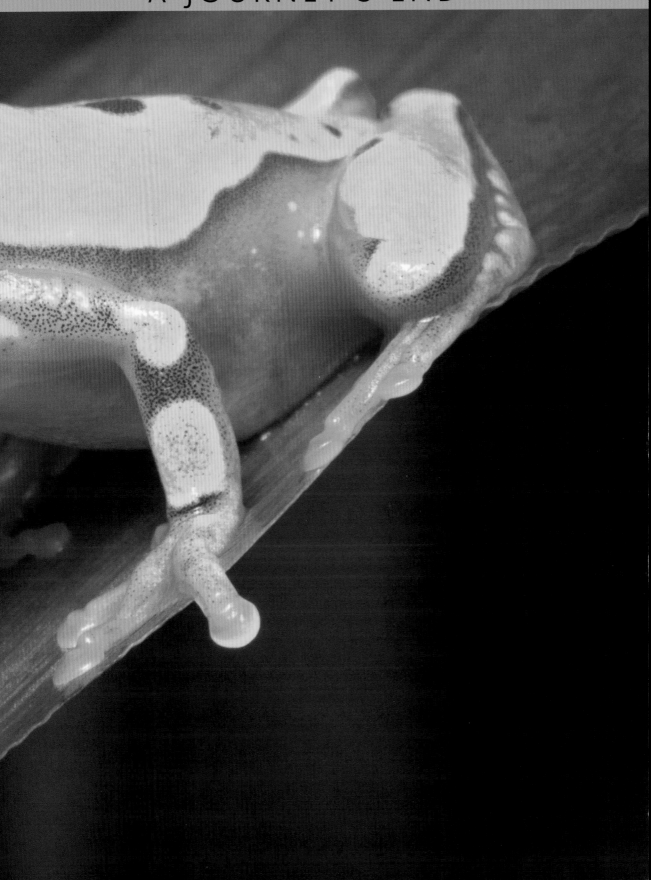

PART THREE

CHAPTER 15

SECOND CHANCES

My journey in search of some of the most elusive creatures on earth has taken me from lung-tingling Andean passes to humid jungles, from flooded marshland to ravaged hillsides, and finally to a bubbling stream in Costa Rica to feast my eyes upon a living emblem of resilience and hope. I have felt the tingle of anticipation as dozens of researchers travelled across 20 countries in search of frogs, salamanders and caecilians unseen in decades, the crushing disappointment of failed searches, and the adrenalin surge of finding the most rare and beautiful of creatures. I have wrestled with the prospect of losing the most important person in my life whilst coordinating searches for species thought to have been extinguished. And as the seed of an idea grew into a global campaign, I felt like a rabbit in the headlights of an expectant media feeding the growing attentions of the millions of people that tuned in for the ride.

But once the dirt has been scraped off the boots and the glare of the media has dimmed, what does it all mean? Why did so many people tune in for the search, and where do the frogs that turned up – and those that are still lost – fit in the grand scheme of things? Essentially, why should we care? First, let's tackle the question of what the frogs – both lost and found – are telling us.

As I compiled the list of lost frogs, salamanders and caecilians in spring through summer of 2010, I was struck by just how many species had not been seen in decades – some even longer than a century. The list now stands at more than 250 amphibian species that have not been recorded this century. I find this figure both alarming – an indication of just how many frogs, salamanders and caecilians are missing – and humbling; a testament to how little we know about our world. Absence is always more difficult to prove than presence, but more than 120 species of amphibians are believed to have gone extinct since 1980, and of more than 7,000 amphibian species that are currently named, a third are at risk of extinction and a further quarter are too little known to be evaluated. After more than 300 million years on the planet, the amphibians – the ultimate survivors – are vanishing from around us, heralding what many experts are calling the sixth mass extinction on earth, and the first since the dinosaurs blinked out of existence.

It is not just the sheer number of amphibian species that are being shed from our planet that has sparked the interest of scientists, conservationists and the public, but the manner in which they have vanished that has whipped up intrigue and alarm, and challenged our very notions about how we protect life on our planet. The sudden, rapid and enigmatic disappearance of frogs from pristine and protected areas, simultaneously on continents separated by vast ocean, was unlike anything our species had seen. While we could point a finger at the causes of previous extinctions on our watch – creatures that had been shot or clubbed out of existence – we were faced with a mass extinction event with no obvious culprit and no obvious solutions. And, what was most worrisome to many people, we didn't know how it would affect *us*.

Since the enigmatic declines of the 1980s, our understanding of what has been driving the loss of amphibians has advanced in leaps and bounds. Perhaps the biggest breakthrough came with the identification in 1999 of the pathogenic amphibian chytrid fungus, which was subsequently implicated in massive die-offs in Central, South and North America, Europe and Australia and has now been identified from more than 500 species in more than 50 countries. Chytridiomycosis is considered to be the most devastating infectious diseases ever recorded among vertebrates, but it is only in recent years that scientists have really started to get a grip on where the fungus may have come from, why it has wreaked such carnage, and why *now*.

※

"It's the most horrific, and yet the most interesting thing out there," says Ann Froschauer, a communications manager with the US Fish and Wildlife Service (whose surname, incidentally, translates as 'Frog bog'). She is talking about fungi; specifically, rogue fungi that have annihilated their hosts. First frogs, and now bats, bees and snakes are being wiped out by killer fungi. "Fungi are dangerous – more so than viruses or bacteria," she warns – but what is it about fungi that make them so different – so deadly?

Let's first consider what a fungus is not: it is neither a plant nor an animal, nor is it a bacteria. Fungi belong to an entirely separate kingdom – one that includes moulds, yeast and mushrooms – and they therefore follow different rules. Fungi are similar to animals in that they need to eat to survive, but fungi can retreat into spores and survive for long periods without feeding. They can also live independently, outside of their host – and can switch to new hosts relatively easily. The amphibian chytrid fungus is thought to be able to survive for years – perhaps even decades – in an environment devoid of frogs. This means that fungi can wipe out their entire host population without wiping out themselves.

It also means they can move independently of their host – hitching a ride on the leg of a bird or on the sole of a muddy boot. Fungi can also reproduce sexually, meaning that when they encounter another fungus of the same species in a new environment, they are able to recombine into a potentially more virulent strain.

Amphibians were the first class of animals to experience such precipitous declines and extinctions at the hands of a deadly fungus – but others are following suit. White-nose Syndrome is a fungal disease that first appeared in bats in New York in early 2007, and has raced through more than 20 states in the US, infecting 10 species and killing an estimated seven million bats. The fungus eats the bat's skin, sometimes puncturing holes in it and sometimes replacing it completely. This mass killer has much in common with chytridiomycosis; the *Washington Post* even goes as far as to call it a 'copycat'. Curiously, the same fungus is found in European bats but without the same devastating impacts. White-nose resembles another fungal killer found recently in six species of snakes in nine US states – the snakes, like the bats, succumb to the fungus while hibernating in underground caves as this is when the immune system is suppressed. A fungus has also been identified as a contributing factor in colony-collapse disorder in bees, and yet another fungus has contributed to the precipitous decline of coral reefs in the Caribbean weakened by rising ocean temperatures. Just in the past months a new chytrid fungus that eats the skin of salamanders has been discovered after it decimated Fire Salamander populations in the Netherlands.

This chilling uptick in the prevalence and impact of fungal diseases is worrying. Matthew Fisher, an epidemiologist at Imperial College in London recently told *Environment 360*: "Fungi have driven more animal species extinct than any other class of pathogens by quite a long way." Fisher and colleagues estimate that fungi have caused more than 80 per cent of known disease-driven animal extinctions – the vast majority of which have occurred in the past two decades.

The increasing devastation caused by fungi in recent years is likely a result of two factors. Firstly, as we move things around the world more frequently and further than ever before, we are introducing pathogens into new areas – and this is often disastrous (just consider the impact of smallpox and other diseases that killed between 10 million and 20 million people when the Europeans colonised the Americas). Secondly, the susceptibility of animals (humans included) to pathogens is increasing as a result of another factor: stress. We are changing our world rapidly – slashing forests, pumping out pesticides and dangerously altering the climate – and with such dramatic change comes stress, which suppresses immune systems. Animals that are immunosuppressed tend to be more vulnerable to fungal attack. We are, in essence, creating a perfect storm to wipe life forms off the face of the earth and, while fungi may be dealing the fatal blow, creatures worldwide are being weakened by the changes we are creating.

A few years ago Arturo Casadevall, a professor at the Albert Einstein College of Medicine, attracted attention when he suggested that the global rise of mammals was thanks to their being warm-blooded, which protected them from heat-intolerant fungi. But as global temperatures rise, mammals (such as ourselves) may lose this advantage. The Centre for Disease Control and Prevention warns that fungal infections pose an increasing threat to public health because opportunistic infections are becoming more problematic as the number of people with weakened immune systems rises, and disease dynamics are affected by climate change, as even small changes in temperature and moisture can affect the growth of fungi. We may not be as far removed from the changes we are wreaking on our environment as we would like to believe.

⚕

Since its discovery in 1999, the amphibian chytrid fungus has become something of a model for studying emerging infectious disease, and has been the subject of intensive research to decipher where it came from, how it kills, how it spreads and how it can be controlled. Recent studies suggest that the fungus may not be as new as previously suspected, but has likely been around for thousands of years, finding its way across the planet and into new areas only recently with globalisation. As the fungus spread – according to a recent study by Ben Phillips and Robert Puschendorf of James Cook University – from North through Central and South America, it adapted from a relatively benign pathogen to a deadly superbug. When the fungus first arrived in Mexico in the late 1960s to early 1970s, it took around nine years for local frog populations to show declines. As the fungus spread southwards, down through Costa Rica, the lag time between arrival and impact got smaller and smaller. By the time it hit Panama in the mid 2000s, the fungus was wiping out entire populations of frogs within a matter of months. It appeared that the fungus, having escaped its niche, had evolved quickly into a deadly pathogen capable of mass killing.

But as scientists furiously sought answers to pressing questions surrounding chytrid and conservationists sought solutions to mitigating its impact, a silver bullet solution was as elusive as the lost frogs themselves. As some of the brightest minds set about trying to unravel the mystery of sudden and rapid declines, the amphibians had a surprise of their own to spring, one that offered a glimmer of hope. Frogs that had not been seen in decades, and had been given up for dead, started to reappear in Australia and the Americas. Some appeared to be persisting at very low abundances while others were recovering to prechytrid levels. Curiously, the reappearance of most species had nothing to do with anything we had done to bring them back. With their reappearance, these Lazarus frogs offered the tantalising prospect of deciphering what enabled these frogs to survive while others around them died, rather like the reappearance of an eyewitness to an unsolved murder.

Frog by frog, some answers began to emerge. Let's start with the Armoured Mist Frog – a species that was once common in waterfalls plunging into rainforests of northeast Australia until its sudden disappearance in 1991. It was presumed to have been simply one more victim of the deadly chytrid fungus – until 2008, when Robert Puschendorf and team stumbled upon a new population in a patch of lowland dry forest. They were surprised not just by the reappearance of the frog, but also by its presence in an entirely new environment, and the fact that the frogs appeared to be healthy and stable despite infection with chytridiomycosis. How was this possible? It was possible because, in the dry forest environment, the frogs were able to raise their body temperature by basking on sun-baked rocks, suppressing the growth of the pathogen, which is intolerant of heat and desiccation.

Were the Armoured Mist Frogs a unique case? To test the idea that other frogs can stave off infection by raising their body temperature, Puschendorf's Australian colleagues, Ross Alford and Jodi Rowley, promptly decked out more than 100 frogs with mini waistbands containing transmitters in order to follow them. After two weeks of "intensive frog-stalking" they found that the warmer frogs were, the less likely they were to be infected by the fungus. Their study supported the idea that frogs could survive attack from the deadly fungus by modifying their behaviour, and suggested that perhaps we should be looking for other frogs that disappeared from cloud and rain forests in drier, warmer environments.

Other forces were at play across the world, and behaviour alone could not explain the survival of some individuals as others died around them. As Vance Vredenburg watched Mountain Yellow-legged Frogs being wiped out from lake after lake high in the Sierra Nevada of California, he noticed that amid the carcasses some frogs were surviving without assistance. Curious as to what separated the victims from the survivors, in 2010 he teamed up with Reid Harris from James Madison University to investigate. Their findings were groundbreaking. The secret to the success of some frogs, they discovered, was the presence of a specific bacteria on the skin of the frogs. Frogs varied naturally in their bacteria-load, and those that were well endowed with a particular bacteria (called *Janthinobacterium lividum,* for those who were wondering) were better able to survive a fungal attack, protected by a substance produced by the bacteria that inhibited the growth of the fungus on the skin.

Could it be that Vredenburg and Harris had uncovered a potential cure for chytrid?

They promptly set about investigating what would happen if you augmented the skin of other frogs with the bacteria – a process known as bioaugmentation, or probiotic therapy. This therapy acts by boosting cutaneous microbial communities, which are one element of an amphibian's defence against the chytrid fungus. Because many frogs do not seem to have evolved adequate innate defences against the fungal pathogen, microbial communities in the skin could provide the helping hand they need to survive infection. According to a recent review by Reid Harris and colleagues, evidence is growing that antifungal skin microbes on amphibians can suppress chytridiomycosis and increase the chances of surviving with the disease. One of the leading experts in bioaugmentation, Reid Harris explains that the process is similar to us eating probiotic yogurt: "When we eat yogurt we're actually augmenting the beneficial bacteria in our own digestive systems." It was an interesting and exciting idea, but did it work? In the laboratory it did. After infection, frogs augmented with bacteria survived whereas those lacking the bacteria died. The proof of the pudding would be testing it in the wild, and so Vredenburg and Harris headed to the high lakes of the Sierra Nevada to augment a portion of frogs with the bacteria, whilst leaving others – the control group – untouched. After a year, the experiment looked promising – those frogs that had been given a bacteria-boost were showing higher survival in the face of infection than those left to their own devices. Thirty-nine per cent of probiotic-treated individuals were recovered compared with no untreated individuals. But when Vredenburg measured the bacteria load of the recovered individuals, he found that the boosted frogs had already shed their beneficial bacteria, and he wasn't sure if they would survive another attack of the fungus. He never had a chance to find out, however – the following year all of the frogs were killed by a harsh winter freeze.

Attempts by another team of scientists to augment the skin of Golden Harlequin Frogs in Panama with the same bacteria met with similar disappointment (all the animals died). In a 2012 review of approaches to combating chytrid that included commercial antifungal products, antimicrobial skin peptides, microbial treatments, and heat therapy, Douglas C Woodhams and co-authors concluded that, "none of the new experimental treatments were considered successful in terms of improving survival", and recommended diverse lines of research in the search for options to treat fungal infection.

Despite initial mixed results in testing the effectiveness of probiotic therapy, Molly Bletz, Reid Harris and co-authors indicated in a 2013 review that, "past probiotic choices for laboratory and field trials have been based on incomplete information and were driven by the urgent need to protect amphibian populations", and proposed that a more systematic approach to identifying probiotics could improve success rates. A recent paper co-authored by 20 heavyweights in conservation science, and led by William Sutherland of Cambridge University, identifies probiotic therapy for amphibians as one of 15 topics that "increasingly may affect conservation of biological diversity, but have yet to be widely considered." They note that probiotic therapy is a particularly promising approach that "could both facilitate reintroduction of amphibians to areas from which they have been extirpated and reduce the magnitude of declines in areas not yet affected by chytridiomycosis".

Currently leading efforts to develop probiotic therapy for chytrid in the wild, and recently appointed Director of International Disease Mitigation with the Amphibian Survival Alliance, is Reid Harris. Harris and team have their sites set on an island containing more than 400 frog species found nowhere else, all of which have to date been chytrid-free: Madagascar. It is a mystery as to why Madagascar has remained chytrid-free, but it is likely that by the time you read this it will no longer be so. Although every effort is being made to prevent the introduction of the fungus (the movement of frogs into and within Madagascar is controlled as much as possible, and scientists in areas with chytrid around the world diligently sterilise boots and equipment to reduce the risk of spreading it), recent tests indicate that the fungus has been detected on frogs in Madagascar – which, according to preliminary vulnerability trials on Malagasy frogs, could be catastrophic. The survival of many of the frog species on the island could depend upon the arsenal of beneficial bacteria that Harris and team have been cultivating. Madagascar is poised to serve as a natural laboratory for testing the effectiveness of probiotic therapy for keeping chytridiomycosis at bay – and this could have far-reaching implications for our ability to treat this devastating disease and reintroduce frogs into areas from which they have been wiped out.

Although probiotic therapy may seem, at the moment, our best prospect for the development of a way of mitigating the impact of chytrid in the wild, there are many scientists who remain cautious when asked if this could provide a 'silver bullet' approach. New Zealander Phil Bishop, Chief Scientist for the Amphibian Survival Alliance, for one is wary about the amount of meddling involved. "New Zealand is a prime example of what can go wrong when you start to move creatures around," he says. "It's important to note that, just because you introduce a type of bacteria that already exists in the environment, it doesn't mean it's *not* going to harm the frogs. We all have *E. coli* in our stomachs, but if we ingest a different strain of *E. coli* we could be puking and shitting for days. We have to be careful." Joe Mendelson of Amphibian Ark also supports the idea of taking a more hands-off approach; of focusing our efforts on recovering those populations that have survived after chytrid has swept through.

Another approach to combating chytrid through augmentation has recently been proposed by a research team in Europe. Rather than tinkering with the frogs themselves, they suggest that the impacts of the fungus could be mitigated through modification of their environment. The proposed strategy is based on the findings of a three-year study to investigate why some populations of Midwife Toads (*Alytes obstetricans*) in the Pyrenees had survived chytridiomycosis while many others were wiped out. The answer, the scientists found, lay not in the toads themselves but in the ponds and lakes in which they were living. "The infected lakes and ponds did not look like the uninfected ones, neither in regard to the vegetation nor in regard to the geological characteristics," Dirk S. Schmeller, the lead scientist on the team told *ScienceDaily* following the publication of their results in January 2014. The ponds differed in one key element – the abundance of microfauna. By feeding on the free-swimming infectious stages – or zoospores – of the fungus, micropredators in the water were keeping infection at bay and giving the toads a fighting chance at survival. The authors suggest that developing methods that facilitate natural augmentation of predatory microorganisms "may hold promise as a field mitigation tool that lacks the downsides associated with introducing nonnative biocontrol agents, such as the use of antifungal chemicals or release of nonnative skin bacteria into the environment". The scientists caution that additional study is required before this can safely be attempted and, at the time of writing, trials have yet to be conducted. What is clear, however, is that factors that impact the microfauna community of lakes and ponds – such as anthropogenic stress – may play a role in determining the outcome of chytridiomycosis, reinforcing the link between ecosystem health and amphibian health, and the role of ecosystem resilience in determining the outcome of colonisation by novel pathogens.

While the search for the silver bullet solution to the chytrid fungus continues, the reappearance and apparent recovery of some frogs from Costa Rica, Panama, Australia and Europe suggests that some frogs are doing something by themselves what we have been unable to help them do so far – beat chytridiomycosis. In order to truly give these frogs a fighting chance at survival in an environment that has not been jerry-rigged to keep them alive, we need to address the root cause of the problem. The impacts of emerging infectious diseases such as chytridiomycosis are being exacerbated by stressors that we are introducing into our environment, in the form of habitat destruction, contamination and climate change. Saving amphibians will require not just good science, but also the will of society to preserve the integrity of the ecosystems upon which we all depend. Amphibians, at the forefront of the species extinction crisis, are natural flagships behind which to rally to promote the preservation of fragile ecosystems bubbling with life. But can we really expect people to care enough about amphibians to rally behind them for this cause?

CHAPTER 16

THE SONG OF THE SPADEFOOT

"It is not half so important to know as to feel"

RACHEL CARSON

If there is one thing that I have learned in my years working in conservation it is this: frogs are not Giant Pandas. Nor are they Polar Bears, Tigers or elephants. Frogs are simply not designed to wrench out our emotions as effectively as these large-bodied mammals, whose charisma has elevated them to emblems of our efforts to try and preserve that which we value. And while creatures further removed from us on the evolutionary tree, like frogs, continue to topple like lemmings over the cliff of existence, our gaze barely falters from the fate of these few 'keepers'. The majority of conservation organisation funds go towards protecting eighty species, predominantly large-bodied mammals, while more than 20,000 species are classified as threatened on the International Union for the Conservation of Nature's Red List. Lest we rely on science to keep us on track, a recent study revealed that scientists are just as prone to flights of fancy when choosing their objects of study, with threatened large mammals appearing in 500 times as many academic papers as threatened amphibians according to one assessment from southern Africa.

Now, I like Giant Pandas and Polar Bears as much as the next person. But if we are to preserve the flourishing processes of life; if we are to maximise evolutionary fodder and deepen the well of living resources upon which to sustain our own existence on a changing planet, shouldn't we be striving to preserve diversity? Shouldn't we be pulling out the stops to lend a helping hand to the unique and the bizarre, the slimy and the scaly, the weird and the wonderful, rather than focusing almost exclusively on creatures with eyelashes? I would argue that we should. But in order to elevate these creatures to priorities for conservation, we need to understand what it is about the Giant Pandas, Polar Bears and Tigers that resonates so deeply with people that, even though few will ever experience these creatures in the wild, they are moved enough by the prospect of their loss to try and save them.

Most people care that Giant Pandas, Polar Bears and Tigers exist because they are embodiments of things that we value; beauty, power, rarity, to name just a few. When we look at a Tiger we see reflected back at us elements of ourselves. When we see a baby panda, that big clumsy bundle of fur stirs in us a deep, primal instinct to protect. We can,

Large-bodied mammals like African Elephants receive the lion's share of conservation attention and support, leaving less charismatic creatures such as frogs out in the cold.

in short, empathise with them. As conservationists we have capitalised on this to craft these creatures into global icons through which we attribute meaning and consciousness to abstract concepts of biodiversity loss and global warming. The Giant Panda has become a symbol of the environmental movement, and the Polar Bear has come to embody the impacts of climate change. It is easier, after all, to relate to a helpless Polar Bear hugging a coffee-table sized block of melting ice than to grapple with the complexities, politics and messiness of climate change. We can offload our sadness, our anger, our guilt, onto a defenceless creature and we can ease our conscience by supporting efforts to save it.

But the emotions that we feel when we see such loaded images have everything to do with our perceptions of the animals themselves – and these, when we have no direct experience of the animals in the wild, are shaped by what we are told or shown. Just a couple of decades ago, Polar Bears were widely held as ruthless marauders to be feared rather than protected – an image fuelled by a dramatic 1987 *National Geographic* documentary entitled 'Polar Bear Alert'. According to Jon Mooallem in his book *Wild Ones,* the documentary shaped the public's perception of the bears to such a degree that, when photographs captured by German photographer Norbert Rosing of a Polar Bear and a dog playing and hugging on the snow were published in *National Geographic* magazine in 1994, they evoked a flurry of angry responses from people convinced that the bears were incapable of such compassion. The photos were promptly forgotten, only to resurface 13 years later on the website of a public radio show in Minnesota to a radically different response. By this time the Polar Bear had been transformed into a victim of climate change; we had been conditioned to feel empathy and compassion towards a creature being driven to homelessness.

Tapping into the magnetism of charismatic creatures – whipping up public 'pandamonium' – can be an effective way of raising both awareness and funds for conservation and, so the argument goes, indirectly generating support for the conservation of ecosystems and creatures that are deemed too uncharismatic, ugly or far removed from us to carry their own fundraising campaign. But, although there is no doubt that the celebrities of the animal world are more adept at loosening the public's purse strings, and although they may serve as important ambassadors for conservation, there *is* reason to question whether the funds they generate are being used most effectively to stem the rapid loss of species and rampant destruction of thriving ecosystems. In truth, the majority of conservation dollars are invested in trying to save those species with donor-appeal rather than species or ecosystems at greatest risk or with significant ecological or evolutionary value – the result being that we are losing at an alarming clip those species that *do* have significant ecological and evolutionary value, and we are continuing to destroy vibrant ecosystems that are the heart and lungs of our planet.

In 2009, TV presenter and conservationist Chris Packham said of Giant Pandas: "Here's a species that of its own accord has gone down an evolutionary cul-de-sac. It's not a strong species. Unfortunately, it's big and cute and it's a symbol of the World Wildlife Fund – and we pour millions of pounds into panda conservation. I reckon we should pull the plug. Let them go with a degree of dignity." There are currently around 1,600 Giant Pandas in the wild and more than 300 in captivity worldwide (it costs about half a million dollars per year for a zoo to borrow a breeding pair of Giant Pandas. Most are on loan, coincidentally, to countries that have signed major trade and foreign investment deals with China). Efforts to boost numbers in the wild have included the reintroduction of two captive-bred pandas into Sichaun Province. The first, Xiang Xiang, was set loose in 2007 only to be fatally beaten up by resident males. Tao Tao had better luck, and has been living in the Liziping Nature Reserve since 2012. China currently plans to reintroduce one captive panda into the wild per year – it's hard to imagine that such a slow drip will do much to boost the viability of wild populations. The biologist and photographer George Shaller recently told *National Geographic Daily News* that officials in China "feel that animals are better off in captivity: They get plenty to eat, they don't get wet and cold – so there's a great reluctance to release them." Lu Zhi, a panda expert from Beijing University, has called efforts to reintroduce pandas to the wild as their habitat is being swallowed up as "pointless as taking off the pants in order to fart." Sir David Attenbourough recently weighed in when he said that the world wouldn't change dramatically if the panda were to disappear, warning that focusing only on saving the appealing creatures was a 'mistake'.

Now, telling a doting public you are pulling the plug on a beloved animal would be like coldly announcing that you are turning off the life support system of a cherished relative. But as controversial as criticisms of panda conservation are, they do raise a very important question; with limited resources and extinctions underway, what should we really be choosing to try to save and what should we be willing to let go?

Perhaps it is time to think outside the panda.

In the past two decades amphibians have been at the forefront of the largest mass extinction event since the dinosaurs disappeared, 65 million years ago. Frogs, salamanders and caecilians have been wrung out of forests and wetlands in all continents on which they live, throwing ecosystems out of whack and shrinking the biological diversity of our planet. Their removal from an ecosystem disrupts the cycle of nutrients, and algal blooms have been documented in tadpole-free streams. Because of their remarkable transformation from aquatic tadpoles to terrestrial adults, amphibians form a key link between water and land; losing one frog is akin to losing two species. As both predators and prey, amphibians are key components of the foodchain, and they keep those things in check that we dislike – insect vectors of disease and crop pests. Their loss has cascading consequences that we only vaguely understand. And yet, their disappearance has created barely a ripple of concern when compared to the loss of charismatic mammals.

The message that amphibians are in trouble seems to have percolated the public conscience to some degree, thanks in large part to the 'canary in the coalmine' analogy, which asserts that amphibians are serving as an early warning of deteriorating ecosystem health. "Ah, yes, they are the canary in the coalmine, don't you know?" people often say

proudly when they learn I am an amphibian specialist. And as conservationists we have clung to this analogy, nodding enthusiastically and stopping just short of patting people on the back when we hear it told back to us. But even though we have an analogy that resonates, we are falling short of a concerted global investment in saving amphibians and the ecosystems that they call home. Although the canary in the coalmine analogy has succeeded in raising awareness about amphibian declines, it speaks volume about our attitude towards amphibians – for nobody ever goes down the mine to save the canary. The whole point is that the canary dies so we don't have to. It speaks to the narcissistic streak in our society, of our propensity to ask first, "what *good* is it?" before deciding whether it is worth saving. Even a number of major conservation organisations are shifting their focus to prioritise the needs of humans over any inherent rights or value of nature. By condoning or promoting arguments for the preservation of nature that are based solely on the economic or utilitarian value of species or ecosystems, are we not helping to foster a values system that ignores any moral responsibility (or even – if we dare to dream for a second – a moral *desire*) to protect other life?

But how *do* we foster a values system that promotes the protection of species and ecosystems regardless of their economic or utilitarian value? Awareness is a good start but it isn't enough by itself. Although an increasing number of people appear to be aware what is happening to amphibians, the investment in trying to save more than 2,000 threatened species pales in comparison to that spent protecting single mammal species ($82 million were spent managing Tiger reserves in 2010 alone, according to the *Economist*). Our attempts to rally support for amphibian conservation using the canary in the coalmine analogy have floundered for a couple of reasons. First, the analogy does not provide any compelling reason for people to care about amphibians – it simply asserts that they are a litmus test for the health of our environment. Second, when the analogy was coined, we didn't know exactly what the loss of amphibians was telling us – we hadn't pinpointed the cause of the disappearances. This early warning was rather like a sign in the middle of nowhere that simply said "Watch out!" It was like being told by your doctor that you are dying without being told what you can do about it. It wasn't obvious to people what they were supposed to do, other than recite the analogy back to amphibian biologists they happened to meet at parties.

A quarter of a century later, we are uniquely placed to tackle the loss of amphibians

LEFT: The Giant Palm Salamander, *Bolitoglossa dofleini*, whose forest home was protected through the creation of a new reserve in the Sierra Caral of Guatemala.

on a global scale should we decide to place importance on their disappearance. We know that frogs and salamanders are being driven to extinction by a lethal cocktail of habitat loss, disease and climate change – and we have been given a second chance to save many species that we thought were lost. We know that nine out of ten threatened amphibians are impacted by habitat loss – and that any strategy to save amphibians needs to include a concerted effort to protect their habitat. We know that these creatures provide an opportunity for countries to meet their targets to stem biodiversity loss by 2020 (after failing to meet their 2010 targets); entire species and ecosystems can be saved through the protection of relatively small parcels of good habitat. And we have an ambitious blueprint for action to halt amphibian declines and extinctions in the form of the *Amphibian Conservation Action Plan*, which was produced at a meeting of more than 80 amphibian experts in Washington, DC in 2005. The newly formed Amphibian Survival Alliance, the world's largest partnership for amphibian conservation, is uniquely placed to engage a diverse suite of partners and spearhead global actions to protect amphibians and their habitats. More than 15 reserves have already been established to protect amphibians in the wild, from Colombia to Madagascar to Sri Lanka, encompassing more than 22,000 hectares. As an example, in 2012 several conservation groups collaborated to create the first reserve of the Sierra Caral of Guatemala, protecting 2,400 hectares of some of the biologically richest forests in the world and the home of 12 threatened amphibian species including the critically endangered and charismatic Guatemala Brook Frog and Giant Palm Salamander. We are building a catalogue of local success stories, but in order to truly scale up amphibian conservation to meet the magnitude of the crisis, in order to channel conservation dollars where they are desperately needed, we must catalyse a groundswell of public support. How exactly we rally a global public behind amphibian conservation is a question I have grappled with over the past several years.

I have had to accept that it is harder to evoke compassion towards an entire class of animals than it is towards one animal; we are hard-wired to empathise with individuals, not statistics. Above a magnitude of one, we become desensitised – it doesn't matter to us whether there are 200 or 2,000 victims – our emotional response to statistics varies little. We have been hampered by our efforts to communicate the startling statistics. While the facts are of course important, by themselves they are simply not enough. We cannot expect people to care that a third of amphibians are threatened with extinction if they do not first care for amphibians. And the number of people that do currently care for amphibians is relatively slim – frogs were born at the wrong end of the evolutionary spectrum to evoke in us anything approaching the empathy we feel toward cute animals with eyelashes. If we conduct the fight for conservation attention and funds on the battlefield of empathy, amphibians will lose almost every time to large mammals. If we want amphibians to receive the attention that they need, we need to change battlefields.

Empathy is a powerful motivator for evoking a desire to protect another being, be it human or animal, but it is not the only motivator of compassionate behaviour. We also act in certain ways because of our sense of identity – who we are, who we want to be, or who we want people to think we are. This sense of identity may lead people to care for the protection of amphibians. Frogs, salamanders and caecilians possess something that the Tiger, the Giant Panda and the Polar Bear do not; something that could be the key to unlocking our desire to save them. Even if in life we often take them for granted, we notice the loss of frogs and newts at the points where their secret worlds intersect with ours. We notice when ponds that once bubbled with life lie still; we notice when the chorus that used to fill the cool evenings in spring falls silent; we notice when delicate newts no longer dot our walk through mossy forests like crumbs scattered by Hansel and Gretel. Their vanishing is written in the silent whispers of lonely trees and in the stillness of clear ponds yearning to herald the onset of spring. And noticing is the first step towards caring.

As widely celebrated as Giant Pandas, Tigers and Polar Bears are, most of our daily lives would change little if they were to disappear from the wild. Many of our lives, on the other hand, even if we are often too busy to be aware, are intricately intertwined with those of amphibians. Their proximity invites us to forge intimate relationships as children: to nurture tadpoles into young froglets and release them into our back gardens. They are members of our community, extensions of our home – they are part of our identity, a link to our past and to our children's present and future.

I have seen first-hand how a sense of pride can elevate the perceived value of amphibians. In Israel, the Hula Painted Frog embodies the pride of a nation that has brought a thriving ecosystem back from the dead. That pride percolates all walks of society: everyone I met during my stay, from taxi drivers to journalists to reserve wardens to citizens to eminent scientists, had their own story about the Hula Painted Frog; *their* Hula Painted Frog. The frog is a beacon of hope in a troubled country: an expression of compassion and deep connection with a unique and rich natural heritage. In Costa Rica, the Golden Toad is an icon for conservation and a catalyst for the creation of Monteverde Cloud Forest Reserve, and in Panama the Golden Harlequin Frog features on the nation's currency. Few things are as powerful as being the sole steward of a unique and rare species – especially one with a good story – to instill a sense of pride.

⚘

I used to believe that the possession of knowledge was enough for people to care about an issue. I was trained as a scientist – to objectively analyse and disseminate data. As long as people *knew* that amphibians were in trouble, they would care enough to do something about it – right? Through the Search for Lost Frogs I learned that the way in which facts are framed and delivered influences how people respond to them. The language we use determines whether people feel powerless or empowered, hopeless or hopeful, connected or detached, apathetic or motivated. By delivering stories about long-lost species and the people on a quest to find them, the Search for Lost Frogs was a vehicle for instilling pride and elevating the perceived value of lost frogs and salamanders around the world. Through the campaign I came to appreciate the power of storytelling as a tool for evoking a visceral response that data alone could not.

Ever since we scratched drawings onto the walls of caves we have been telling stories to connect and to make sense of the world around us. We accept ideas more readily when our minds are in story mode than when they are in an analytical mindset (which they click into when we are presented with statistics); stories unlock our capacity for emotion and are, in essence, a powerful tool for dissolving the invisible line we draw between ourselves and the natural world. Stories, whether visual, written or spoken, can place amphibians and the people working to save them in the context of our lives. Their story becomes our story. The Search for Lost Frogs gave people stories of adventure and discovery, of loss and hope. It brought images of bright orange toads, rainbow toads and yellow and black salamanders into our homes. These images and stories provided an escape from our daily routine and a glimpse into a wilder, more mysterious world, tapping into the inner adventurer within each of us. They were like a jet of air on the embers of curiosity that glow deep within, rekindling lost connections.

After the Search for Lost Frogs media campaign drew to a close I asked Rob McNeil, who was media manager at Conservation International at the outset of the campaign and champion of the idea, why he believed it generated so much attention. "The press campaign really seemed to catch the imagination of lots of people," he said. Although Rob left CI during the campaign to take a job at Oxford University, he continued to follow the coverage,

TOP RIGHT: The Guatemala Brook Frog, *Duellmanohyla soralia*, a critically endangered species from the Sierra Caral of Guatemala.

BELOW RIGHT: Eastern Spadefoot Toad, *Scaphiopus holbrookii*.

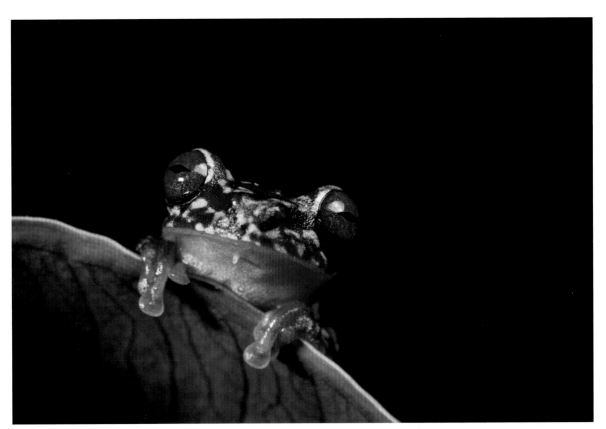

and added, "While it was a disappointment not to be there with the team to celebrate the rediscoveries, it was a fantastic feeling to see them popping up on the news from time to time and to see the real tangible outcomes of our work. It takes these sort of bright ideas to make people realise that conservation really can deliver results – that it is about hope, care and the astonishing array of treasures that evolution has produced for us to marvel at, rather than just a grim fight against the tide of industrialisation. I'm proud of what we did, and if my kids get to grow up in a world where there are a few more weird-ass frogs than there might have been if we didn't do it, then all the better …"

♺

So what is the outlook for amphibians? It really seems to depend upon whom you ask. Some amphibian biologists who have been in the business for a long time refer to themselves as 'extinction biologists' or 'forensic biologists' because of their role documenting the extinction of species. Most of them have watched helplessly as their study animals disappeared. Those born more recently grew up in a world in which amphibians were already disappearing and, conversely, tend to be more optimistic; more inclined to find hope in recent rediscoveries. The differences in attitudes are an expression of what is known as shifting baselines, whereby we measure the world against our own reference points. It is easier to feel that things are getting better when our expectations are low to begin with. But I found one notable exception to this rule: Marty Crump.

"If we could capture what you just said in a powder and sprinkle it on everyone's shoes we may be able to do something about it," Crump says after I have finished telling the story of my search for the Variable Harlequin Frog in Costa Rica. She believes in transmitting the passion and energy that she personifies in order to connect people with nature. Even though Crump has borne witness to the disappearance of the magnificent Golden Toad among other species she held dear, she maintains a relentless optimism that keeps her searching for creatures such as the Chile Darwin's Frog (*Rhinoderma rufum*), a curious frog that broods tadpoles in its mouth and which was last seen 25 years ago. "I'm certainly not going to give up," she says, "I just love being in the field. Part of it is human nature. We get excited about rediscovery. To rediscover a lost species – now that would be fun!"

I am surprised to learn that Crump was not always so enchanted with the creatures she has devoted her life to understand. "As a student, I was so focused on the research that I didn't appreciate the animals themselves," she explains. So what changed? "I can tell you the moment, and exactly who showed me the importance of thinking about conservation," she says. "The late Archie Carr [an American ecologist and pioneering conservationist with a passion for turtles] was a colleague at the University of Florida and a friend. Archie came to the house one day and handed me a jar full of moss and 19 tiny toads. My first daughter, Karen had been born just three days earlier, on 19 May, so there was a toad for every day of the month. He said to me, 'Spadefoot Toads used to be really common here, but they have disappeared – they have been pushed out by development. If you plant all these baby toads in your back garden, when Karen grows up, she will be able to hear Spadefoot Toads singing'. I had been a mother for three days and that made such an impression on me that that is what it is all about: thinking about the next generation. Having children really cemented that idea for me. We have to do it not just for the here and now, but for our kids and our kids' kids."

Carr's message had been impossible to ignore because it spoke to the thing that Crump cared most about in the world. And that is our opportunity and our challenge as conservationists and communicators; to make the most pressing issues resonate on the most visceral level; to appeal to people's existing values and unlock their deepest yearnings to preserve that which they hold dear. Our task is to paint a picture of a better future to strive towards. Only in this way, by turning up with tadpoles ready to plant in the back garden, can we ensure that our children, and our children's children, will grow into a world filled with their song.

CHAPTER 17

THE LAST WORD

When I embarked on my adventures with frogs and newts, perched on the wall of my grandparents' garden and scrambling the scree-smudged moors of the Scottish highlands, I could not have guessed that three decades later I would still be searching for these creatures in places evocative of David Attenborough's silky narration. The more I learned about the incredible diversity of frogs and salamanders beyond the back gardens and misty moors of Scotland, the more it whetted my appetite for exploration. It was the start of a journey through increasingly remote places in search of more exotic creatures.

My journey has been guided by the many people that I have connected with along the way through a shared fascination for frogs and salamanders; individuals who have generously opened the door to hidden worlds in India, Israel, Ecuador, Colombia, Haiti, California and Costa Rica. The frogs and salamanders I found along the way, as they filled the night air with their calls, emerged onto the forest floor like improbably brilliant jewels or ricocheted inside the plastic walls of a rubbish bin, brought direction, purpose and excitement to my journey.

Although my travels have opened my eyes time and time again to incredible wonders, my quest for discovery has also estranged me somewhat from the place that opened my eyes to nature for the first time; the back gardens and boggy vales of Scotland. I have not been back to Drumbeg in more than 25 years, and I sometimes feel pangs of nostalgia for this special time and place. I yearn for the feeling of being so attuned to the rhythm of the land; to feeling the chill of winter soften and anticipating, as the sun sinks later in the day, the emergence of frogs and newts to congregate at secluded ponds. I miss preparing to meet them there. The memories of my intrepid childhood have sharpened with time like the tannins in a good red wine. I can almost taste the moist peaty air as I conjure images of wading through bogs in search of newts. The memories seem to have crystallised in my imagination, but it is over the past 18 months that they have become increasingly vivid, following – and I believe as a result of – a truly life-changing event

⚕

Majadahonda Hospital, Madrid, 10 March 2012

The sharp smell of hand sanitiser jolts back memories, in the way that only smells can, as I sit in the same Madrid hospital in a different but identical room, 18 months after my wife has been released. But I am here now under very different circumstances, to replace old memories with new ones like a fresh lick of paint on an old wall. As I sit next to Iciar in her hospital bed, I look down to see four tiny fingers curled around my thumb. Kena Moore Gomez, just 30 minutes old, opens his large grey-brown eyes and looks into mine, and I am changed in an instant.

⚕

Rock Creek Park, Washington, DC, September 2013

The leaves rattle and shake around me, as if frantically preparing for their autumnal transformation to hues of yellow and orange. A cool breeze signals the end of a humid summer. My thoughts meander like the river upon whose banks I stroll as I weave through Rock Creek Park, a leafy oasis in the outskirts of Washington, DC. Kena, now a year and a half old, sits motionless in his buggy in front of me, captivated by the late evening light as it illuminates twisted trunks and dances on the rippling water.

As we pass the entrance to the National Zoo, nestled in the heart of the park, I decide to take a detour to introduce Kena to what I consider one of the most impressive products of evolution; the great cats. As we approach the Tiger enclosure I see, across a large moat, a large female lying in the shade of a bamboo thicket, motionless apart from the occasional flick of the tail. I park Kena's buggy to face the enclosure, but my avid gesticulating does little to direct his attention away from the ice cream melting down the fingers of the girl next to us. After several long minutes of trying in vain to train his gaze across the moat to the creature beyond, and starting to feel a little foolish, I reverse his buggy and we continue on our way out of the zoo and back to the park.

As I continue along the banks of the river I can't help but wonder why Kena had shown so little interest in the Tiger. Was it too far away? Too inanimate? Too removed from his world by bars and concrete? My thoughts are pierced when Kena rockets forward in his buggy and, pointing to his left, blurts "Bae! Bae!" Bae means, I learned recently, animal. I follow his finger to a Grey Squirrel on a stump of wood some six feet to the left of the trail.

I crouch next to Kena on a copper carpet of leaflitter and watch the squirrel as it rotates an acorn in its mouth with both hands, stopping to nibble it with a cracking sound every couple of turns. Kena looks at me, eyebrows raised and a smile from cheek to cheek, to check that I am seeing what he is seeing, before turning back to wave at the small creature. The squirrel stops turning the acorn and cocks its head towards us, its eyes glinting like small black pearls in a shaft of light. Kena waves with increased vigour.

I sit for a long moment watching Kena watch the squirrel, his face illuminated with pleasure, and consider the irony that, as I had been trying to rouse his interest in a charismatic creature behind bars and concrete, he steered me to an intimate slice of our environment that I would have walked right past. In this moment I feel a curious sensation. As I watch him wave at the squirrel I feel a yearning to be as fully present in the moment as he is; so filled with pure joy and wide-eyed wonder, and a yearning for him to hold onto that unadulterated enchantment. I feel a deep contentment tinged with nostalgia for a moment before it has even ended.

The squirrel is Kena's entry point to nature, an agent for dissolving the invisible line that we draw between ourselves and our natural world. And this, I realise, is what amphibians have been to me. From my grandparent's wall they were my portal to a wild and exciting world, and in the mountains of Drumbeg they were my entry point to a vast and foreboding landscape. Through the frogs and newts I was able to form an intimate association with the land; to bite off and understand a microcosm of a diverse and complex world. They revealed to me, beneath the tea-brown waters, a world teeming with life – an alternate submerged fantasy world. When I hear the calls of frogs fill the night air in Colombia or Costa Rica or Haiti, I am transported back to the boggy vales of Scotland. Like the whistle of a boiling kettle on the kitchen stove, they take me home.

※

As I crouch on the path next to Kena, the evening light slants through the bamboo to cast a warm glow around the soft fur of the squirrel. With a twitch of the tail, the animal turns and bounds off the stump and into the bamboo thicket. After a moment I turn to Kena and say, "Time to go home?" As we walk away from the stump, Kena spins around in his buggy, points to the spot where the squirrel had been, and shouts, "Bae!"

EXPEDITIONS IN SEARCH OF LOST FROGS, ORGANISED BY COUNTRY (SPECIES REDISCOVERIES ARE SHOWN IN BOLD)

AUSTRALIA: An expedition led by Michael McFadden in search of the Gastric Brooding Frog, *Rheobatrachus silus* (last seen, 1985), was unsuccessful in finding the species.

Borneo: Indraneil Das led several unsuccessful expeditions before rediscovering, in June 2011, the **Borneo Rainbow Toad**, *Ansonia latidisca* (last seen, 1924).

BRAZIL: An expedition led by Taran Grant and Patrick Colombo was unsuccessful in finding the Bahia Spinythumb Frog, *Crossodactylus grandis* (last seen, 1960s) and Gruta Button Frog, *Cycloramphus valae* (last seen, 1982)

CAMEROON: An expedition led by Gonwouou Legrand was unsuccessful in tracking down Schneider's Banana Frog, *Afrixalus schneideri* (last seen, 1889)

CAMEROON: Expeditions led by David Gower and Thomas Doherty-Bone were unsuccessful in finding Bornmuller's Caecilian, *Crotaphatrema bornmuelleri* (last seen, 1893); Tchabal Mbabo Caecilian, *Crotaphatrema tchabalmbaboensis* (last seen, 1997); Victoria Caecilian, *Herpele multiplicata* (last seen 1912) and Makumuno Assumbo Caecilian, *Idiocranium russeli* (last seen, 1936)

CHILE: Andrew Charrier, Marty Crump and Dante Fenolio led an expedition in search of Chile Darwin's Frog, *Rhinoderma rufum,* (last seen, 1980), but returned empty handed

COLOMBIA: An expedition led by Alonso Quevedo, Diego Riaño, Robin Moore, Don Church and Wes Sechrest failed to find the Mesopotamia Beaked Toad, *Rhinella rostrata* (last seen, 1914), Sonsón Stubfoot Toad, *Atelopus sonsonensis* (last seen, 1996); Sonsón Frog, *Atopophrynus syntomopu* (last seen, 1980); Chocó Harlequin Frog, *Atelopus chocoensis* (last seen, 1998) and Argella Robber Frog, *Pristimantis bernali* (last seen, 1981), but resulted in the discovery of two species potentially new to science: The Red-Eyed Toad and the 'Monty Burns Toad', a species of beaked toad

COLOMBIA: An expedition led by Gustavo Ballen failed to find the Colombian Stubfoot Toad, *Atelopus minultus* (last seen, 1985)

COLOMBIA: Jonh Jairo Cisneros led an expedition that failed to find the Jambato Toad, *Atelopus ignescens* (last seen, 1988)

COLOMBIA: An expedition led by Alberto Felipe failed to find the Harlequin Frog *Atelopus longibrachius* (last seen, 1990)

COLOMBIA: Jhon Jairo Ospina-Sarria led an expedition that failed to find the Saxiclous Glass Frog, *Centrolene petrophilum* (last seen, 1985)

COSTA RICA: Expeditions led by Alan Pounds failed to locate the Golden Toad, *Incilius periglenes* (last seen, 1989)

COSTA RICA: Adrian Garcia led an expedition that failed to find the Angel Robber Frog, *Craugastor angelicus* (last seen, 1994) and Fleischman's Robber Frog, *Craugastor fleishmanni* (last seen, 1986)

COSTA RICA: An expedition led by Robin Moore tracked down the **Variable Harlequin Frog**, *Atelopus varius*, which disappeared in 1995 and was rediscovered in 2003 by Justin Yeager.

DEMOCRATIC REPUBLIC OF CONGO: An expedition led by Jos Kielgast resulted in the rediscovery of the **Omaniundu Reed Frog**, *Hyperolius sarkuruensis* (last seen, 1979)

ECUADOR: Santiago Ron led an expedition that resulted in the rediscovery of the **Rio Pescado Stubfoot Toad**, *Atelopus balios* (last seen, 1995) but failed to find the Quito Stubfoot Toad, *Atelopus ignescens* (last seen, 1988)

GUATEMALA: An expedition led by Jeff Streicher failed to find Wake's Moss Salamander, *Cryptotriton wakei* (last seen, 1977)

GUATEMALA: Expeditions led by Carlos Vasquez Almazán failed to find Jackson's Climbing Salamander, *Bolitoglossa jacksoni* (last seen, 1977)

HAITI: An expedition led by Blair Hedges and Robin Moore rediscovered five species last seen in 1991: the **La Hotte Glanded Frog**, *Eleutherodactylus gladulifer;* **Hispaniola Crowned Frog**, *Eleutherodactylus corona*; **Ventriloqual Frog**, *Eleutherodactylus dolomedes*; **Mozart's Land Frog**, *Eleutherodactylus amadeus* and **Macaya Breastspot frog**, *Eleutherodactylus thorectes*; and one species last seen in 1996: the **Macaya Burrowing Frog**, *Eleutherodactylus parapelates*; and failed to find the La Selle Grass Frog, *Eleutherodactylus gladuliferoides* (last seen, 1985)

INDIA: Expeditions led by S D Biju rediscovered 36 frog species that included the **Chalazodes Bubble-nest frog**, *Raorchestes chalazodes* (last seen, 1874); **Silent Valley Tropical Frog**, *Micrixalus thampii* (last seen, 1980); **Dehradun Stream Frog**, *Amolops chakrataensis* (last seen, 1985**); Elegant Tropical Frog**, *Micrixalus elegans* (last seen, 1937); and **Anamaiai Dot-frog**, *Ramanella anamaiaiensis* (Last seen, 1938). For further information on species found and still lost, see http://www.lostspeciesindia.org/

INDIA: An expedition led by Ramachandran Kotharambath failed to find the Long-headed Caecilian, *Ichthyphis longicephalus* (last seen, 1979)

INDONESIA: Expeditions led by Mirza Kusrini and Dhinar Arintafika failed to find Jackson's Bubble-nest Frog, *Philautus jacobsoni* (last seen, 1912)

ISRAEL: Expeditions led by Sarig Gafny and Yoram Malka resulted in the rediscovery of the **Hula Painted Frog, *Discoglossus nigriventer*** (last seen, 1955).

IVORY COAST: An expedition led by N'Goran Kouame led to the rediscovery of the **Mt Nimba Reed Frog, *Hyperolius nimbae*** (last seen, 1967), but failed to find the Ivory Coast Toad, *Amietophrynus danielae* (last seen, 1977)

LIBERIA: An expedition led by Annika Hillers in search of the Tlahcuiloh Salamander, *Phrynobatrachus brongersmai* (last seen, 1936) proved inconclusive on account of taxonomic uncertainties.

MEXICO: An expedition led by Sean Rovito resulted in the rediscovery of the **Cave Splayfoot Salamander, *Chiropterotriton mosaueri*** (last seen, 1941), and **Bog Splayfoot Salamander, *Chirpoterotriton magnipes*** (last seen, 2005): a species listed as 'possibly extinct' by the IUCN.

MEXICO: Expeditions led by Georgina Santos Barrera were disrupted by severe weather and failed to find the Guerran Leopard Frog, *Lithobates omiltemanus* (last seen, 1978); Hazel's Treefrog, *Plectrohyla hazelae* (last seen, 1984); Keelsnout Treefrog, *Plectrohyla mykter* (last seen, 1990s); Ahuitzotl Salamander, *Pseudoeurycea ahuitzotl* (last seen, 1990s); Tenchall's False Brook Salamander, *Pseudoeurycea tenchalli* (last seen, 1990s) and Ayotic Minute Salamander, *Thorius infernalis* (last seen, 1990s)

RWANDA: An expedition led by Max Dehling and Ulrich Sinsch failed to find the African Painted Frog, *Callixalus pictus* (last seen, 1950)

SOUTH AFRICA: Expeditions led by Werner Conradie failed to find the **Amatola Toad, *Vandijkophrynus amatolicus*** (last seen, 1998); however, the species was rediscovered in September 2011 by Jeanne Tarrant and Michael Cunningham in the same area as it was last seen.

VENEZUELA: Expeditions led by Enrique La Marca failed to locate the Scarlet Frog, *Atelopus sorianoi* (last seen, 1990) and Yellow Frog of La Carbonera, *Atelopus carbonensis* (last seen, 1995)

ZIMBABWE: An expedition led by James Harvey failed to find the Cave Squeaker, *Arthroleptis troglodytes* (last seen, 1962)

INDEX

ACKNOWLEDGMENTS

I would never have embarked on writing *In Search of Lost Frogs* if it were not for my brother, Richard, who assured me that writing a book was easy. It is not. Not for me, at least. The learning curve was steep, but enriching, and I am grateful for the push to dive in, and for all the encouragement along the way.

I am indebted to my family for their support as I pursued a less than conventional career path; I have been riding with the wind at my back the whole way. As my young fascination with our moist-skinned neighbours evolved into a quest to study and protect them, my long-suffering parents barely batted an eye at the growing menagerie of weird and wonderful creatures inhabiting my bedroom and the occasional salamander hibernating in the fridge. I am grateful to my dad for his eagle-eyed reviews of my draft manuscripts, and my brother Peter for bringing to me the Norman McCaig poem that was perfect for beginning the book. I only wish my mother, Katherine, could read this.

I wrote this book during the first year of my son Kena's life, in the brief windows of time between feeding, walks and naps (his and mine), a feat that would not have been remotely possible without the unwavering love and support of my wonderful wife, Iciar. Although she doesn't have to put up with salamanders in the fridge, she has to endure the challenges of being married to someone who chases and photographs frogs around the world for a living. I acknowledge every day how lucky I am. Kena inspires me every day to try to protect the world he will inherit.

This book represents the culmination of a lot of hard work, only a small fraction of which was mine. I am indebted to all those dedicated individuals who spent weeks and months under some of the most challenging and downright miserable conditions in search of species unseen in decades; their painstaking perseverance, gut-wrenching disappointment and infectious enthusiasm provided the inspiration for this book. I would also like to thank all those that helped me throughout my journey, opening the door to their worlds with generous hospitality, and those who helped to connect me with those people.

I am grateful to David Luxton for helping me navigate my journey into book publishing and providing invaluable feedback that encouraged me to tell the story through my eyes, as well as Lisa Thomas for enthusiastically taking on the project and providing guidance throughout.

My colleagues at Conservation International were instrumental in making the Search for Lost Frogs the success that it became, and it was a pleasure to work with such a talented and passionate group of people. I am grateful to my current partners in crime at the Amphibian Survival Alliance, Global Wildlife Conservation and Rainforest Trust for their tireless efforts to protect our incredible natural heritage, and to long-standing supporters Andrew Sabin, Nancy Wendell and George Meyer for making a difference. We are all in this pond together.

The author and publishers are grateful to the following people for permission to reproduce their photographs: 12 Niall Benvie; 22 David Sewell; 23 US Fish and Wildlife Service (public domain); 28 Hal Cogger; 33 Ignacio De la Riva; 57 Map reproduced from: 'Riding the Wave: Reconciling the Roles of Disease and Climate Change in Amphibian Declines'. Karen R Lips, Jay Diffendorfer, Joseph R Mendelson III, Michael W Sears. 2008. PlOS Biology; 75 Santiago Ron, 81 Santiago Ron; 82 Robert Puschendorf; 87 Poster featuring: the Golden Toad © Public Domain, Gastric-brooding Frog © John Wombey/ARKive, Mesopotamia Beaked Toad, Jackson's Climbing Salamander © Dave Wake, African Painted Frog (Reproduced in *Evolution* Vol 18, No. 3), Rio Pescado Stubfoot Toad © Luis Coloma, Turkestanian Salamander (reproduced with permission from Kuzmin S.L. 1999. *Amphibians of the Former Soviet Union*), Scarlet Harlequin Frog © Enrique La Marca, Hula Painted Frog © Heinrich Mendelssohn, Sambas Stream Frog © Fieldiana Zoology]; 131 N'goran Germaine Kouame; 132 top Jos Kielgast; below Sean Rovito; 168, 171, 172, 173, 174 S.D. Biju; 176 top Eduardo Toral-Contreras; below Indraneil Das; 178 Enrique La Marca; 179 Sam Sweet, 199 Harel Cohen; 243 below Todd Pierson

Excerpts   p.10 Carr, Archie F. "The Paradox Frog". The Windward Road (Gainesville: University Press of Florida, 2013), p. 90; p.64 Leopold, Aldo. 'On a Monument to the Pigeon', from Silent Wings: a Memorial to the Passenger Pigeon, ed. Scott, Walter, E., Wisconsin Society for Ornithology, 1947; p.67 Herald, John. 'Martha, Last of the Passenger Pigeons', reproduced by permission of Brian Hollander and Beverly Traum; p.234 Carson, Rachel, *The Sense of Wonder*, HarperCollins.